MARX'S CONCEPT OF MAN

Other Books by Erich Fromm

MAN FOR HIMSELF

ESCAPE FROM FREEDOM

PSYCHOANALYSIS AND RELIGION

THE FORGOTTEN LANGUAGE

THE SANE SOCIETY

THE ART OF LOVING

ZEN BUDDHISM AND PSYCHOANALYSIS
  (together with D. T. Suzuki and R. de Martino)

SIGMUND FREUD'S MISSION

MAY MAN PREVAIL?

BEYOND THE CHAINS OF ILLUSION

THE DOGMA OF CHRIST, and Other Essays

THE HEART OF MAN

YOU SHALL BE AS GODS

THE REVOLUTION OF HOPE

Erich Fromm

MARX'S CONCEPT OF MAN

With a translation from Marx's
ECONOMIC AND PHILOSOPHICAL
MANUSCRIPTS
by T. B. Bottomore
London School of Economics and
Political Science

With an Afterword by Erich Fromm

FREDERICK UNGAR PUBLISHING CO.
NEW YORK

MILESTONES
OF THOUGHTS
in the History of Ideas

Nineteenth Printing, 1973

Copyright © 1961, 1966 by
Erich Fromm

ISBN 0-8044-5391-8 (cloth)
0-8044-6161-9 (paper)

Library of Congress Catalog Card No. 66-23488

Printed in the United States of America

PREFACE

The bulk of this volume contains an English translation of Karl Marx's main philosophical work, published
for the first time in the United States[1]. Obviously, this
publication is of importance, if for no other reason than
that it will acquaint the American public with one of
the major works of post-Hegelian philosophy, hitherto
unknown in the English-speaking world.

Marx's philosophy, like much of existentialist thinking, represents a protest against man's alienation, his loss
of himself and his transformation into a thing; it is a
movement against the dehumanization and automatiza-
tion of man inherent in the development of Western
industrialism. It is ruthlessly critical of all "answers" to
the problem of human existence which try to present
solutions by negating or camouflaging the dichotomies
inherent in man's existence. Marx's philosophy is rooted
in the humanist Western philosophical tradition, which
reaches from Spinoza through the French and German
enlightenment philosophers of the eighteenth century
to Goethe and Hegel, and the very essence of which is
concern for man and the realization of his potentialities.

For Marx's philosophy, which has found its most
articulate expression in the *Economic and Philosophical
Manuscripts,* the central issue is that of the existence of
the real individual man, who *is* what he *does,* and whose
"nature" unfolds and reveals itself in history. But in contrast to Kierkegaard and others, Marx sees man in his

---

[1] An earlier translation into English, made in Russia, has
been on sale in England since 1959. In Raya Dunayevskaya's
Marxism and Freedom, Bookman Associates, New York, 1958,
some parts of the *Philosophical Manuscripts* (a little less than
one half of what is published here) were for the first time translated and published in the United States.

v

full concreteness as a member of a given society and of a given class, aided in his development by society, and at the same time its captive. The full realization of man's humanity and his emancipation from the social forces that imprison him is bound up, for Marx, with the recognition of these forces, and with social change based on this recognition.

Marx's philosophy is one of protest; it is a protest imbued with faith in man, in his capacity to liberate himself, and to realize his potentialities. This faith is a trait of Marx's thinking that was characteristic of the Western mood from the late Middle Ages to the nineteenth century, and which is so rare today. For this very reason, to many readers who are infected with the contemporary spirit of resignation and the revival of the concept of original sin (in Niebuhrian or Freudian terms), Marx's philosophy will sound dated, old-fashioned, utopian— and for this reason, if not for others, they will reject the voice of faith in man's possibilities, and of hope in his capacity to become what he potentially is. To others, however, Marx's philosophy will be a source of new insight and hope.

I believe that hope and new insight transcending the narrow limits of the positivistic-mechanistic thinking of social science today are needed, if the West is to emerge alive from this century of trial. Indeed while Western thought from the thirteenth to the nineteenth century (or, perhaps, to be exact, up to the outbreak of the First World War in 1914) was one of hope, a hope rooted in Prophetic and Greek-Roman thought, the last forty years have been years of increasing pessimism and hopelessness. The average person runs for shelter; he tries to escape from freedom and he seeks for security in the lap of the big state and the big corporation. If we are not able to emerge from this hopelessness, we may still go on for a time on the basis of our material strength, but in the long historical perspective the West will be condemned to physical or spiritual extinction.

Great as is the importance of Marx's philosophy as a source of philosophical insight and as an antidote against the current—veiled or open—mood of resignation, there is another reason, hardly less important, for its publication in the United States at this time. The world is torn today between two rival ideologies—that of "Marxism" and that of "Capitalism." While in the United States "Socialism" is a word on the Devil's tongue and not one that recommends itself, the opposite is true in the rest of the world. Not only do Russia and China use the term "socialism" to make their systems attractive, but most Asian and African countries are deeply attracted by the ideas of Marxist socialism. To them socialism and Marxism are appealing not only because of the economic achievements of Russia and China, but because of the spiritual elements of justice, equality and universality which are inherent in Marxist socialism (rooted in the Western spiritual tradition). While the truth is that the Soviet Union is a system of a conservative state capitalism and not the realization of Marxian socialism, and while China negates, by the means she employs, that emancipation of the individual person which is the very aim of socialism, they both use the attraction of Marxist thought to recommend themselves to the peoples of Asia and Africa. And how do American public opinion and official policy react? We do everything to support the Russian-Chinese claim by heralding that their system is "Marxist," and by identifying Marxism and socialism with Soviet state capitalism and Chinese totalitarianism. By confronting the uncommitted masses of the world with the alternative between "Marxism" and "socialism" on the one hand, and "capitalism" on the other, (or, as we usually put it, between "slavery" and "freedom" or free enterprise) we give the Soviet Union and the Chinese Communists as much support as we possibly can in the battle for the minds of men.

The alternatives for the underdeveloped countries, whose political development will be decisive for the next hundred years, are not capitalism and socialism, but totalitarian socialism and Marxist humanist socialism, as it tends to develop in various different forms in Poland, Yugoslavia, Egypt, Burma, Indonesia, etc. The West has much to offer as a leader of such a development for the former colonial nations; not only capital and technical advice, but also the Western humanist tradition of which Marxist socialism is the upshot; the tradition of man's freedom, not only *from*, but his freedom *to*—to develop his own human potentialities, the tradition of human dignity and brotherhood. But clearly, in order to exercise this influence and in order to understand the Russian and Chinese claims, we must understand Marx's thought and must discard the ignorant and distorted picture of Marxism which is current in American thinking today. It is my hope that this volume will be a step in that direction.

I have tried in my introduction to present Marx's concept of man in a simple (not, I trust, oversimplified) way, because his style makes his writings not always easy to understand, and I hope that the introduction will be helpful to most readers for an understanding of Marx's text. I have refrained from presenting my disagreements with Marx's thinking, because there are few as far as his humanist existentialism is concerned. A number of disagreements do exist concerning his sociological and economic theories, some of which I have expressed in previous works.[2] They refer mainly to the fact that Marx failed to see the degree to which capitalism was capable of modifying itself and thus satisfying the economic needs of industrialized nations, his failure to see clearly enough the dangers of bureaucratization and centralization, and to envisage the authoritarian systems which could emerge as alternatives to socialism. But since this book deals only with Marx's philosophical and historical thought, it is not the place to discuss the controversial points of his economic and political theory.

However, criticism of Marx is something quite different from the customary fanatical or condescending judgment so characteristic of present-day utterances about him. I am convinced that only if we understand the real meaning of Marxist thought, and hence can differentiate it from Russian and Chinese pseudo-Marxism, will we be able to understand the realities of the present-day world and be prepared to deal realistically and constructively with their challenge. I hope that this volume will contribute not only to a greater understanding of Marx's humanist philosophy, but also that it will help to diminish the irrational and paranoid attitude that sees in Marx a devil and in socialism a realm of the devil.

While the *Economic and Philosophical Manuscripts* constitute the main part of this volume, I have included also small sections of other philosophical writings by Marx to round out the picture. The only larger section I have added comprises various statements dealing with the person of Marx, and which also have never before been published in the United States. I have added this section because Marx's person, like his ideas, has been slandered and vilified by many authors; I believe that

---

[2] Cf., for example, *The Sane Society*, Rinehart & Co., Inc., New York, 1955.

a more adequate picture of Marx, the man, will help to destroy some prejudices with regard to his ideas.[3]

It remains only for me to express my warm appreciation to Mr. T. B. Bottomore of the London School of Economics for his permission to use his excellent new translation of the *Economic and Philosophical Manuscripts*,[4,5] and also to thank him for a number of important critical suggestions he made after reading the manuscript of my introduction.

E. F.

---

[3] A crude example of what has been done in this respect is the recent American publication of a pamphlet by Marx under the title *The World Without Jews*. This title, which makes it appear as if it were given to the pamphlet by Marx himself (the real title is *On the Jewish Problem*), seems to confirm the claim made in publicity for the book that Marx was the founder of Nazi and Soviet anti-Semitism. Anyone who reads the book and who knows Marx's philosophy and literary style will recognize that this claim is absurd and false. It misuses some critical remarks on the Jews, which were made polemically in a brilliant essay dealing with the problem of bourgeois emancipation, in order to make this fantastic accusation against Marx.

[4] Watts & Co., London, will publish at a later date the whole of Mr. Bottomore's translation of the *Economic and Philosophical Manuscripts* (including the mainly economic parts which have been omitted in this volume), together with his own introduction.

[5] Note: All page references to *Economic and Philosophical Manuscripts* are to the Bottomore translation in this volume.

CONTENTS

1

THE FALSIFICATION OF
MARX'S CONCEPTS

It is one of the peculiar ironies of history that there are no limits to the misunderstanding and distortion of theories, even in an age when there is unlimited access to the sources; there is no more drastic example of this phenomenon than what has happened to the theory of Karl Marx in the last few decades. There is continuous reference to Marx and to Marxism in the press, in the speeches of politicians, in books and articles written by respectable social scientists and philosophers; yet with few exceptions, it seems that the politicians and news-papermen have never as much as glanced at a line written by Marx, and that the social scientists are satisfied with a minimal knowledge of Marx. Apparently they feel safe in acting as experts in this field, since nobody with power and status in the social-research empire challenges their ignorant statements.[1]

---

[1] It is a sad comment, yet one which cannot be avoided, that this ignorance and distortion of Marx are to be found more in the United States than in any other Western country. It must be mentioned especially that in the last fifteen years there has been an extraordinary renaissance of discussions on Marx in Germany and France, centered especially around the *Economic and Philosophical Manuscripts* published in this volume. In Germany the participants in this discussion are mainly Protestant theologians. I mention first the extraordinary *Marxismusstudien,* ed. by I. Fetscher, 2 vols. J.C.B. Mohr (Tübingen, 1954 and 1957). Further, the excellent introduc-

Among all the misunderstandings there is probably none more widespread than the idea of Marx's "materialism." Marx is supposed to have believed that the paramount psychological motive in man is his wish for monetary gain and comfort, and that this striving for maximum profit constitutes the main incentive in his personal life and in the life of the human race. Complementary to this idea is the equally widespread assumption that Marx neglected the importance of the individual; that he had neither respect nor understanding for the spiritual needs of man, and that his "ideal" was the well-fed and well-clad, but "soulless" person. Marx's criticism of religion was held to be identical with the denial of all spiritual values, and this seemed all the more apparent to those who assume that belief in God is the condition for a spiritual orientation.

This view of Marx then goes on to discuss his socialist paradise as one of millions of people who submit to an all-powerful state bureaucracy, people who have surrendered their freedom, even though they might have

---

tion by Landshut to the Kroener edition of the *Economic and Philosophical Manuscripts*. Then, the works of Lukacs, Bloch, Popitz and others, quoted later. In the United States a slowly increasing interest in Marx's work has been observed recently. Unfortunately, it is in some part expressed in a number of biased and falsifying books like Schwarzschild's *The Red Prussian*, or in oversimplified and misleading books like the Overstreets' *The Meaning of Communism*. In contrast, Joseph A. Schumpeter, in his *Capitalism, Socialism and Democracy* (Harper & Bros., 1947) offers an excellent presentation of Marxism. Cf. further on the problem of historical naturalism, John C. Bennett's *Christianity and Communism Today* (Association Press, New York). See also the excellent anthologies (and introductions) by Feuer (Anchor Books) and by Bottomore and Rubel, (Watts and Co., London). Specifically, on Marx's view of human nature I want to mention Venable's *Human Nature: The Marxist View*, which,

achieved equality; these materially satisfied "individuals" have lost their individuality and have been successfully transformed into millions of uniform robots and automatons, led by a small elite of better-fed leaders.

Suffice it to say at the outset that this popular picture of Marx's "materialism"—his anti-spiritual tendency, his wish for uniformity and subordination—is utterly false. Marx's aim was that of the spiritual emancipation of man, of his liberation from the chains of economic determination, of restituting him in his human wholeness, of enabling him to find unity and harmony with his fellow man and with nature. Marx's philosophy was, in secular, nontheistic language, a new and radical step forward in the tradition of prophetic Messianism; it was aimed at the full realization of individualism, the very aim which has guided Western thinking from the Renaissance and the Reformation far into the nineteenth century.

This picture undoubtedly must shock many readers because of its incompatibility with the ideas about Marx to which they have been exposed. But before proceed-

---

although knowledgeable and objective, suffers severely from the fact that the author could not make use of the *Economic and Philosophical Manuscripts*. Cf. also, for the philosophical basis of Marx's thought, H. Marcuse's brilliant and penetrating book, *Reason and Revolution* (Oxford University Press, New York, 1941), and the same author's discussion of Marx's theories vs. Soviet Marxism in *Soviet Marxism* (Columbia University Press, New York, 1958). Cf. also my discussion of Marx in *The Sane Society* (Rinehart & Co. Inc., New York, 1955) and my earlier discussion of Marx's theory in *Zeitschrift für Sozialforschung*, Vol. I (Hirschfeld, Leipzig, 1932). In France, the discussion has been led partly by Catholic priests and partly by philosophers, most of them socialists. Among the former I refer especially to J. Y. Calvez' *La Pensée de Karl Marx*, ed. du Seuil, Paris 1956; among the latter, A. Kojève, Sartre, and especially the various works of H. Lefèbvre.

ing to substantiate it, I want to emphasize the irony which lies in the fact that the description given of the aim of Marx and of the content of his vision of socialism, fits almost exactly the reality of present-day Western capitalist society. The majority of people are motivated by a wish for greater material gain, for comfort and gadgets, and this wish is restricted only by the desire for security and the avoidance of risks. They are increasingly satisfied with a life regulated and manipulated, both in the sphere of production and of consumption, by the state and the big corporations and their respective bureaucracies; they have reached a degree of conformity which has wiped out individuality to a remarkable extent. They are, to use Marx's term, impotent "commodity men" serving virile machines. The very picture of mid-twentieth century capitalism is hardly distinguishable from the caricature of Marxist socialism as drawn by its opponents.

What is even more surprising is the fact that the people who accuse Marx most bitterly of "materialism" attack socialism for being unrealistic because it does *not* recognize that the only efficient incentive for man to work lies in his desire for material gain. Man's unbounded capacity for negating blatant contradictions by rationalizations, if it suits him, could hardly be better illustrated. The very same reasons which are said to be proof that Marx's ideas are incompatible with our religious and spiritual tradition and which are used *to defend* our present system *against* Marx, are at the same time employed by the same people to prove that capitalism corresponds to human nature and hence is far superior to an "unrealistic" socialism.

I shall try to demonstrate that this interpretation of Marx is completely false; that his theory does not assume that the main motive of man is one of material gain; that, furthermore, the very aim of Marx is to liberate man from the pressure of economic needs, so that he can be fully human; that Marx is primarily concerned with the emancipation of man as an individual, the overcoming of alienation, the restoration of his capacity to relate himself fully to man and to nature; that Marx's philosophy constitutes a spiritual existentialism in secular language and because of this spiritual quality is opposed to the materialistic practice and thinly disguised materialistic philosophy of our age. Marx's aim, socialism, based on his theory of man, is essentially prophetic Messianism in the language of the nineteenth century.

How can it be, then, that Marx's philosophy is so completely misunderstood and distorted into its opposite? There are several reasons. The first and most obvious one is ignorance. It seems that these are matters which, not being taught at universities and hence not being subjects for examination, are "free" for everybody to think, talk, write about as he pleases, and without any knowledge. There are no properly acknowledged authorities who would insist on respect for the facts, and for truth. Hence everybody feels entitled to talk about Marx without having read him, or at least, without having read enough to get an idea of his very complex, intricate, and subtle system of thought. It did not help matters that Marx's *Economic and Philosophical Manuscripts*, his main philosophical work dealing with his concept of man, of alienation, of emancipation, etc., had not until now been translated into English[2], and hence that some of his ideas were unknown to the English-speaking world.

---

[2] The first English version was published in 1959 in Great Britain by Lawrence and Wishart, Ltd., using a recently published translation by the Foreign Language Publishing House, Moscow. The translation by T. B. Bottomore included in this volume is the first by any Western scholar.

This fact, however, is by no means sufficient to explain the prevailing ignorance, first, because the fact that this work of Marx's had never before been translated into English is in itself as much a symptom as a cause of the ignorance; secondly, because the main trend of Marx's philosophical thought is sufficiently clear in those writings previously published in English to have avoided the falsification which occurred.

Another reason lies in the fact that the Russian Communists appropriated Marx's theory and tried to convince the world that their practice and theory follow his ideas. Although the opposite is true, the West accepted their propagandistic claims and has come to assume that Marx's position corresponds to the Russian view and practice. However, the Russian Communists are not the only ones guilty of misinterpreting Marx. While the Russians' brutal contempt for individual dignity and humanistic values is, indeed, specific for them, the misinterpretation of Marx as the proponent of an economistic-hedonistic materialism has also been shared by many of the anti-Communist and reformist socialists. The reasons are not difficult to see. While Marx's theory was a critique of capitalism, many of his adherents were so deeply imbued with the spirit of capitalism that they interpreted Marx's thought in the economistic and materialistic categories that are prevalent in contemporary capitalism. Indeed, while the Soviet Communists, as well as the reformist socialists, believed they were the enemies of capitalism, they conceived of communism—or socialism —in the spirit of capitalism. For them, socialism is not a society humanly different from capitalism, but rather, a form of capitalism in which the working class has achieved a higher status; it is, as Engels once remarked ironically, "the present-day society without its defects."

So far we have dealt with rational and realistic reasons for the distortion of Marx's theories. But, no doubt, there are also irrational reasons which help to produce this distortion. Soviet Russia has been looked upon as the very incarnation of all evil; hence her ideas have assumed the quality of the devilish. Just as in 1917, within a relatively short time, the Kaiser and the "Huns" were looked upon as the embodiment of evil, and even Mozart's music became part of the devil's territory, so the communists have taken the place of the devil, and their doctrines are not examined objectively. The reason usually given for this hate is the terror which the Stalinists practiced for many years. But there is serious reason to doubt the sincerity of this explanation; the same acts of terror and inhumanity, when practiced by the French in Algiers, by Trujillo in Santo Domingo, by Franco in Spain, do not provoke any similar moral indignation; in fact, hardly any indignation at all. Furthermore, the change from Stalin's system of unbridled terror to Khrushchev's reactionary police state has received insufficient attention, although one would think anyone seriously concerned with human freedom would be aware of and happy with a change which, while by no means sufficient, is a great improvement over Stalin's naked terror. All this gives us cause to wonder whether the indignation against Russia is really rooted in moral and humanitarian feelings, or rather in the fact that a system which has no private property is considered inhuman and threatening.

It is hard to say which of the above-mentioned factors is most responsible for the distortion and misunderstandings of Marx's philosophy. They probably vary in importance with various persons and political groups, and it is unlikely that any one of them is the only responsible factor.

2

MARX'S HISTORICAL MATERIALISM

The first hurdle to be cleared in order to arrive at a proper understanding of Marx's philosophy is the mis-understanding of the concept of *materialism* and *historical materialism*. Those who believe this to be a philosophy claiming that man's material interest, his wish for ever-increasing material gain and comforts, are his main motivation, forget the simple fact that the words "idealism" and "materialism" as used by Marx and all other philosophers have nothing to do with psychic motivations of a higher, spiritual level as against those of a lower and baser kind. In philosophical terminology, "materialism" (or "naturalism") refers to a philosophic view which holds that matter in motion is the fundamental constituent of the universe. In this sense the Greek pre-Socratic philosophers were "materialists," although they were by no means materialists in the above-mentioned sense of the word as a value judgment or ethical principle. By idealism, on the contrary, a philosophy is understood in which it is not the everchanging world of the senses that constitutes reality, but incorporeal essences, or ideas. Plato's system is the first philosophical system to which the name of "idealism" was applied. While Marx was, in the philosophical sense a materialist in ontology, he was not even really interested, in such questions, and hardly ever dealt with them.

However, there are many kinds of materialist and idealist philosophies, and in order to understand Marx's "materialism" we have to go beyond the general definition

8

just given. Marx actually took a firm position *against* a philosophical materialism which was current among many of the most progressive thinkers (especially natural scientists) of his time. This materialism claimed that "the" substratum of all mental and spiritual phenomena was to be found in matter and material processes. In its most vulgar and superficial form, this kind of materialism taught that feelings and ideas are sufficiently explained as results of chemical bodily processes, and "thought is to the brain what urine is to the kidneys."

Marx fought this type of mechanical, "bourgeois" materialism "the abstract materialism of natural science, that excludes history and its process,"[1] and postulated instead what he called in the *Economic and Philosophical Manuscripts* "naturalism or humanism [which] is distinguished from both idealism and materialism, and at the same time constitutes their unifying truth."[2] In fact, Marx never used the terms "historical materialism" or "dialectic materialism"; he did speak of his own "dialectical method" in contrast with that of Hegel and of its "materialistic basis," by which he simply referred to the fundamental conditions of human existence.

This aspect of "materialism," Marx's "materialist method," which distinguishes his view from that of Hegel, involves the study of the real economic and social life of man and of the influence of man's actual way of life on this thinking and feeling. "In direct contrast to German philosophy," Marx wrote, "which descends from heaven to earth, here we ascend from earth to heaven. That is to say, we do not set out from what men imagine, conceive, nor from men as narrated, thought of, or imagined, conceived, in order to arrive at men in the flesh. *We set out*

---

[1] *Capital I*, K. Marx, Charles H. Kerr & Co., Chicago 1906, p. 406.

[2] *Economic and Philosophical Manuscripts*, p. 181.

*from real, active men and on the basis of their real life
process we demonstrate the development of the ideological reflexes and echoes of this life process."*³ Or, as he puts
it in a slightly different way: "Hegel's philosophy of
history is nothing but the philosophical expression of the
Christian-Germanic dogma concerning the contradiction
between spirit and matter, God and the world.... Hegel's
philosophy of history presupposes an abstract or absolute
spirit, which develops in such a way that mankind is only
a mass which carries this spirit, consciously or unconsciously. Hegel assumes that a speculative, esoterical
history precedes and underlies empirical history. The
history of mankind is transformed into the history of the
abstract spirit of mankind, which transcends the real
man."⁴

Marx described his own historical method very succinctly: "The way in which men produce their means of
subsistence depends first of all on the nature of the
actual means they find in existence and have to reproduce. This mode of production must not be considered
simply as being the reproduction of the physical existence of the individuals. Rather, it is a definite form of
activity of these individuals, a definite form of expressing
their life, a definite *mode of life* on their part. As individuals express their life, so they are. What they are, therefore, coincides with their production, both with *what*
they produce and with *how* they produce. The nature of
individuals thus depends on the material conditions
determining their production."⁵

---

³ *German Ideology*, K. Marx and F. Engels, ed. with an
introduction by R. Pascal, New York, International Publishers,
Inc., 1939, p. 14. [My italics—E.F.]

⁴ K. Marx and F. Engels, *Die Heilige Familie* (The Holy
Family), 1845. [My translation—E.F.]

⁵ *German Ideology*, l.c. p. 7.

Marx made the difference between historical materialism and contemporary materialism very clear in his thesis on Feuerbach: "The chief defect of all materialism up to now (including Feuerbach's) is that the object, reality, what we apprehend through our senses, is understood only in the form of the *object* or contemplation (Anschauung); but not as *sensuous human activity*, as *practice*; not subjectively. Hence in opposition to materialism, the active side was developed abstractly by idealism—which of course does not know real sensuous activity as such. Feuerbach wants sensuous objects really distinguished from the objects of thought; but he does not understand human activity itself as *objective* activity."[6] Marx—like Hegel—looks at an object in its movement, in its becoming, and not as a static "object," which can be explained by discovering the physical "cause" of it. In contrast to Hegel, Marx studies man and history by beginning with the real man and the economic and social conditions under which he must live, and not primarily with his ideas. Marx was as far from bourgeois materialism as he was from Hegel's idealism—hence he could rightly say that his philosophy is neither idealism nor materialism but a synthesis: humanism and naturalism.

It should be clear by now why the popular idea of the nature of historical materialism is erroneous. The popular view assumes that in Marx's opinion the strongest psychological motive in man is to gain money and to have more material comfort; if this is the main force within man, so continues this "interpretation" of historical materialism, the key to the understanding of history is the material desires of men; hence, the key to the explanation of history is man's belly, and his greed for

---

[6] "Theses on Feuerbach," *German Ideology*, l.c. p. 197.

material satisfaction. The fundamental misunderstanding on which this interpretation rests is the assumption that historical materialism is a psychological theory which deals with man's drives and passions. But, in fact, historical materialism is not at all a *psychological* theory; it claims that *the way man produces determines his thinking and his desires,* and *not* that his main desires are those for maximal material gain. Economy in this context refers not to a psychic drive, but to the mode of production; not to a subjective, psychological, but to an objective, economic-sociological factor. The only quasi-psychological premise in the theory lies in the assumption that man needs food, shelter, etc., hence needs to produce; hence that the mode of production, which depends on a number of objective factors, comes first, as it were, and determines the other spheres of his activities. The objectively given conditions which determine the mode of production and hence social organization, determine man, his ideas as well as his interests. In fact, the idea that "institutions form men," as Montesquieu put it, was an old insight; what was new in Marx was his detailed analysis of institutions as being rooted in the mode of production and the productive forces underlying it. Certain economic conditions, like those of capitalism, produce as a chief incentive the desire for money and property; other economic conditions can produce exactly the opposite desires, like those of asceticism and contempt for earthly riches, as we find them in many Eastern cultures and in the early stages of capitalism.[7] The passion for money and property, according to Marx,

---

[7] "While the capitalist of the classical type brands individual consumption as a vice against his function, of abstinence from accumulating, the modernized capitalist is capable of looking upon accumulation as abstinence from pleasure." (*Capital I*, l.c. p. 650).

is just as much economically conditioned as the opposite passions.[8]

Marx's "materialistic" or "economic" interpretation of history has nothing whatsoever to do with an alleged "materialistic" or "economic" striving as the most fundamental drive in man. It does mean that man, the real and total man, the "real living individuals"—not the ideas produced by these "individuals" — are the subject matter of history and of the understanding of its laws. Marx's interpretation of history could be called an anthropological interpretation of history, if one wanted to avoid the ambiguities of the words "materialistic" and "economic"; it is the understanding of history based on the fact that men are "the authors *and* actors of their history."[9, 10]

In fact, it is one of the great differences between Marx and most writers of the eighteenth and nineteenth centuries that he does *not* consider capitalism to be the outcome of human nature and the motivation of man in capitalism to be the universal motivation within man.

---

[8] I have tried to clarify this problem in a paper "Über Aufgabe und Methode einer Analytischen Sozialpsychologie" (On the Method and Aim of Analytic Social Psychology), Zeitschrift für Sozialforschung, Vol. I, C.L. Hirschfeld, Leipzig, 1932, p. 28-54.

[9] *Marx-Engels Gesamtausgabe,* Marx-Engels Verlag, ed. D. Rjazanow, Berlin, 1932. I., 6, p. 179. The abbreviation *MEGA* will be used in all following references.

[10] While revising this manuscript I came across an excellent interpretation of Marx, characterized both by thorough knowledge and genuine penetration, by Leonard Krieger, *The Uses of Marx for History* in Political Science Quarterly, Vol. XXXV, 3. "For Marx," Krieger writes, "the common substance of history was the activity of men — 'men as simultaneously the authors and actors of their own history'— and this activity extended equally to all levels: modes of production, social relations and categories." (p. 362). As to

The absurdity of the view that Marx thought the drive
for maximal profit was the deepest motive in man becomes all the more apparent when one takes into account
that Marx made some very direct statements about human drives. He differentiated between constant or "fixed"
drives "which exist under all circumstances and which
can be changed by social conditions only as far as form
and direction are concerned" and "relative" drives which
"owe their origin only to a certain type of social organization." Marx assumed sex and hunger to fall under the
category of "fixed" drives, but it never occurred to him
to consider the drive for maximal economic gain as a
constant drive.[11]

But it hardly needs such proof from Marx's psychological ideas to show that the popular assumption about
Marx's materialism is utterly wrong. Marx's whole criticism of capitalism is exactly that it has made interest
in money and material gain the main motive in man,
and his concept of socialism is precisely that of a society
in which this material interest would cease to be the
dominant one. This will be even clearer later on when
we discuss Marx's concept of human emancipation and
of freedom in detail.

As I emphasized before, Marx starts out with man,
who makes his own history: "The first premise of all
human history is, of course, the existence of living

---

the alleged "materialistic" character of Marx, Krieger writes:
"What intrigues us about Marx is his capacity to find an
essentially ethical rationale running within and across the
centuries at the very same time that he perceives the diversity and complexity of historical existence." (p. 362) [My
italics—E.F.] Or later (p. 368): "There is no more characteristic feature of Marx's philosophical framework than his
categorical reprobation of economic interest as a distortion
vis-à-vis the whole moral man."
    [11] Cf. *MEGA V*, p. 596.

human individuals. Thus the first fact to be established is the physical organization of these individuals and their consequent relation to the rest of nature. Of course, we cannot here go either into the actual physical nature of man, or into the natural conditions in which man finds himself—geological, orohydrographical, climatic and so on. The writing of history must always set out from these natural bases and their modification in the course of history through the action of man. Men can be distinguished from animals by consciousness, by religion or anything else you like. They themselves begin to *produce* their means of subsistence, a step which is conditioned by their physical organization. By producing their means of subsistence men are indirectly producing their actual material life."[12]

It is very important to understand Marx's fundamental idea: man makes his own history; he is his own creator. As he put it many years later in *Capital:* "And would not such a history be easier to compile since, as Vico says, human history differs from natural history in this, that we have made the former, but not the latter."[13] Man gives birth to himself in the process of history. The essential factor in this process of self-creation of the human race lies in its relationship to nature. Man, at the beginning of his history, is blindly bound or chained to nature. In the process of evolution he transforms his relationship to nature, and hence himself.

Marx has more to say in *Capital* about this dependence on nature: "Those ancient social organisms of production are, as compared with bourgeois society, extremely simple and transparent. But they are founded either on the immature development of man individually,

---

[12] *German Ideology,* l.c. p. 7.
[13] *Capital I,* l.c. p. 406.

who has not yet severed the umbilical cord that unites him with his fellow men in a primitive tribal community, or upon direct relations of subjection. They can arise and exist only when the development of the productive power of labor has not risen beyond a low stage, and when, therefore, the social relations within the sphere of material life, between man and man, and between man and nature, are correspondingly narrow. This narrowness is reflected in the ancient worship of Nature, and in the other elements of the popular religions. The religious reflex of the real world can, in any case, only then finally vanish when the practical relations of everyday life offer to man none but perfectly intelligible and reasonable relations with regard to his fellow men and to nature. The life-process of society, which is based on the process of material production, does not strip off its mystical veil until it is treated as production by freely associated men, and is consciously regulated by them in accordance with a settled plan. This, however, demands for society a certain material groundwork or set of conditions of existence which in their turn are the spontaneous product of a long and painful process of development."[14]

In this statement Marx speaks of an element which has a central role in his theory: *labor*. Labor is the factor which meditates between man and nature; labor is man's effort to regulate his metabolism with nature. Labor is the expression of human life and through labor man's relationship to nature is changed, hence through labor man changes himself. More about his concept of labor will be said later on.

I will conclude this section by quoting Marx's most

---

[14] *Capital I*, l.c. p. 91-2.

complete formulation of the concept of historical materialism, written in 1859:

"The general result at which I arrived and which, once won, served as a guiding thread for my studies, can be briefly formulated as follows: in the social production of their life, men enter into definite relations that are indispensable and independent of their will, relations of production which correspond to a definite stage of development of their material productive forces. The sum total of these relations of production constitutes the economic structure of society, the real foundation, on which rises a legal and political superstructure and to which correspond definite forms of social consciousness. The mode of production of material life conditions the social, political and intellectual life process in general. It is not the consciousness of men that determines their social being, but, on the contrary, their social being that determines their consciousness. At a certain stage of their development, the material productive forces of society come in conflict with the existing relations of production, or—what is but a legal expression for the same thing—with the property relations within which they have been at work hitherto. From forms of development of the productive forces these relations turn into their fetters. Then begins an epoch of social revolution. With the change of the economic foundations the entire immense superstructure is more or less rapidly transformed. In considering such transformations a distinction should always be made between the material transformation of the economic conditions of production, which can be determined with the precision of natural science, and the legal, political, religious, esthetic or philosophic—in short, ideological forms in which men become conscious of this conflict and fight it out. Just as our opinion of an individual is not based on what he thinks of himself, so we cannot judge of such a period of transformation by its own consciousness; on the contrary, this consciousness must be explained rather from the contradictions of material life, from the existing conflict between the social productive forces and the relations of production. No social order ever perishes before all the productive forces for which there is room in it have developed; and new, higher relations of production never appear before the material conditions of their existence have matured in the womb of the old society itself. Therefore mankind always sets itself only such tasks as it can solve; since, looking at the matter more closely, it will always be found that the task itself arises only when the material conditions for its solution already exist or are at least in the process of formation. In broad outlines Asiatic, ancient, feudal, and modern bourgeois modes of production can be designated as progressive epochs in the economic formation of society. The bourgeois relations of production are the last antagonistic form of the social process of production—antagonistic not in the sense of individual antagonism, but of one arising from the social conditions of life of the individual; at the same time the productive forces developing in the womb of bourgeois society create the material conditions for the solution of that antagonism. This social formation brings, therefore, the prehistory of human society to a close."[15]

It will be useful again to underscore and elaborate on some specific notions in this theory. First of all, Marx's concept of historical change. Change is due to the contradiction between the productive forces (and

------

[15] "*Preface* to a Contribution to a Critique of Political Economy," Marx, Engels, *Selected Works*, Vol. I, Foreign Languages Publishing House, Moscow, 1955, p. 362-4.

other objectively given conditions) and the existing social organization. When a mode of production or social organization hampers, rather than furthers, the given productive forces, a society, if it is not to collapse, will choose such forms of production as fit the new set of productive forces and develop them. The evolution of man, in all history, is characterized by man's struggle with nature. At one point of history (and according to Marx in the near future), man will have developed the productive sources of nature to such an extent that the antagonism between man and nature can be eventually solved. At this point "the prehistory of man" will come to a close and truly human history will begin.

3

THE PROBLEM OF CONSCIOUSNESS, SOCIAL STRUCTURE AND THE USE OF FORCE

A problem of the greatest importance is raised in the passage just quoted, that of human consciousness. The crucial statement is: "It is not consciousness of men that determines their being, but, on the contrary, their social being that determines their consciousness." Marx gave a fuller statement with regard to the problem of consciousness in *German Ideology:*

"The fact is, therefore, that definite individuals who are productively active in a definite way enter into these definite social and political relations. Empirical observations must in each separate instance bring out empirically, and without any mystification and speculation, the connection of the social and political structure with production. The social structure and the State are continually evolving out of the life-process of definite individuals, but of individuals, not as they may appear in their own or other people's imagination, but as they really are; i.e., as they are effective, produce materially, and are active under definite material limits, presuppositions and conditions independent of their will.

"The production of ideas, of conceptions, of consciousness, is at first directly interwoven with the material activity and the material intercourse of men, the language of real life. Conceiving, thinking, the mental intercourse of men, appear at this stage as the direct afflux from their material behavior. The same applies to mental production as expressed in the language of the politics, laws, morality, religion, metaphysics of a people. Men are the producers of their conceptions, ideas, etc.— real, active men, as they are conditioned by the definite development of their productive forces and of the intercourse corresponding to these, up to its furthest forms. Consciousness can never be anything else than conscious existence, and the existence of men in their actual life-process. If in all ideology men and their circumstances appear upside down as in a *camera obscura*,* this phenomenon arises just as much from their historical life-process as the inversion of objects on the retina does from their physical life-process."[1]

In the first place, it should be noted that Marx, like Spinoza and later Freud, believed that most of what men

---

* An instrument perfected in the late Middle Ages, to throw, by means of mirrors, an image of a scene on a plane surface. It was widely used by artists to establish the correct proportions of a natural object or scene. The image appeared on the paper inverted, though the later use of a lens corrected this.

[1] *German Ideology*, l.c. p. 13-4.

consciously think is "false" consciousness, is ideology and rationalization; that the true mainsprings of man's actions are unconscious to him. According to Freud, they are rooted in man's libidinal strivings; according to Marx, they are rooted in the whole social organization of man which directs his consciousness in certain directions and blocks him from being aware of certain facts and experiences.[2]

It is important to recognize that this theory does not pretend that ideas or ideals are not real or not potent. Marx speaks of awareness, not of ideals. It is exactly the blindness of man's conscious thought which prevents him from being aware of his true human needs, and of ideals which are rooted in them. Only if false consciousness is transformed into true consciousness, that is, only if we are aware of reality, rather than distorting it by

---

[2] Cf. my article in Suzuki, Fromm, de Martino, *Zen Buddhism and Psychoanalysis*, Harper and Brothers, New York, 1960. Cf. also Marx's statement: "Language is as old as consciousness, language is practical consciousness, as it exists for other men, and for that reason is really beginning to exist for me personally as well; for language, like consciousness, only arises from the need, the necessity of intercourse with other men. Where there exists a relationship, it exists for me: the animal has no 'relations' with anything, cannot have any. For the animal, its relation to others does not exist as a relation. Consciousness is therefore from the very beginning a social product, and remains so as long as men exist at all. Consciousness is at first, of course, merely consciousness concerning the immediate sensuous environment and consciousness of the limited connection with other persons and things outside the individual who is growing self-conscious. At the same time it is consciousness of nature, which first appears to men as a completely alien, all-powerful and unassailable force, with which men's relations are purely animal and by which they are overawed like beasts; it is thus a purely animal consciousness of nature (natural religion)."—*German Ideology*, l.c. p. 19.

rationalizations and fictions, can we also become aware
of our real and true human needs.

It should also be noted that for Marx science itself
and all powers inherent in man are part of the productive forces which interact with the forces of nature.
Even as far as the influence of ideas on human evolution is concerned, Marx was by no means as oblivious to
their power as the popular interpretation of his work
makes it appear. His argument was not against ideas, but
against ideas which were not rooted in the human and
social reality, which were not, to use Hegel's term, "a
real possibility." Most of all, he never forgot that not
only do circumstances make man; man also makes circumstances. The following passage should make clear
how erroneous it is to interpret Marx as if he, like many
philosophers of the enlightenment and many sociologists
of today, gave man a passive role in the historical process, as if he saw him as the passive object of circumstances:

"The materialistic doctrine [in contrast to Marx's
view] concerning the changing of circumstances and
education *forgets that circumstances are changed by
men and that the educator himself must be educated.*
This doctrine has therefore to divide society into two
parts, one of which is superior to society [as a whole].

"The coincidence of the changing of circumstances
and of human activity or self-changing can only be
comprehended and rationally understood as *revolutionary practice.*"[3]

---

[3] *German Ideology,* l.c. p. 197-8 [My italics—E.F.] Cf. also
Engels' famous letter to Mehring (July 14, 1893) in which
he states that Marx and he "had neglected [by emphasizing
the formal aspects of the relationship between the socio-
economic structure and ideology to study] *the manner and
mode of how ideas come into being.*"

The last concept, that of "revolutionary practice", leads us to one of the most disputed concepts in Marx's philosophy, that of *force*. First of all, it should be noted how peculiar it is that the Western democracies should feel such indignation about a theory claiming that society can be transformed by the forceful seizure of political power. The idea of political revolution by force is not at all a Marxist idea; it has been the idea of bourgeois society during the last three hundred years. Western democracy is the daughter of the great English, French and American revolutions; the Russian revolution of February, 1917, and the German revolution of 1918 were warmly greeted by the West, despite the fact that they used force. It is clear that indignation against the use of force, as it exists in the Western world today, depends on who uses force, and against whom. Every war is based on force; even democratic government is based on the principle of force, which permits the majority to use force against a minority, if it is necessary for the continuation of the status quo. Indignation against force is authentic only from a pacifist standpoint, which holds that force is either absolutely wrong, or that aside from the case of the most immediate defense its use never leads to a change for the better.

However, it is not sufficient to show that Marx's idea of forceful revolution (from which he excluded as possibilities England and the United States) was in the middle-class tradition; it must be emphasized that Marx's theory constituted an important improvement over the middle-class view, an improvement rooted in his whole theory of history.

Marx saw that political force cannot produce anything for which there has been no preparation in the social and political process. Hence that force, if at all necessary, can give, so to speak, only the last push to a development which has virtually already taken place, but it can never produce anything truly new. "Force," he said, "is the midwife of every old society pregnant with a new one."[4] It is exactly one of his great insights that Marx transcends the traditional middle-class concept—he did *not* believe in the creative power of force, in the idea that political force of itself could create a new social order. For this reason, force, for Marx, could have at most only a transitory significance, never the role of a permanent element in the transformation of society.

4

THE NATURE OF MAN

1. *The Concept of Human Nature*

Marx did not believe, as do many contemporary sociologists and psychologists, that there is no such thing as the nature of man; that man at birth is like a blank sheet of paper, on which the culture writes its text. Quite in contrast to this sociological relativism, Marx started out with the idea that man *qua man* is a recognizable and ascertainable entity; that man can be defined as man not only biologically, anatomically and physiologically, but also psychologically.

Of course, Marx was never tempted to assume that "human nature" was identical with that particular expression of human nature prevalent in his own society. In arguing against Bentham, Marx said: "To know what is useful for a dog, one must study dog nature. This nature itself is not to be deduced from the principle of utility.

---

[4] *Capital I*, l.c., p. 824.

Applying this to man, he that would criticize all human acts, movements, relations, etc., by the principle of utility, *must first deal with human nature in general, and then with human nature as modified in each historical epoch.*"[1] It must be noted that this concept of human nature is not, for Marx—as it was not either for Hegel—an abstraction. It is the *essence* of man—in contrast to the various forms of his historical *existence*—and, as Marx said, "the essence of man is no abstraction inherent in each separate individual."[2] It must also be stated that this sentence from *Capital*, written by the "old Marx," shows the continuity of the concept of man's essence (Wesen) which the young Marx wrote about in the *Economic and Philosophical Manuscripts*. He no longer used the *term* "essence" later on, as being abstract and unhistorical, but he clearly retained the notion of this essence in a more historical version, in the differentiation between "human nature in general" and "human nature as modified" with each historical period.

In line with this distinction between a general human nature and the specific expression of human nature in each culture, Marx distinguishes, as we have already mentioned above, two types of human drives and appetites: the *constant* or fixed ones, such as hunger and the sexual urge, which are an integral part of human nature, and which can be changed only in their form and the direction they take in various cultures, and the *"relative" appetites,* which are not an integral part of human nature but which "owe their origin to certain social structures and certain conditions of production and communication."[3] Marx gives as an example the needs produced

---

[1] *Capital I*, l.c., p. 668.
[2] *German Ideology,* l.c., p. 198.
[3] "Heilige Familie," *MEGA V,* p. 359. [My translation—E.F.]

by the capitalistic structure of society. "The need for money," he wrote in the *Economic and Philosophical Manuscripts*, "is therefore the real need created by the modern economy, and the only need which it creates. . . . This is shown subjectively, partly in the fact that the expansion of production and of needs becomes an *ingenious* and always *calculating* subservience to inhuman, depraved, unnatural, and *imaginary* appetites."[4]

Man's potential, for Marx, is a given potential; man is, as it were, the human raw material which, as such, cannot be changed, just as the brain structure has remained the same since the dawn of history. Yet, man *does* change in the course of history; he develops himself; he transforms himself, he is the product of history; since *he* makes his history, he is his own product. History is the history of man's self-realization; it is nothing but the self-creation of man through the process of his work and his production: "the *whole of what is called world history* is nothing but the creation of man by human labor, and the emergence of nature for man; he therefore has the evident and irrefutable proof of his *self-creation*, of his own *origins*."[5]

2. *Man's self-activity*

Marx's concept of man is rooted in Hegel's thinking. Hegel begins with the insight that appearance and essence do not coincide. The task of the dialectical thinker is "to distinguish the essential from the apparent process of reality, and to grasp their relations."[6] Or, to put it differently, it is the problem of the relationship between es-

---

[4] *E.P. MSS.*, p. 141.

[5] *E.P. MSS.* p. 139.

[6] H. Marcuse, *Reason and Revolution*, Oxford University Press, New York, 1941, p. 146.

sence and existence. In the process of existence, the essence is realized, and at the same time, existing means a
return to the essence. "The world is an estranged and un-
true world so long as man does not destroy its dead objectivity and recognize himself and his own life 'behind'
the fixed form of things and laws. When he finally wins
this *self-consciousness*, he is on his way not only to the
truth of himself, but also of his world. And with the recognition goes the doing. He will try to put this truth into
action, and *make* the world what it *essentially* is, namely,
the fulfillment of man's self-consciousness."[7] For Hegel,
knowledge is not obtained in the position of the subject-
object split, in which the object is grasped as something
separated from and opposed to the thinker. In order to
know the world, man has to *make the world his own.*
Man and things are in a constant transition from one
suchness into another; hence "a thing is for itself only
when it has posited (*gesetzt*) all its determinates and
made them moments of its self-realization, and is thus,
in all changing conditions, always 'returning to itself'."[8]
In this process "entering into itself becomes essence."
This essence, the unity of being, the identity throughout
change is, according to Hegel, a process in which "everything copes with its inherent contradictions and unfolds
itself as a result." "The essence is thus as much historical
as ontological. The essential potentialities of things realize themselves in the same comprehensive process that
establishes their existence. The essence can 'achieve' its
existence when the potentialities of things have ripened
in and through the conditions of reality. Hegel describes
this process as the transition to actuality."[9] In contrast to

---

[7] Marcuse, l.c., p. 113.

[8] Marcuse, l.c., p. 142. Cf. Hegel, *Science and Logic,*
Vol. I, p. 404.

[9] Marcuse, l.c., p. 149.

positivism, for Hegel "facts are facts only if related to that which is not yet fact and yet manifests itself in the given facts as a real possibility. Or, facts are what they are only as moments in a process that leads beyond them to that which is not yet fulfilled in fact."[10]

The culmination of all of Hegel's thinking is the concept of the potentialities inherent in a thing, of the dialectical process in which they manifest themselves, and the idea that this process is one of active movement of these potentialities. This emphasis on the active process within man is already to be found in the ethical system of Spinoza. For Spinoza, all affects were to be divided into passive affects (passions), through which man suffers and does not have an adequate idea of reality, and into active affects (actions) (generosity and fortitude) in which man is free and productive. Goethe, who like Hegel was influenced by Spinoza in many ways, developed the idea of man's productivity into a central point of his philosophical thinking. For him all decaying cultures are characterized by the tendency for pure subjectivity, while all progressive periods try to grasp the world as it is, by one's own subjectivity, but not separate from it.[11] He gives the example of the poet: "as long as he expresses only these few subjective sentences, he can not yet be called a poet, but as soon as he knows *how to appropriate the world for himself, and to express it*, he is a poet. Then he is inexhaustible, and can be ever new, while his purely subjective nature has exhausted itself soon and ceases to have anything to say."[12] "Man", says Goethe, "knows himself only inasmuch as he knows the

---

[10] Marcuse, l.c. p. 152.

[11] Cf. Goethe's conversation with Eckermann, January 29, 1826.

[12] Goethe, conversation with Eckermann on January 29, 1826. [My italics, and translation—E.F.]

world; he knows the world only within himself and he is aware of himself only within the world. Each new object truly recognized, opens up a new organ within ourselves."[13] Goethe gave the most poetic and powerful expression to the idea of human productivity in his *Faust*. Neither possession, nor power, nor sensuous satisfaction, Faust teaches, can fulfill man's desire for meaning in his life; he remains in all this separate from the whole, hence unhappy. Only in being productively active can man make sense of his life, and while he thus enjoys life, he is not greedily holding on to it. He has given up the greed for *having*, and is fulfilled by *being;* he is filled because he is empty; he *is* much, because he *has* little.[14] Hegel gave the most systematic and profound expression to the idea of the productive man, of the individual who is *he*, inasmuch as he is not passive-receptive, but actively related to the world; who is an individual only in this process of grasping the world productively, and thus making it his own. He expressed the idea quite poetically by saying that the subject wanting to bring a content to realization does so by "translating itself from the night of possibility into the day of actuality." For Hegel the development of all individual powers, capacities and potentialities is possible only by continuous action, never by sheer contemplation or receptivity. For Spinoza, Goethe, Hegel, as well as for Marx, man is alive only inasmuch as he is productive, inasmuch as he grasps the world outside of himself in the act of expressing his own specific human powers, and of grasping the world with these powers

---

[13] Quoted by K. Löwith, *Von Hegel zu Nietzsche,* W. Kohlhammer Verlag, Stuttgart, 1941, p. 24. [My translation—E.F.]

[14] Cf. the detailed description of the productive character orientation in E. Fromm, *Man for Himself,* Rinehart & Co. New York, 1947.

Inasmuch as man is not productive, inasmuch as he is receptive and passive, he is nothing, he is dead. In this productive process, man realizes his own essence, he returns to his own essence, which in theological language is nothing other than his return to God.

For Marx man is characterized by the "principle of movement," and it is significant that he quotes the great mystic Jacob Boehme in connection with this point.[15] The principle of movement must not be understood mechanically but as a drive, creative vitality, energy; human passion for Marx "is the essential power of man striving energetically for its object."

The concept of productivity as against that of receptivity can be understood more easily when we read how Marx applied it to the phenomenon of *love*. "Let us assume *man* to be *man*," he wrote, "and his relation to the world to be a human one. Then love can only be exchanged for love, trust for trust, etc. If you wish to influence other people you must be a person who really has a stimulating and encouraging effect upon others. Every one of your relations to man and to nature must be a *specific expression* corresponding to the object of your will, of your *real individual life*. If you love without evoking love in return, i.e., if you are not able, by the *manifestation* of yourself as a loving person, to make yourself a *beloved person*, then your love is impotent and a misfortune."[16] Marx expressed also very specifically the central significance of love between man and woman as the immediate relationship of human being to human being. Arguing against a crude communism which proposed

---

[15] Cf. H. Popitz, *"Der entfremdete Mensch"* (The Alienated Man) Verlag für Recht und Gesellschaft, A.G., Basel, p. 119.

[16] *E.P. MSS.*, p. 168.

the communalization of all sexual relation, Marx wrote: "In the relationship with *woman*, as the prey and the handmaid of communal lust, is expressed the infinite degradation in which man exists for himself; for the secret of this relationship finds its *unequivocal*, incontestable, *open* and revealed expression in the relation of man to woman and in the way in which the *direct* and *natural* species relationship is conceived. The immediate, natural and necessary relation of human being to human being is also the *relation* of *man* to *woman*. In this *natural* species relationship man's relation to nature is directly his relation to man, and his relation to man is directly his relation to nature, to his own *natural* function. Thus, in this relation is *sensuously revealed*, reduced to an observable *fact*, the extent to which human nature has become nature for man and to which nature has become human nature for him. From this relationship man's whole level of development can be assessed. It follows from the character of this relationship how far *man* has become, and has understood himself as, a *species-being*, a *human being*. The relation of man to woman is the *most natural* relation of human being to human being. It indicates, therefore, how far man's *natural* behavior has become *human*, and how far his *human* essence has become a *natural* essence for him, how far his *human nature* has become *nature* for him. It also shows how far man's *needs* have become *human* needs, and consequently how far the other person, as a person, has become one of his needs, and to what extent he is in his individual existence at the same time a social being."[17]

It is of the utmost importance for the understanding of Marx's concept of activity to understand his idea about the relationship between subject and object. Man's

---

[17] *E.P. MSS.*, pp. 126-7.

senses, as far as they are crude animal senses, have only a restricted meaning. "For a starving man the human form of food does not exist, but only its abstract character as food. It could just as well exist in the most crude form, and it is impossible to say in what way this feeding activity would differ from that of animals. The needy man, burdened with cares, has no appreciation of the most beautiful spectacle."[18] The senses which man has, so to speak, naturally, need to be formed by the objects outside of them. Any object can only be confirmation of one of my own faculties. "For it is not only the five senses but also the so-called spiritual senses, the practical senses (desiring, loving, etc.) in brief, human sensibility and the human character of the senses *which can only come into being* through the existence of *its* object, through humanized nature."[19] The objects, for Marx, "confirm and realize his [man's] individuality . . . *The manner in which* these objects become his own depends upon the *nature of the object* and the nature of the corresponding faculty; . . . The *distinctive character* of each faculty is precisely its *characteristic* essence and thus also the characteristic mode of its objectification, of its *objectively real*, living *being*. It is therefore not only in thought, but through *all* the senses that man is affirmed in the objective world."[20]

By relating himself to the objective world, through his powers, the world outside becomes real to man, and in fact it is only "love" which makes man truly believe in the reality of the objective world outside himself.[21] Subject and object cannot be separated. "The eye has become a *human* eye when its *object* has become a

---

[18] *E.P. MSS.*, p. 134.
[19] *E.P. MSS.*, p. 134.
[20] *E.P. MSS.*, p. 133.
[21] *MEGA, Vol. III*, p. 191.

human, social object, created by man and destined for him ... They [the senses] relate themselves to the thing for the sake of the thing, but the thing itself is an *objective human* relation to itself and to man, and vice versa. Need and enjoyment have thus lost their *egoistic* character, and nature has lost its mere *utility* by the fact that its utilization has become *human* utilization. (In effect, I can only relate myself in a human way to a thing when the thing is related in a human way to man.)"[22]

For Marx, "*Communism is the positive* abolition of *private property,*[23] of *human self-alienation,* and thus the real *appropriation* of human nature through and for man. It is, therefore, the return of man himself as a *social,* i. e., really human being, a complete and conscious return which assimilates all the wealth of pre-

---

[22] *E.P. MSS.,* p. 132. This last statement is one which is almost literally the same as has been made in Zen Buddhist thinking, as well as by Goethe. In fact, the thinking of Goethe, Hegel and Marx is closely related to the thinking of Zen. What is common to them is the idea that man overcomes the subject-object split; the object is an object, yet it ceases to be an object, and in this new approach man becomes one with the object, although he and it remain two. Man, in relating himself to the objective world humanly, overcomes self-alienation.

[23] By "private property" as used here and in other statements, Marx never refers to the private property of things for use (such as a house, a table, etc.) Marx refers to the property of the "propertied classes," that is, of the capitalist who, because he owns the means of production, can hire the property-less individual to work for him, under conditions the latter is forced to accept. "Private property" in Marx's usage, then, always refers to private *property within capitalist class society* and thus is a *social and historical category;* the term does not refer to things for use, as for instance, in a socialist society.

vious development. Communism as a fully developed naturalism is humanism and as a fully developed humanism is naturalism. It is the *definitive* resolution of the antagonism between man and nature, and between man and man. It is the true solution of the conflict between existence and essence, between objectification and self-affirmation, between freedom and necessity, between individual and species. It is the solution of the riddle of history and knows itself to be this solution."[24] This active relationship to the objective world, Marx calls "productive life." "It is life creating life. In the type of life activity resides the whole character of a species, its species-character; and free, conscious activity is the species-character of human beings."[25] What Marx means by "species-character" is the essence of man; it is that which is universally human, and which is realized in the process of history by man through his productive activity.

From this concept of human self-realization, Marx arrives at a new concept of wealth and poverty, which is different from wealth and poverty in political economy. "It will be seen from this," says Marx, "how, in place of the *wealth* and *poverty* of political economy, we have the *wealthy* man and the plenitude of *human* need. The wealthy man is at the same time one who needs a complex of human manifestations of life, and whose own self-realization exists as an inner necessity, a *need*. Not only the *wealth* but also the *poverty* of man acquires, in a socialist perspective, a *human* and thus a social meaning. Poverty is the passive bond which leads man to experience a need for the greatest wealth, the *other* person. The sway of the objective entity within me; the sensuous outbreak of my life-activity, is the passion which

---

[24] *E.P. MSS.*, p. 127.
[25] *E.P. MSS.*, p. 101.

here becomes the *activity* of my being."[26] The same idea was expressed by Marx some years earlier: "The existence of what I truly love [specifically he refers here to freedom of the press] is felt by me as a necessity, as a need, without which my essence cannot be fulfilled, satisfied, complete."[27]

"Just as society at its beginnings finds, through the development of *private property* with its wealth and poverty (both intellectual and material), the materials necessary for this *cultural development,* so the fully constituted society produces man in all the plenitude of his being, the wealthy man endowed with all the senses, as an enduring reality. It is only in a social context that subjectivism and objectivism, spiritualism and materialism, activity and passivity, cease to be antinomies and thus cease to exist as such antinomies. The resolution of the *theoretical* contradictions is possible *only* through *practical* means, only through the practical energy of man. Their resolution is not by any means, therefore, only a problem of knowledge, but is a *real* problem of life which philosophy was unable to solve precisely because it saw there a purely theoretical problem."[28]

Corresponding to his concept of the wealthy man is Marx's view of the difference between the sense of *having* and the sense of *being.* "Private property," he says, "has made us so stupid and partial that an object is only *ours* when we have it, when it exists for us as capital or

---

[26] *E.P. MSS.,* pp. 137-8. This dialectic concept of the wealthy man as being the poor man in need of others is, in many ways, similar to the concept of poverty expressed by Meister Eckhart, in his sermon "Blessed Are the Poor," (Meister Eckhart, transl. by R.B. Blakney, Harper and Bros., New York, 1941).

[27] *MEGA I,* i a p. 184.

[28] *E.P. MSS.,* pp. 134-5.

when it is directly eaten, drunk, worn, inhabited, etc., in short, *utilized* in some way. Although private property itself only conceives these various forms of possession as *means of life*, and the life for which they serve as means is the *life* of *private property*—labor and creation of capital. Thus _all_ the physical and intellectual senses have been replaced by the simple alienation of *all* these senses; the sense of *having*. The human being had to be reduced to this absolute poverty in order to be able to give birth to all his inner wealth."[29]

Marx recognized that the science of capitalistic economy, despite its worldly and pleasure-seeking appearance, "is a truly moral science, the most moral of all sciences. Its principal thesis is the renunciation of life and of human needs. The less you eat, drink, buy books, go to the theatre or to balls, or to the public house [*Br.*, pub], and the less you think, love, theorize, sing, paint, fence, etc., the more you will be able to save and the *greater* will become your treasure which neither moth nor rust will corrupt—your *capital*. The less you *are*, the less you express your life, the more you *have*, the greater is your *alienated* life and the greater is the saving of your alienated being. Everything which the economist takes from you in the way of life and humanity, he restores to you in the form of *money* and *wealth*. And everything which you are unable to do, your money can do for you; it can eat, drink, go to the ball and to the theatre. It can acquire art, learning, historical treasures, political power; and it can travel. It *can* appropriate all these things for you, can purchase everything; it is the true *opulence*. But although it can do all this, it only *desires* to create itself, and to buy itself, for everything

---

[29] *E.P. MSS.*, p. 132.

else is subservient to it. When one owns the master, one also owns the servant, and one has no need of the master's servant. Thus all passions and activities must be submerged in *avarice*. The worker must have just what is necessary for him to want to live, and he must want to live only in order to have this."[30]

The aim of society, for Marx, is not the production of useful things as an aim in itself. One easily forgets, he says, "that the production of too many useful things results in too many *useless* people."[31] The contradictions between prodigality and thrift, luxury and abstinence, wealth and poverty, are only apparent because the truth is that all these antinomies are equivalent. It is particularly important to understand this position of Marx today, when both the Communist, and most of the Socialist parties, with some notable exceptions like the Indian, also Burmese and a number of European and American socialists, have accepted the principle which underlies all capitalist systems, namely, that maximum production and consumption are the unquestionable goals of society. One must of course not confuse the aim of overcoming the abysmal poverty which interferes with a dignified life, with the aim of an ever-increasing consumption, which has become the supreme value for both Capitalism and Krushchevism. Marx's position was quite clearly on the side of the conquest of poverty, and equally against consumption as a supreme end.

Independence and *freedom*, for Marx, are based on the act of self-creation. "A being does not regard himself as independent unless he is his own master, and he is only his own master when he owes his existence to him-

---

[30] *E.P. MSS.*, pp. 144-5.
[31] *E.P. MSS.*, p. 145.

self. A man who lives by the favor of another considers himself a dependent being. But I live completely by another person's favor when I owe to him not only the continuance of my life but also *its creation*; when he is its *source*. My life has necessarily such a cause outside itself if it is not my own creation."[32] Or, as Marx put it, man is independent only ". . . if he affirms his individuality as a total man in each of his relations to the world, seeing, hearing, smelling, tasting, feeling, thinking, willing, loving—in short, if he affirms and expresses all organs of his individuality," if he is not only free *from* but also free *to*.

For Marx the aim of socialism was the emancipation of man, and the emancipation of man was the same as his self-realization in the process of productive relatedness and oneness with man and nature. The aim of socialism was the development of the individual personality. What Marx would have thought of a system such as Soviet communism he expressed very clearly in a statement of what he called "crude communism," and which referred to certain communist ideas and practices of his time. This crude communism "appears in a double form; the domination of material property looms so large that it aims to destroy everything which is incapable of being possessed by everyone as private property. It wishes to eliminate talent, etc., by *force*. Immediate physical possession seems to it the unique goal of life and existence. The role of *worker* is not abolished but is extended to all men. The relation of private property remains the relation of the community to the world of things. Finally, this tendency to oppose general private property to private property is expressed in an animal form; *marriage* (which is incontestably a form of *exclusive private prop-*

---

[32] *E.P. MSS.*, p. 138.

erty) is contrasted with the community of women,[33] in which women become communal and common property. One may say that this idea of the *community of women* is the *open secret* of this entirely crude and unreflective communism. Just as women are to pass from marriage to universal prostitution, so the whole world of wealth (i.e., the objective being of man) is to pass to the relation of universal prostitution with the community. This communism, which negates the *personality* of man in every sphere, is only the logical expression of private property, which *is* this negation. Universal *envy* setting itself up as a power is only a camouflaged form of cupidity which reestablishes itself and satisfies itself in a different way. The thoughts of every individual private property are *at least* directed against any *wealthier* private property, in the form of envy and the desire to reduce everything to a common level; so that this envy and levelling in fact constitute the essence of competition. Crude communism is only the culmination of such envy and levelling-down on the basis of a *preconceived* minimum. How little this abolition of private property represents a genuine appropriation is shown by the abstract negation of the whole world of culture and civilization, and the regression to the *unnatural* simplicity of the poor and wantless individual who has not only not surpassed private property but has not yet even attained to it. The community is only a community of *work* and of *equality of wages* paid out by the communal capital, by the *community* as universal capitalist. The two sides of the relation are raised to a *supposed* universality; *labor* as a condition in which everyone is placed, and *capital*

---

[33] Marx refers here to speculations among certain eccentric communist thinkers of his time who thought that if everything is common property women should be too.

as the acknowledged universality and power of the community."[34]

Marx's whole concept of the self-realization of man can be fully understood only in connection with his concept of work. First of all, it must be noted that labor and capital were not at all for Marx only economic categories; they were anthropological categories, imbued with a value judgment which is rooted in his humanistic position. Capital, which is that which is accumulated, represents the past; labor, on the other hand is, or ought to be when it is free, the expression of life. "In bourgeois society," says Marx in the *Communist Manifesto*," . . . the past dominates the present. In communist society the present dominates the past. In bourgeois society, capital is independent and has individuality, while the living person is dependent and has no individuality." Here again, Marx follows the thought of Hegel, who understood labor as the "act of man's self-creation." Labor, to Marx, is an activity, not a commodity. Marx originally called man's function "self-activity," not labor, and spoke of the "abolition of labor" as the aim of socialism. Later, when he differentiated between free and alienated labor, he used the term "emancipation of labor."

"Labor is, in the first place, a process in which both man and nature participate, and in which man of his own accord starts, regulates, and controls the material reactions between himself and nature. He opposes himself to nature as one of her own forces, setting in motion arms and legs, head and hands, the natural forces of his body, in order to appropriate nature's productions in a form adapted to his own wants. By thus acting on the external world and changing it, he at the same time changes his own nature. He develops his slumbering

---

[34] *E.P. MSS.*, pp. 124-6.

powers and compels them to act in obedience to his sway. We are not now dealing with those primitive instinctive forms of labor that remind us of the mere animal. An immeasurable interval of time separates the state of things in which a man brings his labor power to market for sale as a commodity, from that state in which human labor was still in its first instinctive stage. We presuppose labor in a form that stamps it as exclusively human. A spider conducts operations that resemble those of a weaver, and a bee puts to shame many an architect in the construction of her cells. But what distinguishes the worst architect from the best of bees is this, that the architect raises his structure in imagination before he erects it in reality. At the end of every labor process, we get a result that already existed in the imagination of the laborer at its commencement. He not only effects a change of form in the material on which he works, but he also realizes a purpose of his own that gives the law to his modus operandi, and to which he must subordinate his will. And this subordination is no mere momentary act. Besides the exertion of the bodily organs, the process demands that, during the whole operation, the workman's will be steadily in consonance with his purpose. This means close attention. The less he is attracted by the nature of the work, and the mode in which it is carried on, and the less, therefore, he enjoys it as something which gives play to his bodily and mental powers, the more close his attention is forced to be."[35]

Labor is the self-expression of man, an expression of his individual physical and mental powers. In this process of genuine activity man develops himself, becomes himself; work is not only a means to an end—the product—

---

[35] *Capital I*, l.c. p. 197-8.

but an end in itself, the meaningful expression of human energy; hence work is enjoyable.

Marx's central criticism of capitalism is not the injustice in the distribution of wealth; it is the perversion of labor into forced, alienated, meaningless labor, hence the transformation of man into a "crippled monstrosity." Marx's concept of labor as an expression of man's individuality is succinctly expressed in his vision of the complete abolition of the lifelong submersion of a man in one occupation. Since the aim of human development is that of the development of the total, universal man, man must be emancipated from the crippling influence of specialization. In all previous societies, Marx writes, man has been "a hunter, a fisherman, a shepherd, or a critical critic, and must remain so if he does not want to lose his means of livelihood; while in communist society, where nobody has one exclusive sphere of activity but each can become accomplished in any branch he wishes, society regulates the general production and thus makes it possible for me to do one thing today and another tomorrow, to hunt in the morning, fish in the afternoon, rear cattle in the evening, criticize after dinner, just as I have a mind, without ever becoming hunter, fisherman, shepherd or critic."[36]

There is no greater misunderstanding or misrepresentation of Marx than that which is to be found, implicitly or explicitly, in the thought of the Soviet Communists, the reformist socialists, and the capitalist opponents of socialism alike, all of whom assume that Marx wanted only the economic improvement of the working class, and that he wanted to abolish private property so that the worker would own what the capitalist now has. The truth is that for Marx the situation of a worker in a Rus-

---

[36] *German Ideology*, l.c. p. 22.

sian "socialist" factory, a British state-owned factory, or an American factory such as General Motors, would appear essentially the same. This, Marx expresses very clearly in the following:

"An enforced *increase in wages* (disregarding the other difficulties, and especially that such an anomaly could only be maintained by force) would be nothing more than a *better remuneration of slaves,* and would not restore, either to the worker or to the work, their human significance and worth.

"Even the *equality of incomes* which Proudhon demands would only change the relation of the present-day worker to his work into a relation of all men to work. Society would then be conceived as an abstract capitalist."[37]

The central theme of Marx is the transformation of alienated, meaningless labor into productive, free labor, not the better payment of alienated labor by a private or "abstract" state capitalism.

5

ALIENATION

The concept of the active, productive man who grasps and embraces the objective world with his own powers cannot be fully understood without the concept of the *negation of productivity: alienation.* For Marx the history of mankind is a history of the increasing development of man, and at the same time of increasing alienation. His concept of socialism is the emancipation from alienation, the return of man to himself, his self-realization.

---

[37] *E.P. MSS.,* p. 107.

Alienation (or "estrangement") means, for Marx, that man does *not* experience himself as the acting agent in his grasp of the world, but that the world (nature, others, and he himself) remain alien to him. They stand above and against him as objects, even though they may be objects of his own creation. Alienation is essentially experiencing the world and oneself passively, receptively, as the subject separated from the object.

The whole concept of alienation found its first expression in Western thought in the Old Testament concept of idolatry.[1] The essence of what the prophets call "idolatry" is not that man worships many gods instead of only one. It is that the idols are the work of man's own hands —they are things, and man bows down and worships things; worships that which he has created himself. In doing so he transforms himself into a thing. He transfers to the things of his creation the attributes of his own life, and instead of experiencing himself as the creating person, he is in touch with himself only by the worship of the idol. He has become estranged from his own life forces, from the wealth of his own potentialties, and is in touch with himself only in the indirect way of submission to life frozen in the idols.[2]

---

[1] The connection between alienation and idolatry has also been emphasized by Paul Tillich in *Der Mensch im Christentum und im Marxismus,* Düsseldorf, 1953, p. 14. Tillich also points out in another lecture, "Protestantische Vision," that the concept of alienation in substance is to be found also in Augustine's thinking. Löwith also has pointed out that what Marx fights against are not the gods, but the idols, [cf. *Von Hegel zu Nietzsche,* l.c. p. 378].

[2] This is, incidentally, also the psychology of the fanatic. He is empty, dead, depressed, but in order to compensate for the state of depression and inner deadness, he chooses an idol, be it the state, a party, an idea, the church, or God. He makes this idol into the absolute, and submits to it in an

The deadness and emptiness of the idol is expressed in the Old Testament: "Eyes they have and they do not see, ears they have and they do not hear," etc. The more man transfers his own powers to the idols, the poorer he himself becomes, and the more dependent on the idols, so that they permit him to redeem a small part of what was originally his. The idols can be a god-like figure, the state, the church, a person, possessions. Idolatry changes its objects; it is by no means to be found only in those forms in which the idol has a so-called religious meaning. Idolatry is always the worship of something into which man has put his own creative powers, and to which he now submits, instead of experiencing himself in his creative act. Among the many forms of alienation, the most frequent one is alienation in language. If I express a feeling with a word, let us say, if I say "I love you," the word is meant to be an indication of the reality which exists within myself, the power of my loving. The *word* "love" is meant to be a symbol of the *fact* love, but as soon as it is spoken it tends to assume a life of its own, it becomes a reality. I am under the illusion that the saying of the word is the equivalent of the experience, and soon I say the word and feel nothing, except the *thought* of love which the word expresses. The alienation of language shows the whole complexity of alienation. Language is one of the most precious human achievements; to avoid alienation by not speaking would be foolish—yet one must be always aware of the danger of the spoken word, that it threatens to substitute

---

absolute way. In doing so his life attains meaning, and he finds excitement in the submission to the chosen idol. His excitement, however, does not stem from joy in productive relatedness; it is intense, yet cold excitement built upon inner deadness or, if one would want to put it symbolically, it is "burning ice."

itself for the living experience. The same holds true for all other achievements of man; ideas, art, any kind of man-made objects. They are man's creations; they are valuable aids for life, yet each one of them is also a trap, a temptation to confuse life with things, experience with artifacts, feeling with surrender and submission.

The thinkers of the eighteenth and nineteenth centuries criticized their age for its increasing rigidity, emptiness, and deadness. In Goethe's thinking the very same concept of productivity that is central in Spinoza as well as in Hegel and Marx, was a cornerstone. "The divine," he says, "is effective in that which is alive, but not in that which is dead. It is in that which is becoming and evolving, but not in that which is completed and rigid. That is why *reason*, in its tendency toward the divine, deals only with that which is becoming, and which is alive, while the *intellect* deals with that which is completed and rigid, in order to use it."[3]

We find similar criticisms in Schiller and Fichte, and then in Hegel and in Marx, who makes a general criticism that in his time "truth is without passion, and passion is without truth."[4]

Essentially the whole existentialist philosophy, from Kierkegaard on, is, as Paul Tillich puts it, "an over one-hundred-years-old movement of rebellion against the dehumanization of man in industrial society." Actually, the concept of alienation is, in nontheistic language, the equivalent of what in theistic language would be called "sin": man's relinquishment of himself, of God within himself.

---

[3] Eckermann's conversation with Goethe, February 18, 1829, published in Leipzig, 1894, page 47. [My translation —E.F.]

[4] *18th Brumaire of Louis Bonaparte.*

The thinker who coined the concept of alienation was Hegel. To him the history of man was at the same time the history of man's alienation (Entfremdung). "What the mind really strives for," he wrote in *The Philosophy of History*, "is the realization of its notion; but in doing so it hides that goal from its own vision and is proud and well satisfied in this alienation from its own essence."[5] For Marx, as for Hegel, the concept of alienation is based on the distinction between existence and essence, on the fact that man's existence is alienated from his essence, that in reality he is not what he potentially is, or, to put it differently, that *he is not what he ought to be, and that he ought to be that which he could be.*

For Marx the process of alienation is expressed in work and in the division of labor. Work is for him the active relatedness of man to nature, the creation of a new world, including the creation of man himself. (Intellectual activity is of course, for Marx, always work, like manual or artistic activity.) But as private property and the division of labor develop, labor loses its character of being an expression of man's powers; labor and its products assume an existence separate from man, his will and his planning. "The object produced by labor, its product, now stands opposed to it as an *alien being*, as a *power independent* of the producer. The product of labor is labor which has been embodied in an object and turned into a physical thing; this product is an *objectification* of labor."[6] Labor is alienated because the work has ceased to be a part of the worker's nature and "consequently, he does not fulfill himself in his work but denies himself, has a feeling of misery rather than well-being, does not

---

[5] *The Philosophy of History*, translated by J. Sibree, The Colonial Press, New York, 1899.

[6] *E.P. MSS.*, p. 95.

develop freely his mental and physical energies but is physically exhausted and mentally debased. The worker therefore feels himself at home only during his leisure time, whereas at work he feels homeless."[7] Thus, in the act of production the relationship of the worker to his own activity is experienced "as something alien and not belonging to him, activity as suffering (passivity), strength as powerlessness, creation as emasculation."[8] While man thus becomes alienated from himself, the product of labor becomes "an alien object which dominates him. This relationship is at the same time the relationship to the sensuous external world, to natural objects, as an alien and hostile world."[9] Marx stresses two points: 1) in the process of work, and especially of work under the conditions of capitalism, man is estranged from his own creative powers, and 2) the *objects* of his own work become alien beings, and eventually rule over him, become powers independent of the producer. "The laborer exists for the process of production, and not the process of production for the laborer."[10]

A misunderstanding of Marx on this point is widespread, even among socialists. It is believed that Marx spoke primarily of the *economic* exploitation of the worker, and the fact that his share of the product was not as large as it should be, or that the product should belong to him, instead of to the capitalist. But as I have shown before, the state as a capitalist, as in the Soviet Union, would not have been any more welcome to Marx than the private capitalist. He is not concerned primarily with the equalization of income. He is concerned with

[7] *E.P. MSS.*, p. 98.
[8] *E.P. MSS.*, p. 99.
[9] *E.P. MSS.*, p. 99.
[10] *Capital I*, l.c. p. 536.

the liberation of man from a kind of work which destroys his individuality, which transforms him into a thing, and which makes him into the slave of things. Just as Kierkegaard was concerned with the salvation of the individual, so Marx was, and his criticism of capitalist society is directed not at its method of distribution of income, but its mode of production, its destruction of individuality and its enslavement of man, not by the capitalist, but the enslavement of man—worker *and* capitalist—by things and circumstances of their own making.

Marx goes still further. In unalienated work man not only realizes himself as an individual, but also as a species-being. For Marx, as for Hegel and many other thinkers of the enlightenment, each individual represented the species, that is to say, humanity as a whole, the universality of man: the development of man leads to the unfolding of his whole humanity. In the process of work he "no longer reproduces himself merely intellectually, as in consciousness, but actively and in a real sense, and he sees his own reflection in a world which he has constructed. While, therefore, alienated labor takes away the object of production from man, it also takes away his *species life*, his real objectivity as a species-being, and changes his advantage over animals into a disadvantage in so far as his inorganic body, nature, is taken from him. Just as alienated labor transforms free and self-directed activity into a means, so it transforms the species life of man into a means of physical existence. Consciousness, which man has from his species, is transformed through alienation so that species life becomes only a means for him."[11]

As I indicated before, Marx assumed that the alienation of work, while existing throughout history, reaches

---

[11] *E.P. MSS.*, pp. 102-3.

its peak in capitalist society, and that the working class
is the most alienated one. This assumption was based on
the idea that the worker, having no part in the direction
of the work, being "employed" as part of the machines
he serves, is transformed into a thing in its dependence
on capital. Hence, for Marx, "the emancipation of society from private property, from servitude, takes the
political form of the *emancipation of the workers*; not in
the sense that only the latter's emancipation is involved,
but because this emancipation includes the *emancipation
of humanity as a whole*. For all human servitude is involved in the relation of the worker to production, and
all types of servitude are only modifications or consequences of this relation."[12]

Again it must be emphasized that Marx's aim is not
limited to the emancipation of the working class, but
the emancipation of the human being through the resti-
tution of the unalienated and hence free activity of all
men, and a society in which man, and not the production
of things, is the aim, in which man ceases to be "a crippled monstrosity, and becomes a fully developed human
being."[13] Marx's concept of the alienated product of labor
is expressed in one of the most fundamental points developed in *Capital*, in what he calls "the fetishism of
commodities." Capitalist production transforms the relations of individuals into qualities of things themselves,
and this transformation constitutes the nature of the commodity in capitalist production. "It cannot be otherwise
in a mode of production in which the laborer exists to
satisfy the need of self-expansion of existing values, instead of on the contrary, material wealth existing to satisfy the needs of development on the part of the laborer.

---

[12] *E.P. MSS.*, p. 107.
[13] *Capital I*, l.c. p. 396.

As in religion man is governed by the products of his own brain, so in capitalist production he is governed by the products of his own hands."[14] "Machinery is adapted to the weakness of the human being, in order to turn the weak human being into a machine."[15]

The alienation of work in man's production is much greater than it was when production was by handicraft and manufacture. "In handicrafts and manufacture, the workman makes use of a tool; in the factory the machine makes use of him. There the movements of the instrument of labor proceed from him; here it is the movement of the machines that he must follow. In manufacture, the workmen are parts of a living mechanism; in the factory we have a lifeless mechanism, independent of the workman, who becomes its mere living appendage."[16] It is of the utmost importance for the understanding of Marx to see how the concept of alienation was and remained the focal point in the thinking of the young Marx who wrote the *Economic and Philosophical Manuscripts*, and of the "old" Marx who wrote *Capital*. Aside from the examples already given, the following passages, one from the *Manuscripts*, the other from *Capital*, ought to make this continuity quite clear:

"This fact simply implies that the object produced by labor, its product, now stands opposed to it as an *alien being*, as a *power independent* of the producer. The product of labor is labor which has been embodied in an object and turned into a physical thing; this product is an *objectification* of labor. The performance of work is at the same time its objectification. The performance of work appears in the sphere of political economy as a

---

[14] *Capital I,* l.c. p. 680-1.

[15] *E.P. MSS.,* p. 143.

[16] *Capital I,* l.c. p. 461-2.

vitiation of the worker, objectification as a *loss* and as *servitude to the object*, and appropriation as *alienation*."[17]

This is what Marx wrote in *Capital*: "Within the capitalist system all methods for raising the social productiveness of labor are brought about at the cost of the individual laborer; all means for the development of production transform themselves into means of domination over, and exploitation of, the producers; they mutilate the laborer into a fragment of a man, degrade him to the level of an appendage of a machine, destroy every remnant of charm in his work and turn it into a hated toil; they estrange from him the intellectual potentialities of the labor process in the same proportion as science is incorporated in it as an independent power."[18]

Again the role of private property (of course not as property of objects of use, but as capital which hires labor) was already clearly seen in its alienating functioning by the young Marx: *"Private property,"* he wrote, "is therefore the product, the necessary result, of *alienated labor*, of the external relation of the worker to nature and to himself. *Private property* is thus derived from the analysis of the concept of *alienated labor*; that is, alienated man, alienated labor, alienated life, and estranged man."[19]

It is not only that the world of things becomes the ruler of man, but also that the *social and political circumstances* which he creates become his masters. "This consolidation of what we ourselves produce, which turns into an objective power above us, growing out of our control, thwarting our expectations, bringing to naught

---

[17] *E.P. MSS.*, p. 95.
[18] *Capital I*, l.c. p. 708.
[19] *E.P. MSS.*, pp. 105-6.

our calculations, is one of the chief factors in historical development up to now."[20] The alienated man, who believes that he has become the master of nature, has become the slave of things and of circumstances, the powerless appendage of a world which is at the same time the frozen expression of his own powers.

For Marx, alienation in the process of work, from the product of work and from circumstances, is inseparably connected with alienation from oneself, from one's fellow man and from nature. "A direct consequence of the alienation of man from the product of his labor, from his life activity and from his species life is that *man is alienated* from other men. When man confronts himself, he also confronts *other* men. What is true of man's relationship to his work, to the product of his work and to himself, is also true of his relationship to other men, to their labor and to the objects of their labor. In general, the statement that man is alienated from his species life means that each man is alienated from others, and that each of the others is likewise alienated from human life."[21] The alienated man is not only alienated from other men; he is alienated from the essence of humanity, from his "species-being," both in his natural and spiritual qualities. This alienation from the human essence leads to an existential egotism, described by Marx as man's human essence becoming "a *means* for his *individual existence*. It [alienated labor] alienates from man his own body, external nature, his mental life and his *human* life."[22]

Marx's concept touches here the Kantian principle that man must always be an end in himself, and never a

[20] *German Ideology*, l.c. p. **23.**

[21] *E.P. MSS.*, p. 103.

[22] *E.P. MSS.*, p. 103.

means to an end. But he amplifies this principle by stating that man's human essence must never become a means for individual existence. The contrast between Marx's view and Communist totalitarianism could hardly be expressed more radically; humanity in man, says Marx, must not even become a *means* to his individual existence; how much less could it be considered a means for the state, the class, or the nation.

Alienation leads to the perversion of all values. By making economy and its values—"gain, work, thrift, and sobriety"[23]—the supreme aim of life, man fails to develop the truly moral values, "the riches of a good conscience, of virtue, etc., but how can I be virtuous if I am not alive, and how can I have a good conscience if I am not aware of anything?"[24] In a state of alienation each sphere of life, the economic and the moral, is independent from the other, "each is concentrated on a specific area of alienated activity and is itself alienated from the other."[25]

Marx recognized what becomes of human needs in an alienated world, and he actually foresaw with amazing clarity the completion of this process as it is visible only today. While in a socialist perspective the main importance should be attributed "to the *wealth* of human needs, and consequently also to a *new mode of production* and to a new *object* of production," to "a new manifestation of *human* powers and a new enrichment of the human being,"[26] in the alienated world of capitalism needs are not expressions of man's latent powers, that is, they are not *human* needs; in capitalism "every man speculates upon creating a *new* need in another in order

[23] *E.P. MSS.*, p. 146.
[24] *E.P. MSS.*, p. 146.
[25] *E.P. MSS.*, p. 146
[26] *E.P. MSS.*, p. 140.

to force him to a new sacrifice, to place him in a new dependence, and to entice him into a new kind of pleasure and thereby into economic ruin. Everyone tries to establish over others an *alien* power in order to find there the satisfaction of his own egoistic need. With the mass of objects, therefore, there also increases the realm of alien entities to which man is subjected. Every new product is a new *potentiality* of mutual deceit and robbery. Man becomes increasingly poor as a man; he has increasing need of *money* in order to take possession of the hostile being. The power of his *money* diminishes directly with the growth of the quantity of production, i.e., his need increases with the increasing *power* of money. The need for money is therefore the real need created by the modern economy, and the only need which it creates. The *quantity* of money becomes increasingly its only important quality. Just as it reduces every entity to its abstraction, so it reduces itself in its own development to a *quantitative* entity. Excess and immoderation become its true standard. This is shown subjectively, partly in the fact that the expansion of production and of needs becomes an *ingenious* and always *calculating* subservience to inhuman, depraved, unnatural, and *imaginary* appetites. Private property does not know how to change crude need into *human* need; its *idealism* is *fantasy, caprice* and *fancy*. No eunuch flatters his tyrant more shamefully or seeks by more infamous means to stimulate his jaded appetite, in order to gain some favor, than does the eunuch of industry, the entrepreneur, in order to acquire a few silver coins or to charm the gold from the purse of his dearly beloved neighbor. (Every product is a bait by means of which the individual tries to entice the essence of the other person, his money. Every real or potential need is a weakness which will draw the bird into the lime. Universal exploitation of human communal life. As every imperfection of man is a bond with heaven, a point at which his heart is accessible to the priest, so every want is an opportunity for approaching one's neighbor with an air of friendship, and saying, 'Dear friend, I will give you what you need, but you know the *conditio sine qua non*. You know what ink you must use in signing yourself over to me. I shall swindle you while providing your enjoyment.') The entrepreneur accedes to the most depraved fancies of his neighbor, plays the role of pander between him and his needs, awakens unhealthy appetites in him, and watches for every weakness in order, later, to claim the remuneration for this labor of love."[27] The man who has thus become subject to his alienated needs is "a *mentally* and *physically dehumanized* being . . . the *self-conscious* and *self-acting commodity*."[28] This commodity-man knows only one way of relating himself to the world outside, by having it and by consuming (using) it. The more alienated he is, the more the sense of having and using constitutes his relationship to the world. "The less you *are*, the less you express your life, the more you *have*, the greater is your *alienated* life and the greater is the saving of your alienated being."[29]

There is only one correction which history has made in Marx's concept of alienation; Marx believed that the working class was the most alienated class, hence that the emancipation from alienation would necessarily start with the liberation of the working class. Marx did not foresee the extent to which alienation was to become the fate of the vast majority of people, especially of the ever-

---

[27] *E.P. MSS.*, pp. 140-2.
[28] *E.P. MSS.*, p. 111.
[29] *E.P. MSS.*, p. 144.

increasing segment of the population which manipulate symbols and men, rather than machines. If anything, the clerk, the salesman, the executive, are even more alienated today than the skilled manual worker. The latter's functioning still depends on the expression of certain personal qualities like skill, reliability, etc., and he is not forced to sell his "personality," his smile, his opinions in the bargain; the symbol manipulators are hired not only for their skill, but for all those personality qualities which make them "attractive personality packages," easy to handle and to manipulate. They are the true "organization men"—more so than the skilled laborer—their idol being the corporation. But as far as consumption is concerned, there is no difference between manual workers and the members of the bureaucracy. They all crave for things, new things, to have and to use. They are the passive recipients, the consumers, chained and weakened by the very things which satisfy their synthetic needs. They are not related to the world productively, grasping it in its full reality and in this process becoming one with it; they worship things, the machines which produce the things—and in this alienated world they feel as strangers and quite alone. In spite of Marx's underestimating the role of the bureaucracy, his general description could nevertheless have been written today: "Production does not simply produce man as a *commodity*, the *commodity-man*, man in the role of *commodity*; it produces him in keeping with this role as a *spiritually* and physically *dehumanized* being—[the] immorality, deformity, and hebetation of the workers and the capitalists. Its product is the *self-conscious* and *self-acting commodity* . . . the human commodity."[30]

---

[30] *E.P. MSS.*, p. 111.

To what extent things and circumstances of our own making have become our masters, Marx could hardly have foreseen; yet nothing could prove his prophecy more drastically than the fact that the whole human race is today the prisoner of the nuclear weapons it has created, and of the political institutions which are equally of its own making. A frightened mankind waits anxiously to see whether it will be saved from the power of the things it has created, from the blind action of the bureaucracies it has appointed.

6

MARX'S CONCEPT OF SOCIALISM

Marx's concept of socialism follows from his concept of man. It should be clear by now that according to this concept, socialism is *not* a society of regimented, automatized individuals, regardless of whether there is equality of income or not, and regardless of whether they are well fed and well clad. It is not a society in which the individual is subordinated to the state, to the machine, to the bureaucracy. Even if the state as an "abstract capitalist" were the employer, even if "the entire social capital were united in the hands either of a single capitalist or a single capitalist corporation,"[1] this would not be socialism. In fact, as Marx says quite clearly in the *Economic and Philosophical Manuscripts,* "communism as such is not the aim of human development." What, then, is the aim?

Quite clearly the aim of socialism is *man.* It is to

---

[1] *Capital I,* l.c. p. 689.

create a form of production and an organization of society in which man can overcome alienation from his product, from his work, from his fellow man, from himself and from nature; in which he can return to himself and grasp the world with his own powers, thus becoming one with the world. Socialism for Marx was, as Paul Tillich put it, "a resistance movement against the destruction of love in social reality."[2]

Marx expressed the aim of socialism with great clarity at the end of the third volume of *Capital*: "In fact, the realm of freedom does not commence until the point is passed where labor under the compulsion of necessity and of external utility is required. In the very nature of things it lies beyond the sphere of material production in the strict meaning of the term. Just as the savage must wrestle with nature, in order to satisfy his wants, in order to maintain his life and reproduce it, so civilized man has to do it, and he must do it in all forms of society and under all possible modes of production. With his development the realm of natural necessity expands, because his wants increase; but at the same time the forces of production increase, by which these wants are satisfied. The freedom in this field cannot consist of anything else but of the fact that *socialized man, the associated producers, regulate their interchange with nature rationally, bring it under their common control, instead of being ruled by it as by some blind power;* they accomplish their task with the least expenditure of energy and under conditions most adequate to their human nature and most worthy of it. *But it always remains a realm of necessity.* Beyond it begins that development of human power, which is its own end, the true realm of freedom,

---

[2] *Protestantische Vision*, Ring Verlag, Stuttgart, 1952, p. 6. [My translation—E.F.]

which, however, can flourish only upon that realm of
necessity as its basis."[3]

Marx expresses here all essential elements of socialism. First, man produces in an associated, not competi-
tive way; he produces rationally and in an unalienated
way, which means that he brings production under his
control, instead of being ruled by it as by some blind
power. This clearly excludes a concept of socialism in
which man is manipulated by a bureaucracy, even if
this bureaucracy rules the whole state economy, rather
than only a big corporation. It means that the individual
participates actively in the planning *and* in the execu-
tion of the plans; it means, in short, the realization of
political and industrial democracy. Marx expected that
by this new form of an unalienated society man would
become independent, stand on his own feet, and would
no longer be crippled by the alienated mode of production and consumption; that he would truly be the
master and the creator of his life, and hence that he
could begin to make *living* his main business, rather
than producing the *means* for living. Socialism, for Marx,
was never as such the fulfillment of life, but the *condition* for such fulfillment. When man has built a rational, nonalienated form of society, he will have the
chance to begin with what is the aim of life: the "development of human power, which is its own end, the
true realm of freedom." Marx, the man who every year
read all the works of Aeschylus and Shakespeare, who
brought to life in himself the greatest works of human
thought, would never have dreamt that his idea of
socialism could be interpreted as having as its aim the
well-fed and well-clad "welfare" or "workers'" state. Man,

[3] *Capital* III, translated by Ernest Untermann, Charles H.
Kerr & Co., Chicago 1909, p. 954.

in Marx's view, has created in the course of history a culture which he will be free to make his own when he is freed from the chains, not only of economic poverty, but of the spiritual poverty created by alienation. Marx's vision is based on his faith in man, in the inherent and real potentialities of the essence of man which have developed in history. He looked at socialism as the *condition* of human freedom and creativity, not as in itself constituting the goal of man's life.

For Marx, socialism (or communism) is not flight or abstraction from, or loss of the objective world which men have created by the objectification of their faculties. It is not an impoverished return to unnatural, primitive simplicity. It is rather the first real emergence, the genuine actualization of man's nature as something real. Socialism, for Marx, is a society which permits the actualization of man's essence, by overcoming his alienation. It is nothing less than creating the conditions for the truly free, rational, active and independent man; it is the fulfillment of the prophetic aim: the destruction of the idols.

That Marx could be regarded as an enemy of freedom was made possible only by the fantastic fraud of Stalin in presuming to talk in the name of Marx, combined with the fantastic ignorance about Marx that exists in the Western world. For Marx, the aim of socialism was freedom, but freedom in a much more radical sense than the existing democracy conceives of it—freedom in the sense of independence, which is based on man's standing on his own feet, using his own powers and relating himself to the world productively. "Freedom," said Marx, "is so much the essence of man that even its opponents realize it. . . . No man fights freedom; he fights at most the freedom of others. Every kind of freedom has therefore always existed, only at one time as a special privilege, another time as a universal right."[4]

Socialism, for Marx, is a society which serves the needs of man. But, many will ask, is not that exactly what modern capitalism does? Are not our big corporations most eager to serve the needs of man? And are the big advertising companies not reconnaissance parties which, by means of great efforts, from surveys to "motivation analysis," try to find out what the needs of man are? Indeed, one can understand the concept of socialism only if one understands Marx's distinction between the *true* needs of man, and the synthetic, *artificially produced* needs of man.

As follows from the whole concept of man, his *real needs* are rooted in his nature; this distinction between real and false needs is possible only on the basis of a picture of the nature of man and the true human needs rooted in his nature. Man's true needs are those whose fulfillment is necessary for the realization of his essence as a human being. As Marx put it: "The existence of what I truly love is felt by me as a necessity, as a need, without which my essence cannot be fulfilled, satisfied, complete."[5] Only on the basis of a specific concept of man's nature can Marx make the difference between true and false needs of man. Purely subjectively, the false needs are experienced as being as urgent and real as the true needs, and from a purely subjective viewpoint, there could not be a criterion for the distinction. (In modern terminology one might differentiate between neurotic and rational [healthy] needs).[6] Often man is conscious

---

[4] Quoted by R. Dunayevskaya, *Marxism and Freedom*, with a preface by H. Marcuse, Bookman Associates, New York, 1958, p. 19.

[5] *MEGA I*, 1 a, p. 184.

[6] Cf. my *Man for Himself*, Rinehart & Co., Inc., New York, 1947.

only of his false needs and unconscious of his real ones. The task of the analyst of society is precisely to awaken man so that he can become aware of the illusory false needs and of the reality of his true needs. The principal goal of socialism, for Marx, is the recognition and realization of man's true needs, which will be possible only when production serves man, and capital ceases to create and exploit the false needs of man.

Marx's concept of socialism is a protest, as is all existentialist philosophy, against the alienation of man; if, as Aldous Huxley put it, "our present economic, social and international arrangements are based, in large measure, upon organized lovelessness,"[7] then Marx's socialism is a protest against this very lovelessness, against man's exploitation of man, and against his exploitativeness towards nature, the wasting of our natural resources at the expense of the majority of men today, and more so of the generations to come. The unalienated man, who is the goal of socialism as we have shown before, is the man who does not "dominate" nature, but who becomes one with it, who is alive and responsive toward objects, so that objects come to life for him.

Does not all this mean that Marx's socialism is the realization of the deepest religious impulses common to the great humanistic religions of the past? Indeed it does, provided we understand that Marx, like Hegel and like many others, expresses his concern for man's soul, not in theistic, but in philosophical language.

Marx fought against religion exactly because it is alienated, and does not satisfy the true needs of man. Marx's fight against God is, in reality, a fight against the idol that is called God. Already as a young man he

---

[7] A. Huxley, *The Perennial Philosophy*, Harper and Brothers, New York, 1944, p. 93.

wrote as the motto for his dissertation "Not those are godless who have contempt for the gods of the masses but those who attribute the opinions of the masses to the gods." Marx's atheism is the most advanced form of rational mysticism, closer to Meister Eckhart or to Zen Buddhism than are most of those fighters for God and religion who accuse him of "godlessness."

It is hardly possible to talk about Marx's attitude toward religion without mentioning the connection between his philosophy of history, and of socialism, with the Messianic hope of the Old Testament prophets and the spiritual roots of humanism in Greek and Roman thinking. The Messianic hope is, indeed, a feature unique in Occidental thought. The prophets of the Old Testament are not only, like Lao Tzu or Buddha, *spiritual* leaders; they are also *political* leaders. They show man a vision of how he ought to be, and confront him with the alternatives between which he must choose. Most of the Old Testament prophets share the idea that history has a meaning, that man perfects himself in the process of history, and that he will eventually create a social order of peace and justice. But peace and justice for the prophets do not mean the absence of war and the absence of injustice. Peace and justice are concepts which are rooted in the whole of the Old Testament concept of man. Man, before he has consciousness of himself, that is, before he is human, lives in unity with nature (Adam and Eve in Paradise). The first act of Freedom, which is the capacity to say "no," opens his eyes, and he sees himself as a stranger in the world, beset by conflicts with nature, between man and man, between man and woman. The process of history is the process by which man develops his specifically human qualities, his powers of love and understanding; and once he has achieved full humanity he can return to the lost unity between himself and the world. This new unity, however, is different from the preconscious one which existed before history began. It is the at-onement of man with himself, with nature, and with his fellow man, based on the fact that man has given birth to himself in the historical process. In Old Testament thought, God is revealed in history ("the God of Abraham, the God of Isaac, the God of Jacob"), and in *history*, not in a state *transcending* history, lies the salvation of man. This means that man's spiritual aims are inseparably connected with the transformation of society; politics is basically not a realm that can be divorced from that of moral values and of man's self-realization.

Related thoughts arose in Greek (and Hellenistic) and Roman thinking. From Zeno, the founder of Stoic philosophy, to Seneca and Cicero, the concepts of natural law and of the equality of man exercised a powerful influence on the minds of men and, together with the prophetic tradition, are the foundations of Christian thinking.

While Christianity, especially since Paul, tended to transform the historical concept of salvation into an "other-worldly," purely spiritual one, and while the Church became the substitute for the "good society," this transformation was by no means a complete one. The early Church fathers express a radical criticism of the existing state; Christian thought of the late Middle Ages criticizes secular authority and the state from the standpoint of divine *and* natural law. This viewpoint stresses that society and the state must not be divorced from the spiritual values rooted in revelation and reason ("intellect" in the scholastic meaning of the word). Beyond this, the Messianic idea was expressed even in more radical forms in the Christian sects before the Reformation, and in the thinking of many Christian groups after the Reformation, down to the Society of Friends of the present time.

The mainstream of Messianic thinking after the Reformation, however, was expressed no longer in religious thought, but in philosophical, historical and social thought. It was expressed somewhat obliquely in the great utopias of the Renaissance, in which the new world is not in a distant future, but in a distant place. It was expressed in the thinking of the philosophers of the enlightenment and of the French and English Revolutions. It found its latest and most complete expression in Marx's concept of socialism. Whatever direct influence Old Testament thinking might have had on him through socialists like Moses Hess, no doubt the prophetic Messianic tradition influenced him indirectly through the thought of the enlightenment philosophers and especially through the thought stemming from Spinoza, Goethe, Hegel. What is common to prophetic, thirteenth-century Christian thought, eighteenth-century enlightenment,[8] and nineteenth-century socialism, is the idea that State (society) and spiritual values cannot be divorced from each other; that politics and moral values are indivisible. This idea was attacked by the secular concepts of the Renaissance (Machiavelli) and again by the secularism of the modern state. It seems that Western man, whenever he was under the influence of gigantic material conquests, gave himself unrestrictedly to the

[8] Cf. Carl L. Becker, *The Heavenly City of the Eighteenth-Century Philosophers,* Yale University Press, New Haven, 1932 and 1959; A.P. d'Entrèves, *The Medieval Contribution to Political Thought,* Oxford University Press, 1939; Hans Baron, *Fifteenth-Century Civilization and the Renaissance,* in Cambridge Modern History, Vol. 8; Harold J. Laski, *Political Theory in the Later Middle Ages,* The New Cambridge Modern History, Vol. I.

new powers he had acquired and, drunk with these new powers, forgot *himself*. The elite of these societies became obsessed with the wish for power, luxury, and the manipulation of men, and the masses followed them. This happened in the Renaissance with its new science, the discovery of the globe, the prosperous City States of Northern Italy; it happened again in the explosive development of the first and the present second industrial revolutions.

But this development has been complicated by the presence of another factor. If the state or the society is meant to serve the realization of certain spiritual values, the danger exists that a supreme authority tells man—and forces him—to think and behave in a certain way. The incorporation of certain objectively valid values into social life tends to produce authoritarianism. The spiritual authority of the Middle Ages was the Catholic Church. Protestantism fought this authority, at first promising greater independence for the individual, only to make the princely state the undisputed and arbitrary ruler of man's body and soul. The rebellion against princely authority occurred in the name of the nation, and for a while the national state promised to be the representative of freedom. But soon the national state devoted itself to the protection of the material interests of those who owned capital, and could thus exploit the labor of the majority of the population. Certain classes of society protested against this new authoritarianism and insisted on the freedom of the individual from the interference of secular authority. This postulate of liberalism, which tended to protect "freedom from," led, on the other hand, to the insistence that state and society must not attempt to realize "freedom to," that is to say, liberalism had to insist not only on separation from State and Church, but had also to deny that it was the function of the state to help realize certain spiritual and moral values; these values were supposed to be entirely a matter for the individual.

Socialism (in its Marxist and other forms) returned to the idea of the "good society" as the condition for the realization of man's spiritual needs. It was antiauthoritarian, both as far as the Church *and* the State are concerned, hence it aimed at the eventual disappearance of the state and at the establishment of a society composed of voluntarily cooperating individuals. Its aim was a reconstruction of society in such a way as to make it the basis for man's true return to himself, *without* the presence of those authoritarian forces which restricted and impoverished man's mind.

Thus, Marxist and other forms of socialism are the heirs of prophetic Messianism, Christian Chiliastic sectarianism, thirteenth-century Thomism, Renaissance Utopianism, and eighteenth-century enlightenment.[9] It is the synthesis of the prophetic-Christian idea of society as the plane of spiritual realization, and of the idea of individual freedom. For this reason, it is opposed to the Church because of its restriction of the mind, and to liberalism because of its separation of society and moral values. It is opposed to Stalinism and Krushchevism, for their authoritarianism as much as their neglect of humanist values.

Socialism is the abolition of human self-alienation, the return of man as a real human being. "It is the *definitive* resolution of the antagonism between man and nature, and between man and man. It is the true solution of the conflict between existence and essence, be-

---

[9] I shall deal with this development in detail in a forthcoming book in the World Perspective Religious Series, ed. by Ruth Nanda Anshen, Harper & Brothers, New York.

tween objectification and self-affirmation, between freedom and necessity, between individual and species. It
is a solution of the riddle of history and knows itself to
be this solution". [10,11] For Marx, socialism meant the social
order which permits the return of man to himself, the
identity between existence and essence, the overcoming
of the separateness and antagonism between subject and
object, the humanization of nature; it meant a world in
which man is no longer a stranger among strangers, but
is in *his* world, where he is at home.

7

THE CONTINUITY IN MARX'S THOUGHT

Our presentation of Marx's concept of human nature,
alienation, activity, etc., would be quite one-sided and,
in fact, misleading if they were right who claim that the
ideas of the "young Marx" contained in the *Economic
and Philosophical Manuscripts* were abandoned by the
older and mature Marx as remnants of an idealistic past
connected with Hegel's teaching. If those who make this
claim were right, one might still prefer the young to the
old Marx, and wish to connect socialism with the former

---

[10] *E.P. MSS.*, p. 127.

[11] The idea of the relation between Messianic prophet
ism and Marx's socialism has been stressed by a number of
authors. The following may be mentioned here: Karl Löwith
Meaning in History, Chicago University Press, 1949; Paul
Tillich in writings quoted here. Lukacs, in *Geschichte und
Klassenbewusstsein* speaks of Marx as of an eschatological
thinker. Cf. also statements by Alfred Weber, J.A. Schumpeter, and a number of other authors, quoted in *Marxismusstudien.*

rather than with the latter. However, there is fortunately no such need to split Marx into two. The fact is that the basic ideas on man, as Marx expressed them in the *Economic and Philosophical Manuscripts,* and the ideas of the older Marx as expressed in *Capital,* did not undergo a basic change; that Marx did not renounce his earlier views, as the spokesmen of the above-mentioned thesis claim.

First of all, who are those who claim that the "young Marx" and the "old Marx" have contradictory views on man? This view is presented mainly by the Russian Communists; they can hardly do anything else, since their thinking, as well as their social and political sys· tem, is in every way a contradiction of Marx's human· ism. In their system, man is the servant of the state and of production, rather than being the supreme aim of all social arrangements. Marx's aim, the development of the individuality of the human personality, is negated in the Soviet system to an even greater extent than in contemporary capitalism. The materialism of the Communists is much closer to the mechanistic materialism of the nineteenth-century bourgeoisie that Marx fought against, than to Marx's historical materialism.

The Communist party of the Soviet Union expressed this view by forcing G. Lukacs, who was the first one to revive Marx's humanism, to a "confession" of his errors when Lukacs was in Russia in 1934, after being forced to escape from the Nazis. Similarly, Ernst Bloch, who presents the same emphasis on Marx's humanism in his brilliant book *Das Prinzip Hoffnung* (The Principle Hope),[1] suffered severe attacks from Communist party writers, despite the fact that his book contains a number

---

[1] Ernst Bloch, *Das Prinzip Hoffnung,* Suhrkamp Verlag Frankfurt am Main, 1959, 2 volumes.

of admiring remarks about Soviet Communism. Aside from the Communist writers, Daniel Bell has recently taken the same position by claiming that the view of Marx's humanism based on the *Economic and Philosophical Manuscripts* "is not the historical Marx." "While one may be sympathetic to such an approach," says Bell, "it is only further myth-making to read this concept back as a central theme of Marx."[2]

It is indeed true that the classic interpreters of Marx, whether they were reformists like Bernstein, or orthodox Marxists like Kautsky, Plechanow, Lenin or Bucharin, did not interpret Marx as being centered around his humanist existentialism. Two facts mainly explain this phenomenon. First, the fact that the *Economic and Philosophical Manuscripts* were not published before 1932, and were unknown until then even in manuscript form; and the fact that *German Ideology* was never published in full until 1932, and for the first time in part only in 1926.[3] Naturally, these facts contributed a great deal to the distorted and one-sided interpretation of Marx's ideas by the above-mentioned writers. But the fact that these writings of Marx were more or less unknown until the early twenties and the thirties, respectively, is by no means a sufficient explanation for the neglect of Marxist humanism in the "classic" interpretation, since *Capital* and other published writings of Marx, such as the *Critique of Hegel's Philosophy of Law* (published in 1844) could have given a sufficient basis to visualize Marx's humanism. The more relevant explanation lies in the fact that the philosophical thinking of the time from the death of Marx to the 1920's was dominated by positi-

---

[2] This and all following quotations from D. Bell are from his paper "The Meaning of Alienation" in *Thought*, 1959.
[3] In *Marx-Engels Archiv I*, ed. by Rjazanow.

vistic-mechanistic ideas which influenced thinkers like
Lenin and Bucharin. It must also not be forgotten that,
like Marx himself, the classic Marxists were allergic to
terms which smacked of idealism and religion, since
they were well aware that these terms were to a large
extent, used to hide basic economic and social realities.

For Marx this allergy to idealistic *terminology* was
all the more understandable, since he was deeply rooted
in the spiritual, though nontheistic tradition, which
stretches not only from Spinoza and Goethe to Hegel,
but which also goes back to Prophetic Messianism. These
latter ideas were quite consciously alive in socialists like
St. Simon and Moses Hess, and certainly formed a great
part of the socialist thinking of the nineteenth-century
and even of the thinking of leading socialists up to the
First World War (such as Jean Jaurès).

The spiritual-humanistic tradition, in which Marx
still lived and which was almost drowned by the mech-
anistic-materialistic spirit of successful industrialism, experienced a revival, although only on a small scale in
individual thinkers, at the end of the First World War,
and on a larger scale during and after the Second World
War. The dehumanization of man as evidenced in the
cruelties of the Stalinist and Hitler regimes, in the bru-
tality of indiscriminate killing during the war, and also
the increasing dehumanization brought about by the
new gadget-minded consumer and organization man,
lead to this new expression of humanistic ideas. In other
words, the protest against alienation expressed by Marx,
Kierkegaard and Nietzsche, then muted by the apparent
success of capitalist industrialism, raised its voice again
after the human failure of the dominant system, and
led to a re-interpretation of Marx, based on the *whole*
Marx and his humanist philosophy. I have mentioned
already the Communist writers who are outstanding in

this humanist revisionism. I should add here the Yugoslav Communists who, although they have not as far as I know raised the philosophical point of alienation, have emphasized as their main objection to Russian Communism their concern for the individual as against the machinery of the state, and have developed a system of decentralization and individual initiative which is in radical contrast to the Russian ideal of centralization and of complete bureaucratization.

In Poland, East Germany and Hungary, the political opposition to the Russians was closely allied to the representatives of humanist socialism. In France, Germany and to a smaller extent in England, there is lively discussion going on regarding Marx which is based on a thorough knowledge and understanding of his ideas. Of literature in German, I mention only the papers contained in the *Marxismusstudien*,[4] written largely by Protestant theologians; French literature is even larger, and written by Catholics[5] as well as by Marxists and non-Marxist philosophers.[6]

The revival of Marxist humanism in English-speaking countries has suffered from the fact that the *Economic and Philosophical Manuscripts* had never been translated into English until recently. Nevertheless, men like T. B. Bottomore and others share the ideas on Marxist humanism represented by the aforementioned writers.

---

[4] J.C.B. Mohr, Tübingen, Vol. I and II, 1954, 1957.

[5] The main work on this theme is by a Jesuit priest, Jean-Yves Calvez, *La Pensée de Karl Marx*. Editions du Seuil. Paris, 1956.

[6] I will mention only the works of H. Lefèbvre, Navill, Goldmann, and of A. Kojève, J.-P. Sartre, M. Merlean-Ponty. Cf. the excellent paper "Der Marxismus im Spiegel der Französischen Philosophie" by I. Fetscher, in *Marxismusstudien*, l.c. Vol. I, p. 173 ff.

In the United States, the most important work which has opened up an understanding of Marx's humanism is Herbert Marcuse's *Reason and Revolution;*[7] Raya Dunayevskaya's *Marxism and Freedom,* with a preface by H. Marcuse,[8] is also a significant addition to Marxist-humanist thought.

Pointing to the fact that the Russian Communists were forced to postulate the split between the young and the old Marx, and adding the names of a number of profound and serious writers who negate this Russian position does not, however, constitute a proof that the Russians (and D. Bell) are wrong. While it would transcend the limits of this volume to attempt as full a refutation of the Russian position as is desirable, I shall try, nevertheless, to demonstrate to the reader why the Russian position is untenable.

There are some facts which, superficially appraised, might seem to support the Communist position. In *German Ideology,* Marx and Engels no longer used the terms "species" and "human essence" ("Gattung" and "menschliches Wesen"), which are used in the *Economic and Philosophical Manuscripts.* Furthermore, Marx said later (in the preface to *The Critique of Political Economy,* 1859) that in *German Ideology* he and Engels "resolved to work out in common the opposition of our view to the ideological view of German philosophy, in fact, to settle accounts with our erstwhile philosophical conscience."[9] It has been claimed that this "settling of

---

[7] Oxford University Press, New York, 1941.

[8] Bookman Associates, New York, 1958.

[9] When outside circumstances made the publication of this work (*German Ideology*) impossible, "we abandoned the manuscript to the gnawing criticism of the mice all the more willingly as we had achieved our main purpose—self-clarification."

accounts" with their erstwhile philosophical conscience meant that Marx and Engels had abandoned the basic ideas expressed in the *Economic and Philosophical Manuscripts*. But even a superficial study of *German Ideology* reveals that this is not true. While *German Ideology* does not use certain terms such as "human essence," etc., it nevertheless continues the main trend of thought of the *Economic and Philosophical Manuscripts*, especially the *concept of alienation*.

Alienation, in *German Ideology*, is explained as the result of the division of labor which "implies the contradiction between the interest of the separate individual or the individual family and the communal interest of all individuals who have intercourse with one another."[10] In the same paragraph the concept of alienation is defined, as in the *Economic and Philosophical Manuscripts*, in these words: "man's own deed becomes an alien power opposed to him, which enslaves him instead of being controlled by him."[11] Here, too, we find the definition of alienation with reference to circumstances already quoted above: "This crystallization of social activity, this consolidation of what we ourselves produce into an objective power above us, growing out of our control, thwarting our expectations, bringing to naught our calculations, is one of the chief factors in historical development up till now."[12, 13]

---

[10] *German Ideology*, l.c. p. 22.

[11] *German Ideology*, l.c. p. 22.

[12] *German Ideology*, l.c. p. 22-3.

[13] It is significant that Marx corrected Engel's expression "self-activity" into "activity" when Engels used it with reference to *previous* history. It shows how important it was for Marx to keep the term "self-activity" for a non-alienated society. See *MEGA I*, Vol. V, p. 61.

Fourteen years later, in his polemic with Adam Smith (in 1857-8), Marx used the same allegedly "idealistic" arguments which he used in the *Economic and Philosophical Manuscripts*, arguing that the need to work does not constitute in itself a restriction of freedom (provided it is not alienated work). Marx speaks of the "self-realization" of the person, "hence [of] true freedom."[14] Eventually, the same idea that the aim of human evolution is the unfolding of man, the creation of the "wealthy" man who has overcome the contradiction between himself and nature and achieved true freedom, is expressed in many passages of *Capital*, written by the mature and old Marx. As quoted earlier, Marx wrote in the third volume of *Capital:* "Beyond it [the realm of necessity] *begins that development of human power, which is its own end, the true realm of freedom, which, however, can flourish only upon that realm of necessity as its basis.* The shortening of the working day is its fundamental premise."[15]

In other parts of *Capital*, he speaks of the importance of producing "fully developed human beings,"[16] the full development of the human race,"[17] and "man's necessity to develop himself,"[18] and of the "fragment of a man" as the result of the process of alienation.[19]

Since D. Bell is one of the few American writers interested in Marx's concept of alienation, I want to demonstrate why his position, which is in effect the same

---

[14] Cf. the brilliant article by Th. Ramm, "Die Künftige Gesellschaftsordnung nach der Theorie von Marx und Engels," *Marxissmusstudien II,* l.c. p. 77 ff.

[15] Cf. *Capital III,* l.c. p. 945-6 [My italics—E.F.]

[16] Cf. *Capital I,* l.c. p. 529-30.

[17] *Capital I,* p. 554-5.

[18] *Capital I,* p. 563.

[19] *Capital I,* l.c. p. 708.

as that taken by the Russian Communists, for exactly the opposite motives, is also untenable. Bell's main claim is that to interpret Marx from the standpoint of the humanist writers quoted above is further myth-making. He claims that "Marx had repudiated the idea of alienation, divorced from the economic system, and, by so doing, closed off a road which would have given us a broader, more useful analysis of society and personality than the Marxiam dogmatics which have prevailed."

This statement is both ambiguous and erroneous. It sounds as if Marx, in his late writings, had repudiated the idea of alienation in its human meaning, and transformed it into a "purely economic category," as Bell says later on. Marx never repudiated the idea of alienation in its human sense, but he claimed that *it cannot be divorced from the concrete and real life process* of the alienated individual. This is something quite different from putting up the straw man of the "old Marx" who repudiates the "young Marx's" concept of human alienation. Bell must make this error because he accepts the whole cliché of the conventional interpretation of Marx. "For Marx the only social reality is not Man, nor the individual, but economic *classes of men*. Individuals and their motives count for naught. The only form of consciousness which can be translated into action — and which can explain history, past, present and future — is class consciousness." In trying to show that Marx was not interested in the individual, but only in the mass, just as he was allegedly no longer interested in human, but only in economic factors, Bell does not see—or does not mention—that Marx criticized capitalism precisely because it destroys individual personality (as he criticized "crude communism" for the same reason), and that the statement that history can be explained only by class-consciousness is a statement of fact, as far as previous history is concerned, not an expression of Marx's disregard of the individual.

Unfortunately Bell misquotes a Marx text which is of decisive importance in order to prove his thesis. He says of Marx: "But in saying there is no human nature 'inherent in each separate individual' (as Marx does in the sixth thesis on Feuerbach) but only *classes*, one introduces a new person, a new abstraction."

What *does* Marx say in the sixth thesis on Feuerbach? "Feuerbach resolves the essence of religion into the essence of *man*. *But the essence of man is no abstraction inherent in each separate individual.* In its reality it is the *ensemble* (aggregate) of social relations. Feuerbach, who does not enter more deeply into the criticism of this real essence, is therefore forced: 1) to abstract from the process of history and to establish religious temperament as something independent and to postulate an abstract — *isolated* — human individual. 2) The essence of man can therefore be understood only as 'genus,' the inward, dumb generality which *naturally* unites the many individuals."[20] Marx does not say, as Bell quotes, that "there is no human nature inherent in each separate individual," but something quite different, namely, that "the essence of man is no *abstraction* inherent in each individual." It is the essential point of Marx's "materialism" against Hegel's idealism. Marx never gave up his concept of man's nature" (as we have shown by quoting the statement from *Capital*) but this nature is not a purely biological one, and not an abstraction; it is one which can be understood only historically, because it unfolds in history. The nature (essence) of man can be inferred from its many manifestations (and distortions)

---

[20] Marx and Engels, *German Ideology*, l.c. p. 198-9 [partly my italics—E.F.]

in history; it cannot be seen as *such*, as a statistically existing entity "behind" or "above" each separate man, but as that in man which exists as a potentiality and unfolds and changes in the historical process.

In addition to all this Bell has not properly understood the concept of alienation. He defines it as "the radical dissociation into a *subject* that strives to control his own fate and an *object* which is manipulated by others." As follows from my own discussion, as well as that of most serious students of the concept of alienation, this is a completely inadequate and misleading definition. In fact, it is just as inadequate as Bell's assertion that Zen Buddhism (like other "modern tribal and communal philosophies" of "reintegration") aims "at losing one's sense of self" and thus is ultimately antihuman because they [the philosophers of reintegration, including Zen] are anti-individual. There is no space to refute this cliché, except to suggest a more careful and less biased reading of Marx and of Zen Buddhist texts.

To sum up this point of the alleged difference between the young and the mature Marx: it is true that Marx (like Engels), in the course of a lifetime, changed some of his ideas and concepts. He became more adverse to the use of terms too close to Hegelian idealism; his language became less enthusiastic and eschatological; probably he was also more discouraged in the later years of his life than he was in 1844. But in spite of certain changes in concepts, in mood, in language, the core of the philosophy developed by the young Marx was never changed, and it is impossible to understand his concept of socialism, and his criticism of capitalism as developed in his later years, except on the basis of the concept of man which he developed in his early writings.

8

MARX, THE MAN

The misunderstanding and the misinterpretation of Marx's writings are paralleled only by the misinterpretation of his personality. Just as in the case of his theories, the distortion of his personality also follows a cliché repeated by journalists, politicians, and even social scientists who should know better. He is described as a "lonely" man, isolated from his fellows, aggressive, arrogant, and authoritarian. Anyone who has even a slight knowledge of Marx's life would have great difficulty in accepting this because he would find it difficult to reconcile it with the picture of Marx the husband, the father, and the friend.

There are perhaps few marriages known to the world which were a human fulfillment in such an extraordinary way as was that of Karl and Jenny Marx. He, the son of a Jewish lawyer, fell in love as an adolescent with Jenny von Westphalen, the daughter of a Prussian feudal family, and a descendant of one of the oldest Scottish families. They married when he was twenty-four years of age, and he survived her death by only a little over a year. This was a marriage in which, despite the differences in background, despite a continual life of material poverty and sickness, there was unwavering love and mutual happiness, possible only in the case of two people with an extraordinary capacity for love, and deeply in love with each other.

His youngest daughter, Eleanor, described the relationship between her parents in a letter referring to a day shortly before her mother's death, and over a year before the death of her father. "Moor" [Marx's nickname], she writes, "got the better of his illness again. Never shall I forget the morning he felt himself strong enough to go into mother's room. When they were together they were young again—she a young girl and he a loving youth, both on life's threshold, not an old, disease-ridden man and an old, dying woman parting from each other for life."[1]

Marx's relationship to his children was as free from any taint of domination, and as full of productive love, as that to his wife. One needs only to read the description given by his daughter Eleanor of his walks with his children, when he told them tales, tales measured by miles, not chapters. "Tell us another mile," was the cry of the girls. "He read the whole of Homer, the whole Nibelungenlied, Gudrun, Don Quixote, the Arabian Nights, etc. As to Shakespeare, he was the Bible of our house, and seldom out of our hands or mouths. By the time I was six, I knew scene upon scene of Shakespeare by heart."[2]

His friendship with Frederick Engels is perhaps even more unique than his marriage and his relationship to his children. Engels himself was a man of extraordinary human and intellectual qualities. He always recognized and admired Marx's superior talent. He devoted his life to Marx's work, and yet he was never reluctant to make his own contribution, and did not underestimate it. There was hardly ever any friction in the relationship between these two men, no competitiveness, but a sense

[1] Reminiscences of Marx and Engels, Foreign Languages Publishing House, Moscow, p. 127.
[2] Reminiscences of Marx and Engels, l.c. p. 252.

of comradeship rooted in as deep a love for each other as one ever might find between two men.

Marx was the productive, nonalienated, independent man whom his writings visualized as the man of a new society. Productively related to the whole world, to people, and to ideas, he *was* what he *thought*. A man who read Aeschylus and Shakespeare every year in the original languages, and who during his saddest time, that of the illness of his wife, plunged into mathematics and studied calculus, Marx was a humanist through and through. Nothing was more wonderful to him than man, and he expressed that feeling in a frequently repeated quotation from Hegel: "even the criminal thought of a malefactor has more grandeur and nobility than the wonders of heaven." His answers to the questionnaire made up for him by his daughter Laura reveal a great deal of the man: his idea of misery was submission; the vice he detested most was servility, and his favorite maxims were "nothing human is alien to me" and "one must doubt of everything."

Why was this man supposed to be arrogant, lonely, authoritarian? Aside from the motive of slander, there were some reasons for this misunderstanding. First of all, Marx (like Engels) had a sarcastic style, especially in writing, and was a fighter with a good deal of aggressiveness. But, more importantly, he was a man with a complete inability to tolerate sham and deception, and with an utter seriousness about the problems of human existence. He was incapable of accepting dishonest rationalizations, or fictitious statements about important matters, politely and with a smile. He was incapable of any kind of insincerity, whether it referred to personal relations or to ideas. Since most people prefer to think in fictions rather than in realities, and to deceive themselves and others about the facts underlying individual and social life, they must indeed regard Marx as one who was arrogant or cold, but this judgment says more about them than it does about Marx.

If and when the world returns to the tradition of humanism and overcomes the deterioration of Western culture, both in its Soviet and in its capitalist form, it will see, indeed, that Marx was neither a fanatic nor an opportunist—that he represented the flowering of Western humanity, that he was a man with an uncompromising sense of truth, penetrating to the very essence of reality, and never taken in by the deceptive surface; that he was of an unquenchable courage and integrity; of a deep concern for man and his future; unselfish, and with little vanity or lust for power; always alive, always stimulating, and bringing to life whatever he touched. He represented the Western tradition in its best features: its faith in reason and in the progress of man. He represented, in fact, the very concept of man which was at the center of his thinking. The man who *is* much, and *has* little; the man who is rich because he has need of his fellow man.

ECONOMIC AND PHILOSOPHICAL MANUSCRIPTS

KARL MARX

Translated by
T. B. BOTTOMORE

TRANSLATOR'S NOTE

The *Economic and Philosophical Manuscripts* comprise four manuscripts which Marx wrote in the period April - August 1844. The manuscripts are now in the keeping of the International Institute of Social History, Amsterdam. They were first published in a full and accurate version, prepared by D. Riazanov, by the Marx-Engels Institute (now the Institute of Marxism-Leninism) Moscow, in *Karl Marx, Friedrich Engels: Historisch-kritische Gesamtausgabe,* Marx-Engels-Verlag, Berlin 1932, Abt. I, Band III. This edition, from which the present translation is made, will be referred to as the MEGA.

The first manuscript comprises 18 sheets (36 pages). Each page is divided by two vertical lines to form three columns, and these are entitled, respectively, "Wages," "Profit of Capital," and "Rent of Land." The text, under these three headings, constitutes the first three sections of the published manuscript. From page XXII of the manuscript onwards, however, Marx begins to write on a different subject, ignoring the division of the pages into three columns; this section was given the title "Alienated Labor" by the editors of the MEGA. The manuscript breaks off on page XXVII.

The second manuscript comprises two sheets (4 pages). The text begins in the middle of a sentence, and this is evidently the concluding portion of a manuscript which has been lost.

The third manuscript comprises 34 sheets (68 pages). Marx's pagination is faulty; page XXI is followed by page XXIII, and page XXIV is followed by page XXVI.

The last twenty-three pages are blank. The manuscript begins with two short sections which refer to a lost manuscript, and which the editors of the MEGA entitled "Private Property and Labor" and "Private Property and Communism" respectively. There follows the critique of Hegel's philosophy, which the editors placed at the end of the published version, following the indications given in the "Preface"; and the "Preface" itself (beginning on page XXXIX) which was clearly intended to introduce the whole work. On pages XLI-XLIII is another independent section, to which the editors gave the title "Money."

The fourth manuscript, comprising two sheets (4 pages) was found sewn into the third manuscript. The text is a paraphrase of the final chapter, "Absolute Knowledge," of Hegel's *Phenomenology of Spirit;* and it was published by the editors of the MEGA in the Appendix to Abt. I, Band III. Much of the text is used in the criticism of Hegel's philosophy in the third manuscript.

Each manuscript is separately paginated in Roman numerals by Marx, and these page numbers are indicated in the translation.

My footnotes to *the translation* are indicated by *"Tr. Note";* in many cases they utilize the references and critical notes appended to the MEGA edition.

These manuscripts, like other early writings of Marx, employ many terms borrowed from Hegel and Feuerbach. In particular, the section in the third manuscript devoted to a criticism of Hegel's philosophy employs many terms to which Hegel gave a technical meaning. In making my translation I have consulted the standard translations of Hegel's writings, and I have derived much help from a recent study of Hegel by J. N. Findlay, *Hegel: A Re-Examination* (London, Allen & Unwin, 1958). Here I need only mention that I have translated

Wesen by several terms, "being," "essence," "life," according to the context; that I have translated *aufheben* either as "annul," "abolish" (negative sense) or as "supersede" (positive sense), according to the context; and that I have translated both *Entäusserung* and *Entfremdung* as "alienation" (or sometimes "estrangement") since Marx indicates no systematic distinction between them.

One final note: Marx's own emphasis in his manuscripts is transcribed here by the corresponding use of italics.

PREFACE TO
ECONOMIC AND PHILOSOPHICAL MANUSCRIPTS

I have already announced in the *Deutsch-Französi-sche Jahrbücher*[1] a critique of jurisprudence and political science in the form of a critique of the *Hegelian* philosophy of right. However, in preparing the work for publication it became apparent that a combination of the criticism directed solely against the speculative theory with the criticism of the various subjects would be quite unsuitable; it would hamper the development of the argument and make it more difficult to follow. Moreover, I could only have compressed such a wealth of diverse subjects into a *single* work by writing in an aphoristic style, and such an aphoristic presentation would have given the *impression* of arbitrary systematization. I shall, therefore, publish my critique of law, morals, politics, etc. in a number of independent brochures; and finally I shall endeavor, in a separate work, to present the interconnected whole, to show the relationships between the parts, and to provide a critique of the speculative treatment of this material. That is why, in the present work, the relationships of political economy with the state, law, morals, civil life, etc. are touched upon only to the extent that political economy itself expressly deals with these subjects.

It is hardly necessary to assure the reader who is

---

[1] *Deutsch-Französische Jahrbücher*, edited by K. Marx and A. Ruge (Paris 1844). Only one issue was published, in February 1844. Marx refers to his essay "Zur Kritik der Hegelschen Rechtsphilosophie," on pages 71 et seq.—*Tr. Note*

familiar with political economy that my conclusions are the fruit of an entirely empirical analysis, based upon a careful critical study of political economy.

It goes without saying that in addition to the French and English socialists I have also used German socialist writings. But the *original* and important German works on this subject—apart from the writings of Weitling — are limited to the essays published by Hess in the *Einundzwanzig Bogen*,[2] and Engels' "Umrisse zur Kritik der Nationalökonomie" in the *Deutsch-Französische Jahrbücher*. In the latter publication I myself have indicated in a very general way the basic elements of the present work.

The *positive*, humanistic and naturalistic criticism begins with Feuerbach. The less blatant Feuerbach's writings, the more certain, profound, extensive and lasting is their influence; they are the only writings since Hegel's *Phenomenology* and *Logic* which contain a real theoretical revolution.

Unlike the *critical theologians* of our time I have considered the final chapter of the present work, a critical exposition of the *Hegelian dialectic* and general philosophy, to be absolutely essential, for the task has not yet been accomplished. This *lack of thoroughness* is not accidental, for the *critical* theologian remains a *theologian.* He must either begin from certain presuppositions of philosophy accepted as authoritative or else, if in the course of criticism and as a result of other people's discoveries doubts have arisen in his mind concern-

---

[2] *Einundzwanzig Bogen aus der Schweiz,* edited by Georg Herwegh. First part, Zurich and Winterthur 1843. Marx refers to the articles by Hess, "Sozialismus und Kommunismus" on pages 74 et seq.; "Die Eine und ganze Freiheit" on pages 92 et seq.; and "Philosophie der Tat" on pages 309 et seq.—*Tr. Note*

ing the philosophical presuppositions, he abandons them
in a cowardly and unjustified manner, *abstracts* from
them, and shows both his servile dependence upon them
and his resentment of this dependence in a negative,
unconscious and sophistical way.

Looked at more closely, *theological criticism,* which
was at the beginning of the movement a genuinely progressive factor, is seen to be, in the last analysis, no
more than the culmination and consequence of the old
philosophical, and especially *Hegelian, transcendental-
ism* distorted into a *theological caricature.* I shall describe elsewhere at greater length, this interesting act
of historical justice, this nemesis which now destines
theology, ever the infected spot of philosophy, to por-
tray in itself the negative dissolution of philosophy, i. e.
the process of its decay.

First Manuscript
ALIENATED LABOR

(XXII) We have begun from the presuppositions of political economy. We have accepted its terminology and its laws. We presupposed private property, the separation of labor, capital and land, as also of wages, profit and rent, the division of labor, competition, the concept of exchange value, etc. From political economy itself, in its own words, we have shown that the worker sinks to the level of a commodity, and to a most miserable commodity; that the misery of the worker increases with the power and volume of his production; that the necessary result of competition is the accumulation of capital in a few hands, and thus a restoration of monopoly in a more terrible form; and finally that the distinction between capitalist and landlord, and between agricultural laborer and industrial worker, must disappear and the whole of society divide into the two classes of property *owners* and propertyless *workers*.

Political economy begins with the fact of private property; it does not explain it. It conceives the *material process* of private property, as this occurs in reality, in general and abstract formulas which then serve it as laws. It does not *comprehend* these laws; that is, it does not show how they arise out of the nature of private property. Political economy provides no explanation of the basis of the distinction of labor from capital, of capital from land. When, for example, the relation of wages to profits is defined, this is explained in terms of the interests of capitalists; in other words, what should be explained is assumed. Similarly, competition is referred to at every point and is explained in terms of external conditions. Political economy tells us nothing about the extent to which these external and apparently accidental conditions are simply the expression of a necessary development. We have seen how exchange itself seems an accidental fact. The only moving forces which political economy recognizes are *avarice* and the *war between the avaricious, competition.*

Just because political economy fails to understand the interconnections within this movement it was possible to oppose the doctrine of competition to that of monopoly, the doctrine of freedom of the crafts to that of the guilds, the doctrine of the division of landed property to that of the great estates; for competition, freedom of crafts, and the division of landed property were conceived only as accidental consequences brought about by will and force, rather than as necessary, inevitable and natural consequences of monopoly, the guild system and feudal property.

Thus we have now to grasp the real connection between this whole system of alienation—private property, acquisitiveness, the separation of labor, capital and land, exchange and competition, value and the devaluation of man, monopoly and competition—and the system of *money.*

Let us not begin our explanation, as does the economist, from a legendary primordial condition. Such a primordial condition does not explain anything; it merely removes the question into a gray and nebulous distance. It asserts as a fact or event what it should deduce, namely, the necessary relation between two things; for example, between the division of labor and exchange. In the same way theology explains the origin of evil by the fall of man; that is, it asserts as a historical fact what it should explain.

We shall begin from a *contemporary* economic fact. The worker becomes poorer the more wealth he produces and the more his production increases in power and extent. The worker becomes an ever cheaper commodity the more goods he creates. The *devaluation* of the human world increases in direct relation with the *increase in value* of the world of things. Labor does not only create goods; it also produces itself and the worker as a *commodity*, and indeed in the same proportion as it produces goods.

This fact simply implies that the object produced by labor, its product, now stands opposed to it as an *alien being*, as a *power independent* of the producer. The product of labor is labor which has been embodied in an object and turned into a physical thing; this product is an *objectification* of labor. The performance of work is at the same time its objectification. The performance of work appears in the sphere of political economy as a *vitiation* of the worker, objectification as a *loss* and as *servitude to the object*, and appropriation as *alienation*.

So much does the performance of work appear as vitiation that the worker is vitiated to the point of starvation. So much does objectification appear as loss of the object that the worker is deprived of the most essential things not only of life but also of work. Labor itself becomes an object which he can acquire only by the greatest effort and with unpredictable interruptions. So much does the appropriation of the object appear as alienation that the more objects the worker produces the fewer he can possess and the more he falls under the domination of his product, of capital.

All these consequences follow from the fact that the worker is related to the *product of his labor* as to an *alien* object. For it is clear on this presupposition that the more the worker expends himself in work the more powerful becomes the world of objects which he creates in face of himself, the poorer he becomes in his inner life, and the less he belongs to himself. It is just the same as in religion. The more of himself man attributes to God the less he has left in himself. The worker puts his life into the object, and his life then belongs no longer to himself but to the object. The greater his activity, therefore, the less he possesses. What is embodied in the product of his labor is no longer his own. The greater this product is, therefore, the more he is diminished. The *alienation* of the worker in his product means not only that his labor becomes an object, assumes an *external* existence, but that it exists independently, *outside himself*, and alien to him, and that it stands opposed to him as an autonomous power. The life which he has given to the object sets itself against him as an alien and hostile force.

(XXIII) Let us now examine more closely the phenomenon of *objectification*, the worker's production and the *alienation* and *loss* of the object it produces, which is involved in it. The worker can create nothing without *nature*, without the *sensuous external world*. The latter is the material in which his labor is realized, in which it is active, out of which and through which it produces things.

But just as nature affords the *means of existence* of labor in the sense that labor cannot *live* without objects upon which it can be exercised, so also it provides the *means of existence* in a narrower sense; namely the means of physical existence for the *worker* himself. Thus, the more the worker *appropriates* the external world of sensuous nature by his labor the more he deprives himself of *means of existence*, in two respects: first, that the sensuous external world becomes progressively less an object belonging to his labor or a means of existence of his labor, and secondly, that it becomes progressively less a means of existence in the direct sense, a means for the physical subsistence of the worker.

In both respects, therefore, the worker becomes a slave of the object; first, in that he receives an *object of work*, i.e., receives *work*, and secondly that he receives *means of subsistence*. Thus the object enables him to exist, first as a *worker* and secondly, as a *physical subject*. The culmination of this enslavement is that he can only maintain himself as a *physical subject* so far as he is a *worker*, and that it is only as a *physical subject* that he is a worker.

(The alienation of the worker in his object is expressed as follows in the laws of political economy: the more the worker produces the less he has to consume; the more value he creates the more worthless he becomes; the more refined his product the more crude and misshapen the worker; the more civilized the product the more barbarous the worker; the more powerful the work the more feeble the worker; the more the work manifests intelligence the more the worker declines in intelligence and becomes a slave of nature.)

Political economy conceals the alienation in the nature of labor insofar as it does not examine the direct relationship between the worker (work) and production. Labor certainly produces marvels for the rich but it produces privation for the worker. It produces palaces, but hovels for the worker. It produces beauty, but deformity for the worker. It replaces labor by machinery, but it casts some of the workers back into a barbarous kind of work and turns the others into machines. It produces intelligence, but also stupidity and cretinism for the workers.

The direct relationship of labor to its products is the relationship of the worker to the objects of his production. The relationship of property owners to the objects of production and to production itself is merely a *consequence* of this first relationship and confirms it. We shall consider this second aspect later.

Thus, when we ask what is the important relationship of labor, we are concerned with the relationship of the *worker* to production.

So far we have considered the alienation of the worker only from one aspect; namely, *his relationship with the products of his labor.* However, alienation appears not only in the result, but also in the *process,* of *production,* within *productive activity* itself. How could the worker stand in an alien relationship to the product of his activity if he did not alienate himself in the act of production itself? The product is indeed only the *résumé* of activity, of production. Consequently, if the product of labor is alienation, production itself must be active alienation—the alienation of activity and the activity of alienation. The alienation of the object of labor merely summarizes the alienation in the work activity itself.

What constitutes the alienation of labor? First, that the work is *external* to the worker, that it is not part of his nature; and that, consequently, he does not fulfill himself in his work but denies himself, has a feeling of misery rather than well being, does not develop freely his mental and physical energies but is physically exhausted and mentally debased. The worker therefore feels himself at home only during his leisure time, whereas at work he feels homeless. His work is not voluntary but imposed, *forced labor.* It is not the satisfaction of a need, but only a *means* for satisfying other needs. Its alien character is clearly shown by the fact that as soon as there is no physical or other compulsion it is avoided

like the plague. External labor, labor in which man alienates himself, is a labor of self-sacrifice, of mortification.
Finally, the external character of work for the worker is
shown by the fact that it is not his own work but work
for someone else, that in work he does not belong to himself but to another person.

Just as in religion the spontaneous activity of human
fantasy, of the human brain and heart, reacts independently as an alien activity of gods or devils upon the individual, so the activity of the worker is not his own
spontaneous activity. It is another's activity and a loss of
his own spontaneity.

We arrive at the result that man (the worker) feels
himself to be freely active only in his animal functions—
eating, drinking and procreating, or at most also in his
dwelling and in personal adornment—while in his human
functions he is reduced to an animal. The animal becomes human and the human becomes animal.

Eating, drinking and procreating are of course also
genuine human functions. But abstractly considered,
apart from the environment of other human activities,
and turned into final and sole ends, they are animal
functions.

We have now considered the act of alienation of
practical human activity, labor, from two aspects: (1)
the relationship of the worker to the *product of labor* as
an alien object which dominates him. This relationship
is at the same time the relationship to the sensuous external world, to natural objects, as an alien and hostile
world; (2) the relationship of labor to the *act of production* within *labor*. This is the relationship of the worker
to his own activity as something alien and not belonging
to him, activity as suffering (passivity), strength as powerlessness, creation as emasculation, the *personal* physical
and mental energy of the worker, his personal life (for

what is life but activity?) as an activity which is directed against himself, independent of him and not belonging to him. This is *self-alienation* as against the above-mentioned alienation of the *thing*.

(XXIV) We have now to infer a third characteristic of *alienated labo*r from the two we have considered.

Man is a species-being[1] not only in the sense that he makes the community (his own as well as those of other things) his object both practically and theoretically, but also (and this is simply another expression for the same thing) in the sense that he treats himself as the present, living species, as a *universal* and consequently free being.

Species-life, for man as for animals, has its physical basis in the fact that man (like animals) lives from inorganic nature, and since man is more universal than an animal so the range of inorganic nature from which he lives is more universal. Plants, animals, minerals, air, light, etc. constitute, from the theoretical aspect, a part of human consciousness as objects of natural science and art; they are man's spiritual inorganic nature, his intellectual means of life, which he must first prepare for enjoyment and perpetuation. So also, from the practical aspect they form a part of human life and activity. In practice man lives only from these natural products, whether in the form of food, heating, clothing, housing, etc. The universality of man appears in practice in the universality which makes the whole of nature into his inorganic body: (1) as a direct means of life; and equally (2) as the material object and instrument of his life activity. Nature is the *in-*

---

[1] The term "species-being" is taken from Feuerbach's *Das Wesen des Christentums* (The Essence of Christianity). Feuerbach used the notion in making a distinction between consciousness in man and in animals. Man is conscious not merely of himself as an individual but of the human species or "human essence."—*Tr. Note*

organic body of man; that is to say, nature excluding the human body itself. To say that man *lives* from nature means that nature is his *body* with which he must remain in a continuous interchange in order not to die. The statement that the physical and mental life of man, and nature, are interdependent means simply that nature is interdependent with itself, for man is a part of nature.

Since alienated labor: (1) alienates nature from man; and (2) alienates man from himself, from his own active function, his life activity; so it alienates him from the species. It makes *species-life* into a means of individual life. In the first place it alienates species-life and individual life, and secondly, it turns the latter, as an abstraction, into the purpose of the former, also in its abstract and alienated form.

For labor, *life activity, productive life,* now appear to man only as *means* for the satisfaction of a need, the need to maintain his physical existence. Productive life is, however, species-life. It is life creating life. In the type of life activity resides the whole character of a species, its species-character; and free, conscious activity is the species-character of human beings. Life itself appears only as a *means of life.*

The animal is one with its life activity. It does not distinguish the activity from itself. It is *its activity.* But man makes his life activity itself an object of his will and consciousness. He has a conscious life activity. It is not a determination with which he is completely identified. Conscious life activity distinguishes man from the life activity of animals. Only for this reason is he a species-being. Or rather, he is only a self-conscious being, i.e. his own life is an object for him, because he is a species-being. Only for this reason is his activity free activity. Alienated labor reverses the relationship, in that man because he is a self-conscious being makes his life activity, his *being*, only a means for his *existence*.

The practical construction of an *objective world*, the *manipulation* of inorganic nature, is the confirmation of man as a conscious species-being, i.e. a being who treats the species as his own being or himself as a species-being. Of course, animals also produce. They construct nests, dwellings, as in the case of bees, beavers, ants, etc. But they only produce what is strictly necessary for themselves or their young. They produce only in a single direction, while man produces universally. They produce only under the compulsion of direct physical need, while man produces when he is free from physical need and only truly produces in freedom from such need. Animals produce only themselves, while man reproduces the whole of nature. The products of animal production belong directly to their physical bodies, while man is free in face of his product. Animals construct only in accordance with the standards and needs of the species to which they belong, while man knows how to produce in accordance with the standards of every species and knows how to apply the appropriate standard to the object. Thus man constructs also in accordance with the laws of beauty.

It is just in his work upon the objective world that man really proves himself as a *species-being*. This production is his active species life. By means of it nature appears as *his* work and his reality. The object of labor is, therefore, the *objectification of man's species life*; for he no longer reproduces himself merely intellectually, as in consciousness, but actively and in a real sense, and he sees his own reflection in a world which he has constructed. While, therefore, alienated labor takes away the object of production from man, it also takes away his *species life*, his real objectivity as a species-being, and changes his advantage over animals into a disadvantage in so far as his inorganic body, nature, is taken from him.

Just as alienated labor transforms free and self-directed activity into a means, so it transforms the species life of man into a means of physical existence.

Consciousness, which man has from his species, is transformed through alienation so that species life becomes only a means for him.

(3) Thus alienated labor turns the *species life of man*, and also nature as his mental species-property, into an *alien* being and into a *means* for his *individual existence*. It alienates from man his own body, external nature, his mental life and his *human* life.

(4) A direct consequence of the alienation of man from the product of his labor, from his life activity and from his species life is that *man is alienated* from other *men*. When man confronts himself he also confronts *other* men. What is true of man's relationship to his work, to the product of his work and to himself, is also true of his relationship to other men, to their labor and to the objects of their labor.

In general, the statement that man is alienated from his species life means that each man is alienated from others, and that each of the others is likewise alienated from human life.

Human alienation, and above all the relation of man to himself, is first realized and expressed in the relationship between each man and other men. Thus in the relationship of alienated labor every man regards other men according to the standards and relationships in which he finds himself placed as a worker.

(XXV) We began with an economic fact, the alienation of the worker and his production. We have expressed this fact in conceptual terms as *alienated labor*, and in analyzing the concept we have merely analyzed an economic fact.

Let us now examine further how this concept of alienated labor must express and reveal itself in reality. If the product of labor is alien to me and confronts me as an alien power, to whom does it belong? If my own activity does not belong to me but is an alien, forced activity, to whom does it belong? To a being *other* than myself. And who is this being? The *gods*? It is apparent in the earliest stages of advanced production, e.g., temple building, etc. in Egypt, India, Mexico, and in the service rendered to gods, that the product belonged to the gods. But the gods alone were never the lords of labor. And no more was *nature*. What a contradiction it would be if the more man subjugates nature by his labor, and the more the marvels of the gods are rendered superfluous by the marvels of industry, he should abstain from his joy in producing and his enjoyment of the product for love of these powers.

The *alien* being to whom labor and the product of labor belong, to whose service labor is devoted, and to whose enjoyment the product of labor goes, can only be *man* himself. If the product of labor does not belong to the worker, but confronts him as an alien power, this can only be because it belongs to *a man other than the worker*. If his activity is a torment to him it must be a source of enjoyment and pleasure to another. Not the gods, nor nature, but only man himself can be this alien power over men.

Consider the earlier statement that the relation of man to himself is first realized, objectified, through his relation to other men. If therefore he is related to the product of his labor, his objectified labor, as to an *alien*, hostile, powerful and independent object, he is related in

such a way that another alien, hostile, powerful and independent man is the lord of this object. If he is related
to his own activity as to unfree activity, then he is
related to it as activity in the service, and under the
domination, coercion and yoke, of another man.

Every self-alienation of man, from himself and from
nature, appears in the relation which he postulates between other men and himself and nature. Thus religious
self-alienation is necessarily exemplified in the relation
between laity and priest, or, since it is here a question of
the spiritual world, between the laity and a mediator. In
the real world of practice this self-alienation can only be
expressed in the real, practical relation of man to his
fellow-men. The medium through which alienation occurs is itself a *practical* one. Through alienated labor,
therefore, man not only produces his relation to the object and to the process of production as to alien and
hostile men; he also produces the relation of other men
to his production and his product, and the relation between himself and other men. Just as he creates his own
production as a vitiation, a punishment, and his own
product as a loss, as a product which does not belong to
him, so he creates the domination of the non-producer
over production and its product. As he alienates his own
activity, so he bestows upon the stranger an activity
which is not his own.

We have so far considered this relation only from
the side of the worker, and later on we shall consider it
also from the side of the non-worker.

Thus, through alienated labor the worker creates the
relation of another man, who does not work and is outside the work process, to this labor. The relation of the
worker to work also produces the relation of the capitalist (or whatever one likes to call the lord of labor) to
work. *Private property* is therefore the product, the nec-

essary result, of *alienated labor*, of the external relation
of the worker to nature and to himself.

Private property is thus derived from the analysis of
the concept of *alienated labor*; that is, alienated man,
alienated labor, alienated life, and estranged man.

We have, of course, derived the concept of *alienated
labor (alienated life)* from political economy, from an
analysis of the *movement of private property*. But the
analysis of this concept shows that although private property appears to be the basis and cause of alienated labor,
it is rather a consequence of the latter, just as the gods
are *fundamentally* not the cause but the product of con-
fusions of human reason. At a later stage, however, there
is a reciprocal influence.

Only in the final stage of the development of private
property is its secret revealed, namely, that it is on one
hand the *product* of alienated labor, and on the other
hand the *means* by which labor is alienated, the *realization of this alienation*.

This elucidation throws light upon several unresolved
controversies:

(1) Political economy begins with labor as the real
soul of production and then goes on to attribute nothing
to labor and everything to private property. Proudhon,
faced by this contradiction, has decided in favor of
labor against private property. We perceive, however,
that this apparent contradiction is the contradiction of
alienated labor with itself and that political economy has
merely formulated the laws of alienated labor.

We also observe, therefore, that *wages* and *private
property* are identical, for wages, like the product or object of labor, labor itself remunerated, are only a necessary consequence of the alienation of labor. In the wage
system labor appears not as an end in itself but as the
servant of wages. We shall develop this point later on

and here only bring out some of the (XXVI) consequences.

An enforced *increase in wages* (disregarding the other difficulties, and especially that such an anomaly could only be maintained by force) would be nothing more than a *better remuneration of slaves*, and would not restore, either to the worker or to the work, their human significance and worth.

Even the *equality of incomes* which Proudhon demands would only change the relation of the present day worker to his work into a relation of all men to work. Society would then be conceived as an abstract capitalist.

(2) From the relation of alienated labor to private property it also follows that the emancipation of society from private property, from servitude, takes the political form of the *emancipation of the workers*; not in the sense that only the latter's emancipation is involved, but because this emancipation includes the emancipation of humanity as a whole. For all human servitude is involved in the relation of the worker to production, and all the types of servitude are only modifications or consequences of this relation.

As we have discovered the concept of *private property* by an *analysis* of the concept of *alienated labor*, so with the aid of these two factors we can evolve all the categories of political economy, and in every category, e.g., trade, competition, capital, money, we shall discover only a particular and developed expression of these fundamental elements.

However, before considering this structure let us attempt to solve two problems.

(1) To determine the general nature of *private property* as it has resulted from alienated labor, in its relation to *genuine human and social property*.

(2) We have taken as a fact and analyzed the *aliena-*

tion of labor. How does it happen, we may ask, that *man alienates his labor?* How is this alienation founded in the nature of human development? We have already done much to solve the problem in so far as we have *transformed* the question concerning the *origin of private property* into a question about the relation between *alienated labor* and the process of development of mankind. For in speaking of private property one believes oneself to be dealing with something external to mankind. But in speaking of labor one deals directly with mankind itself. This new formulation of the problem already contains its solution.

ad (1) *The general nature of private property and its relation to genuine human property.*

We have resolved alienated labor into two parts, which mutually determine each other, or rather constitute two different expressions of one and the same relation. *Appropriation* appears as *alienation* and *alienation* as *appropriation*, alienation as genuine acceptance in the community.

We have considered one aspect, *alienated* labor, in its bearing upon the *worker* himself, i.e., *the relation of alienated labor to itself*. And we have found as the necessary consequence of this relation the *property relation* of the *non-worker* to the *worker* and to *labor*. *Private property* as the material summarized expression of alienated labor includes both relations; *the relation of the worker to labor, to the product of his labor and to the non-worker*, and the relation of the *non-worker to the worker and to the product of the latter's labor*.

We have already seen that in relation to the worker, who *appropriates* nature by his labor, appropriation appears as alienation, self-activity as activity for another and of another, living as the sacrifice of life, and production of the object as loss of the object to an alien power, an alien man. Let us now consider the relation of this *alien* man to the worker, to labor, and to the object of labor.

It should be noted first that everything which appears to the worker as an *activity of alienation*, appears to the non-worker as a *condition of alienation*. Secondly, the *real, practical* attitude of the worker in production and to the product (as a state of mind) appears to the non-worker who confronts him as a *theoretical* attitude.

(XXVII) Thirdly, the non-worker does everything against the worker which the latter does against himself, but he does not do against himself what he does against the worker.

Let us examine these three relationships more closely.[2]

---

[2] The manuscript breaks off unfinished at this point.— *Tr. Note*

Second Manuscript
(THE RELATIONSHIP OF PRIVATE PROPERTY)

(XL) . . . forms the interest on his capital. The worker is the subjective manifestation of the fact that capital is man wholly lost to himself, just as capital is the objective manifestation of the fact that labor is man lost to himself. However, the *worker* has the misfortune to be a *living* capital, a capital with needs, which forfeits its interest and consequently its livelihood every moment that it is not at work. As capital, the *value* of the worker varies according to supply and demand, and his *physical existence*, his *life*, was and is considered as a supply of goods, similar to any other goods. The worker produces capital and capital produces him. Thus he produces himself, and man as a *worker*, as a *commodity*, is the product of the whole process. Man is simply a *worker*, and as a worker his human qualities only exist for the sake of capital which is *alien* to him. Since labor and capital are alien to each other, and thus related only in an external and accidental manner, this alien character must *appear* in reality. As soon as it occurs to capital—either necessarily or voluntarily—not to exist any longer for the worker, he no longer exists for himself; he has *no* work, *no* wage, and since he exists only as a *worker* and not as a *human being*, he may as well let himself be buried, starve, etc. The worker is only a worker when he exists as capital *for himself*, and he only exists as capital when *capital* is there *for him*. The existence of capital is *his* existence, his life, since it determines the content of his

110

life independently of him. Political economy thus does not recognize the unoccupied worker, the working man so far as he is outside this work relationship. Swindlers, thieves, beggars, the unemployed, the starving, poverty stricken and criminal working man, are figures which do not exist for political economy, but only for other eyes; for doctors, judges, gravediggers, beadles, etc. They are ghostly figures beyond its realm. The needs of the worker are thus reduced to the need to maintain him *during work*, so that the race of workers does not die out. Consequently, wages have exactly the same significance as the *maintenance* of any other productive instrument, and as the *consumption of capital* in general so that it can reproduce itself with interest. It is like the oil which is applied to a wheel to keep it running. Wages thus form part of the necessary *costs* of capital and of the capitalist, and they must not exceed this necessary amount. Thus it was quite logical for the English factory lords, before the Amendment Bill of 1834, to deduct from wages the public alms which workers received from the poor law taxes, and to treat them as an integral part of their wages.

Production does not only produce man as a *commodity*, the *human commodity*, man in the form of a *commodity*; in conformity with this situation it produces him as a *mentally* and *physically dehumanized* being.—Immorality, miscarriage, helotism of workers and capitalists. —Its product is the *self-conscious* and *self-acting commodity* . . . the human commodity. . . . It is a great step forward by Ricardo, Mill, etc., as against Smith and Say, to declare the *existence* of human beings — the greater or lesser human productivity of the commodity—as *indifferent* or indeed *harmful*. The true end of production is not the number of workers a given capital maintains, but the amount of interest it earns, the total annual

saving. It was likewise a great and logical advance in
recent (XLI) English political economy that, while establishing *labor* as the only principle of political economy, it clearly distinguished the inverse relation between
wages and interest on capital and observed that as a rule
the capitalist could *only* increase his gains by the depression of wages and vice versa. The *normal* relation is seen
to be not the defrauding of the consumer, but the mutual
cheating of capitalist and worker. The relation of private
property includes within itself, in a latent state, the
relation of private property as *labor*, the relation of private property as capital, and the mutual *influence* of these
two. On the one hand, there is the production of human
activity as *labor*, that is, as an activity which is alien to
itself, to man and to nature, and thus alien to consciousness and to the realization of human life; the *abstract*
existence of man as a mere *working man* who therefore
plunges every day from his fulfilled nothingness into
absolute nothingness, into social, and thus real, non-
existence. On the other hand, there is the production of
objects of human labor as *capital*, in which every natural and social characteristic of the object is *dissolved*,
in which private property has lost its natural and social
quality (and has thereby lost all political and social dis-
guise and no longer even *appears* to be involved with
human relationships), and in which the *same* capital
remains the *same* in the most varied natural and social
conditions, which have no relevance to its *real* content.
This contradiction, at its highest point, is necessarily the
summit and the decline of the whole relation.

It is, therefore, another great achievement of recent
English political economy to have defined ground rent
as the difference between the returns on the worst and
the best cultivated land, to have demolished the romantic illusions of the landowner—his alleged social impor-

tance and the identity of his interests with those of society at large (a view which Adam Smith held even after the Physiocrats)—and to have anticipated and prepared the development in reality which will transform the land-owner into an ordinary, prosaic capitalist and thereby simplify the contradiction, bring it to a head and pre-pare its solution. *Land* as *land, ground rent* as *ground rent*, have lost their status distinction and have become dumb *capital* and *interest*, or rather, capital and interest which only talk money.

The *distinction* between capital and land, profit and ground rent, and the distinction of both from wages, *industry, agriculture, immoveable* and *moveable* private property, is a *historical* distinction, not one inscribed in the nature of things. It is a *fixed* stage in the formation and development of the antithesis between capital and labor. In industry, etc. as opposed to immoveable landed property, only the mode of origin and the antithesis to agriculture through which industry has developed, is ex-pressed. As a *particular* kind of labor, as a more *signifi-cant, important* and *comprehensive* distinction it exists only so long as industry (town life) is established *in op-position* to landed property (aristocratic feudal life) and still bears the characteristics of this contradiction in itself in the form of monopolies, crafts, guilds, corporations, etc. In such a situation, labor still appears to have a *social* meaning, still has the significance of *genuine* com-munal life, and has not yet progressed to *neutrality* in relation to its content, to full self-sufficient being, i.e., to abstraction from all other existence and thus to *liberated* capital.

(XLII) But the necessary *development* of labor is liberated *industry*, constituted for itself alone, and *liber-ated capital*. The power of industry over its opponent is shown by the rise of *agriculture* as a real industry, whereas formerly most of the work was left to the soil itself and to the *slave* of the soil through whom the land cultivated itself. With the transformation of the slave into a *free* worker, i.e., into a *hireling*, the landowner himself is transformed into a lord of industry, a capitalist.

This transformation takes place at first through the medium of the tenant farmer. But the tenant is the representative, the revealed *secret*, of the landowner. Only through him does the landowner have an *economic* existence, as a property owner; for the ground rent of his land only exists as a result of the competition between tenants. Thus the landowner *has* already become to a large extent, in the person of the tenant farmer, a *common* capitalist. And this must be fulfilled in reality; the capitalist directing agriculture (the tenant) must become a landowner, or vice versa. The *industrial trade* of the tenant is that of the landowner, for the existence of the former establishes that of the latter.

Recollecting their contrasting origins and descent the landowner recognizes the capitalist as his insubordinate, liberated and enriched slave of yesterday, and sees himself as a *capitalist* who is threatened by him. The capitalist sees the landowner as the idle, cruel and egotistical lord of yesterday; he knows that he injures him as a capitalist, and yet that industry is responsible for his present social significance, for his possession and pleasures. He regards the landowner as the antithesis of *free* enterprise and of *free capital* which is independent of every natural limitation. This opposition is extremely bitter and each side expresses the truth about the other. It is only necessary to read the attacks upon immoveable property by representatives of moveable property, and vice versa, in order to obtain a clear picture of their respective worthlessness. The landowner emphasizes the noble lineage of his property, feudal souvenirs, reminis-

censes, the poetry of recollection, his open-hearted character, his political importance, etc. and when he talks
in economic terms asserts that agriculture *alone* is productive. At the same time he portrays his opponent as a
sly, bargaining, deceitful, mercenary, rebellious, heartless
and soulless individual, an extortionate, pimping, servile,
smooth, flattering, dessicated rogue, without honor, principles, poetry or anything else, who is alienated from the
community which he freely trades away, and who breeds,
nourishes and cherishes competition and along with it
poverty, crime and the dissolution of all social bonds.
(See among others the Physiocrat, Bergasse, whom Ca-
mille Desmoulins lashes in his journal *Révolutions de
France et de Brabant*; see also von Vincke, Lancizolle,
Haller, Leo, Kosegarten,[1] and Sismondi).

Moveable property, for its part, points to the miracle
of modern industry and development. It is the child, the
legitimate, native-born son, of the modern age. It pities
its opponent as a simpleton, *ignorant* of his own nature
(and this is entirely true) who wishes to replace moral
capital and free labor by crude, immoral coercion and
serfdom. It depicts him as a Don Quixote who, under
the appearance of *directness, decency,* the *general interest,* and *stability,* conceals his incapacity for development, greedy self-indulgence, selfishness, sectional interest and evil intention. It exposes him as a cunning

---

[1] See the garrulous Old-Hegelian theologian Funke who,
according to Herr Leo, related with tears in his eyes how a
slave had refused, when serfdom was abolished, to cease
being a *noble possession.* See also Justus Moser's *Patriotische
Phantasien,* which are distinguished by the fact that they
never for a moment abandon the ingenuous, petty-bourgeois
"home-made", ordinary, limited horizon of the philistine, and
yet remain pure fantasy. This contradiction has made them
so acceptable to the German mind.

monopolist; it pours cold water upon his reminiscences, his poetry and his romanticism, by a historical and satirical recital of the baseness, cruelty, degradation, prostitution, infamy, anarchy and revolt, of which the romantic castles were the workshops.

It (moveable property) claims to have won political freedom for the people, to have removed the chains which bound civil society, to have linked together different worlds, to have established commerce which promotes friendship between peoples, to have created a pure morality and an agreeable culture. It has given the people, in place of their crude wants, civilized needs and the means of satisfying them. But the landowner—this idle grain speculator—raises the price of the people's basic necessities of life and thereby forces the capitalist to raise wages without being able to increase productivity, so hindering and ultimately arresting the growth of national income and the accumulation of capital upon which depends the creation of work for the people and of wealth for the country. He brings about a general decline, and parasitically exploits *all* the advantages of modern civilization without making the least contribution to it, and without abandoning any of his feudal prejudices. Finally, let him—for whom cultivation and the land itself exist only as a heaven-sent source of money— regard the *tenant farmer* and say whether he himself is not a *straightforward, fantastic, cunning* scoundrel, who in his heart and in reality has long been captivated by *free* industry and by the *delights* of trade, however much he may resist them and prattle about historical reminiscences or moral and political aims. Everything which he can really bring forward in justification is true only of the *cultivator of the land* (the capitalist and the laborers) of whom the landowner is rather the *enemy*; thus he

testifies against himself. *Without* capital, landed property is lifeless and worthless matter. It is indeed the civilized victory of moveable property to have discovered and
created human labor as the source of wealth, in place
of the lifeless thing. (See Paul Louis Courier, Saint-
Simon, Ganilh, Ricardo, Mill, MacCulloch, Destutt de
Tracy, and Michel Chevalier.)

From the *real* course of development (to be inserted
here) there follows the necessary victory of the *capitalist*,
i.e., of developed private property, over undeveloped,
immature private property, the *landowner*. In general,
movement must triumph over immobility, overt self-
conscious baseness over concealed, unconscious baseness,
avarice over *self-indulgence*, the avowedly restless and
able self-interest of *enlightenment* over the local, world-
ly-wise, simple, idle and fantastic *self-interest of supersti-
tion*, and *money* over the other forms of private property.

The states which have a presentiment of the danger
represented by fully developed free industry, pure morality, and trade which promotes the amity of peoples, attempt, but quite in vain, to arrest the capitalization of
landed property.

Landed property, as distinct from capital, is private
property, capital, which is still afflicted by *local* and political prejudices; it is capital which has not yet emerged
from its involvement with the world, *undeveloped* capital. In the course of its *formation on a world scale* it
must achieve its abstract, i.e., *pure* expression.

The relations of private property are capital, labor,
and their interconnections.

The movements through which these elements have
to go are:

First—*unmediated* and *mediated unity of the two.*
   Capital and labor are at first still united; later
   indeed separated and alienated, but reciprocally

developing and promoting each other as *positive* conditions.

Opposition between the two—they mutually exclude each other; the worker recognizes the capitalist as his own non-existence and vice versa; each seeks to rob the other of his existence.

Opposition of each *to* itself. Capital = accumulated labor = labor. As such it divides into *capital itself* and *interest*; the latter divides into *interest* and *profit*. Complete sacrifice of the capitalist. He sinks into the working class, just as the worker—but only exceptionally—becomes a capitalist. Labor as a moment of capital, its *cost*. Thus wages a sacrifice of capital.

Labor divides into *labor itself* and *wages of labor*. The worker himself a capital, a commodity.

Clash of reciprocal contradictions.[2]

[2] The second manuscript ends here.—*Tr. Note*

Third Manuscript
(PRIVATE PROPERTY AND LABOR)

(I) *ad* page XXXVI. The *subjective essence* of private property, *private* property as activity for itself, as *subject*, as *person*, is labor. It is evident, therefore, that only the political economy which recognized labor as its principle (Adam Smith) and which no longer regarded private property as merely a *condition* external to man, can be considered as both a product of the real *dynamism* and *development* of private property,[1] a product of modern *industry*, and a force which has accelerated and extolled the dynamism and development of industry and has made it a power in the domain of *consciousness*.

Thus, in the view of this enlightened political economy which has discovered the *subjective essence* of wealth within the framework of private property, the partisans of the monetary system, and of the mercantilist system, who consider private property as a *purely objective* being for man, are *fetishists* and *Catholics*. Engels is right, therefore, in calling Adam Smith the *Luther of political economy*. Just as Luther recognized religion and *faith* as the essence of the real *world*, and for that reason took up a position against Catholic paganism; just as he annulled *external* religiosity while making religiosity the *inner* essence of man; just as he negated the distinction between priest and layman because he transferred the priest into the heart of the layman; so

---

[1] It is the independent movement of private property become conscious of itself; modern industry as Self.

wealth external to man and independent of him (and thus only to be acquired and conserved from outside) is annulled. That is to say, its *external* and *mindless* objectivity is annulled by the fact that private property is incorporated in man himself, and man himself is recognized as its essence. But as a result, man himself is brought into the sphere of private property, just as, with Luther, he is brought into the sphere of religion. Under the guise of recognizing man, political economy, whose principle is labor, carries to its logical conclusion the denial of man. Man himself is no longer in a condition of external tension with the external substance of private property; he has himself become the tension-ridden being of private property. What was previously a phenomenon of *being external to oneself*, a real external manifestation of man, has now become the act of objectification, of alienation. This political economy seems, therefore, at first, to recognize man with his independence, his personal activity, etc. It incorporates private property in the very essence of man, and it is no longer, therefore, conditioned by the local or national *characteristics of private property* regarded as *existing* outside itself. It manifests a cosmopolitan, universal activity which is destructive of every limit and every bond, and substitutes itself as the *only policy*, the *only* universality, the *only* limit and the *only* bond. But in its further development it is obliged to discard this hypocrisy and to show itself in all its cynicism. It does this, without any regard for the apparent contradictions to which its doctrine leads, by showing in a more *one-sided* fashion, and thus with greater *logic* and *clarity*, that *labor* is the sole *essence of wealth*, and by demonstrating that this doctrine, in contrast with the original conception, has consequences which are *inimical to man*. Finally, it gives the death blow to *ground rent*, that last individual and natural form of private property and source of wealth existing independently of the movement of labor which was the expression of feudal property, but has become entirely its economic expression and is no longer able to put up any resistance to political economy. (The Ricardo School.) Not only does the *cynicism* of political economy increase from Smith, through Say, to Ricardo, Mill, etc. inasmuch as for the latter the consequences of *industry* appeared more and more developed and contradictory; from a positive point of view they become more alienated, and more consciously alienated, from man, in comparison with their predecessors. This is *only* because their science develops with greater logic and truth. Since they make private property in its active form the subject, and since at the same time they make man as a non-being into a being, the contradiction in reality corresponds entirely with the contradictory essence which they have accepted as a principle. The divided (II) *reality* of *industry* is far from refuting, but instead confirms, its *self-divided* principle. Its principle is in fact the principle of this division.

The physiocratic doctrine of Quesnay forms the transition from the mercantilist system to Adam Smith. *Physiocracy* is in a direct sense the *economic* decomposition of feudal property, but for this reason it is equally directly the *economic transformation*, the reestablishment, of this same feudal property, with the difference that its language is no longer feudal but economic. All wealth is reduced to *land* and *cultivation* (agriculture). Land is not yet *capital* but is still a *particular* mode of existence of capital, whose value is claimed to reside in, and derive from, its natural particularity; but land is nonetheless a natural and universal *element*, whereas the mercantilist system regarded only precious metals as wealth. The *object* of wealth, its matter, has therefore been given the greatest universality within *natural limits* —inasmuch as it is also, as *nature*, directly objective wealth. And it is only by labor, by agriculture, that land exists for man. Consequently, the subjective essence of wealth is already transferred to labor. But at the same time agriculture is the *only productive labor*. Labor is therefore not yet taken in its universality and its abstract form; it is still bound to a particular *element of nature as its matter*, and is only recognized in a particular *mode of existence determined by nature*. Labor is still only a *determinate, particular* alienation of man, and its product is also conceived as a determinate part of wealth due more to nature than to labor itself. Land is still regarded here as something which exists naturally and independently of man, and not yet as capital; i.e., as a factor of labor. On the contrary, labor appears to be a factor of *nature*. But since the fetishism of the old external wealth, existing only as an object, has been reduced to a very simple natural element, and since its essence has been partially, and in a certain way, recognized in its subjective existence, the necessary advance has been made in recognizing the *universal nature* of wealth and in raising labor in its absolute form, i.e., in abstraction, to the *principle*. It is demonstrated against the physiocrats that from the economic point of view (i.e., from the only valid point of view) agriculture does not differ from any other industry; and that it is not, therefore, a specific kind of labor, bound to a particular element, or a particular manifestation of labor, but *labor in general* which is the *essence* of wealth.

Physiocracy denies *specific*, external, purely objective wealth, in declaring that labor is its essence. For the physiocrats, however, labor is in the first place only the *subjective essence* of landed property. (They begin from that kind of property which appears historically as the predominant recognized type.) They merely turn landed property into alienated man. They annul its feudal character by declaring that *industry* (agriculture) is its *essence*; but they reject the industrial world and accept the feudal system by declaring that *agriculture* is the *only* industry.

It is evident that when the *subjective essence*—industry in opposition to landed property, industry forming itself as industry—is grasped, this essence includes within itself the opposition. For just as industry incorporates the superseded landed property, its subjective essence incorporates the subjective essence of the latter.

Landed property is the first form of private property, and industry first appears historically in simple opposition to it, as a particular form of private property (or rather, as the liberated slave of landed property); this sequence is repeated in the scientific study of the *subjective* essence of private property, and labor appears at first only as *agricultural labor* but later establishes itself as *labor in general*.

(III) All wealth has become *industrial* wealth, the *wealth* of labor, and *industry* is realized labor; just as the *factory system* is the realized essence of *industry* (i.e., of labor), and as *industrial capital* is the realized objective form of private property. Thus we see that it is only at this stage that private property can consolidate its rule over man and become, in its most general form, a world-historical power.

(PRIVATE PROPERTY AND COMMUNISM)

ad page XXXIX. But the antithesis between *propertylessness* and *property* is still an indeterminate antithesis, which is not conceived in its *active reference* to its intrinsic relations, not yet conceived as a contradiction, so long as it is not understood as an antithesis between *labor* and *capital*. Even without the advanced development of private property, e.g., in ancient Rome, in Turkey, etc. this antithesis may be expressed in a primitive form. In this form it does not yet *appear* as established by private property itself. But labor, the subjective essence of private property as the exclusion of property, and capital, objective labor as the exclusion of labor, constitute *private property* as the developed relation of the contradiction and thus a dynamic relation which drives towards its resolution.

ad ibidem The supersession of self-estrangement follows the same course as self-estrangement. *Private property* is first considered only from its objective aspect, but with labor conceived as its essence. Its mode of existence is therefore *capital* which it is necessary to abolish "as such" (Proudhon). Or else the *specific form* of labor (labor which is brought to a common level, sub-divided, and thus unfree) is regarded as the source of the *noxiousness* of private property and of its existence alienated from man. Fourier, in accord with the Physiocrats, regards *agricultural labor* as being at least the exemplary kind of labor. Saint-Simon asserts on the contrary that *industrial labor* as such is the essence of labor, and consequently he desires the *exclusive* rule of the industrialists and an amelioration of the condition of the workers. Finally, *communism* is the *positive* expression of the abolition of private property, and in the first place of universal private property. In taking this relation in its *universal aspect* communism is (1) in its first form, only the generalization and fulfilment of the relation. As such it appears in a double form; the domination of material property looms so large that it aims to destroy everything which is incapable of being possessed by everyone as private property. It wishes to eliminate talent, etc. by *force.* Immediate physical possession seems to it the unique goal of life and existence. The role of *worker* is not abolished, but is extended to all men. The relation of private property remains the relation of the community to the world of things. Finally, this tendency to oppose general private property to private property is expressed in an animal form; *marriage* (which is incontestably a form of *exclusive private property*) is contrasted with the community of women, in which women become communal and common property. One may say that this idea of the *community of women* is the *open secret* of this entirely crude and unreflective communism. Just as women are to pass from marriage to universal prostitution, so the whole world of wealth (i.e., the objective being of man) is to pass from the relation of exclusive marriage with the private owner to the relation of universal prostitution with the community. This communism, which negates the *personality* of man in every sphere, is only the logical expression of private property, which is this negation. Universal *envy* setting itself up as a power is only a camouflaged form of cupidity which re-establishes itself and satisfies itself in a different way. The thoughts of every individual private property are *at least* directed against any *wealthier* private property, in the form of envy and the desire to reduce everything to a common level; so that this envy and leveling in fact constitute the essence of competition. Crude communism is only the culmination of such envy and leveling-down on the basis of a *preconceived* minimum. How little this abolition of private property represents a genuine appropriation is shown by the abstract negation of the whole world of culture and civilization, and the regression to the *unnatural* (IV) simplicity of the poor and wantless individual who has not only not surpassed private property but has not yet even attained to it.

The community is only a community of *work* and of *equality of wages* paid out by the communal capital, by the *community* as universal capitalist. The two sides of the relation are raised to a *supposed* universality; *labor* as a condition in which everyone is placed, and *capital* as the acknowledged universality and power of the community.

In the relationship with *woman*, as the prey and the handmaid of communal lust, is expressed the infinite degradation in which man exists for himself; for the secret of this relationship finds its *unequivocal*, incontestable, *open* and revealed expression in the relation of man to woman and in the way in which the *direct* and *natural* species relationship is conceived. The immediate, natural and necessary relation of human being to human being is also the *relation* of *man* to *woman*. In this *natural* species relationship man's relation to nature is directly his relation to man, and his relation to man is directly his relation to nature, to his own *natural* function. Thus, in this relation is *sensuously revealed*, reduced to an observable *fact*, the extent to which human nature has become nature for man and to which nature has become human nature for him. From this relationship man's whole level of development can be assessed. It follows from the character of this relationship how far *man* has become, and has understood himself as, a *species-being*, a *human being*. The relation of man to woman is the *most natural* relation of human being to human being. It indicates, therefore, how far man's *natural* behavior has become *human*, and how far his *human* essence has become a *natural* essence for him, how far his *human nature* has become *nature for him*. It also shows how far man's *needs* have become *human* needs, and consequently how far the other person, as a person, has become one of his needs, and to what extent he is in his individual existence at the same time a social being. The first positive annulment of private property, crude communism, is therefore only a *phenomenal form* of the infamy of private property representing itself as positive community.

(2) Communism (a) still political in nature, democratic or despotic; (b) with the abolition of the state, yet still incomplete and influenced by private property, that is, by the alienation of man. In both forms communism is already aware of being the reintegration of man, his return to himself, the supersession of man's self-alienation. But since it has not yet grasped the positive nature of private property, or the *human* nature of needs, it is still captured and contaminated by private property. It has well understood the concept, but not the essence.

(3) *Communism* is the *positive* abolition of *private property*, of *human self-alienation*, and thus the real *appropriation* of *human* nature through and for man. It is, therefore, the return of man himself as a *social*, i.e., really human, being, a complete and conscious return which assimilates all the wealth of previous development. Communism as a fully-developed naturalism is humanism and as a fully-developed humanism is naturalism. It is the *definitive* resolution of the antagonism between man and nature, and between man and man. It is the true solution of the conflict between existence and essence, between objectification and self-affirmation, between freedom and necessity, between individual and species. It is the solution of the riddle of history and knows itself to be this solution.

(V) Thus the whole historical development, both the *real* genesis of communism (the birth of its empirical existence) and its thinking consciousness, is its comprehended and conscious process of becoming; whereas the other, still undeveloped communism seeks in certain historical forms opposed to private property, a *historical* justification founded upon what already exists, and to this end tears out of their context isolated elements of this development (Cabet and Villegardelle are pre-eminent among those who ride this hobby horse) and asserts them as proofs of its historical pedigree. In doing so, it makes clear that by far the greater part of this development contradicts its own assertions, and that if it has ever existed its past existence refutes its pretension to *essential being*.

It is easy to understand the necessity which leads the whole revolutionary movement to find its empirical, as well as its theoretical, basis in the development of *private property*, and more precisely of the economic system.

This material, directly *perceptible* private property is the material and sensuous expression of *alienated human* life. Its movement—production and consumption—is the *sensuous* manifestation of the movement of all previous production, i.e., the realization or reality of man. Religion, the family, the state, law, morality, science, art, etc. are only *particular* forms of production and come under its general law. The positive supersession of *private property* as the appropriation of *human* life, is therefore the *positive* supersession of all alienation, and the return of man from religion, the family, the state, etc. to his *human*, i.e., *social* life. Religious alienation as such occurs only in the sphere of *consciousness*, in the inner life of man, but economic alienation is that of *real life* and its supersession therefore affects both aspects. Of course, the development in different nations has a different beginning according to whether the actual and *established* life of the people is more in the realm of mind or more in the external world, is a real or ideal life. Communism begins where atheism begins (Owen), but atheism is at the outset still far from being *communism;* indeed it is still for the most part an abstraction. Thus the philanthropy of atheism is at first only an abstract *philosophical* philanthropy, whereas that of communism is at once *real* and oriented towards *action.*

We have seen how, on the assumption that private property has been positively superseded, man produces man, himself and then other men; how the object which is the direct activity of his personality is at the same time his existence for other men and their existence for him. Similarly, the material of labor and man himself as a subject are the starting point as well as the result of this movement (and because there must be this starting point private property is a historical necessity). Therefore, the *social* character is the universal character of the whole movement; *as* society itself produces *man* as *man,* so it is *produced* by him. Activity and mind are social in their content as well as in their *origin;* they are *social* activity and *social* mind. The *human* significance of nature only exists for *social* man, because only in this case is nature a *bond* with other *men,* the basis of his existence for others and of their existence for him. Only then is nature the *basis* of his own *human* experience and a vital element of human reality. The *natural* existence of man has here become his *human* existence and nature itself has become human for him. Thus *society* is the accomplished union of man with nature, the veritable resurrection of nature, the realized naturalism of man and the realized humanism of nature.

(VI) Social activity and social mind by no means exist *only* in the form of activity or mind which is directly communal. Nevertheless, communal activity and mind, i.e., activity and mind which express and confirm themselves directly in a *real association* with other men, occur everywhere where this *direct* expression of sociability arises from the content of the activity or corresponds to the nature of mind.

Even when I carry out *scientific* work, etc. an activity which I can seldom conduct in direct association with other men, I perform a *social*, because *human*, act. It is not only the material of my activity—such as the language itself which the thinker uses—which is given to me as a social product. *My own existence* is a social activity. For this reason, what I myself produce I produce for society, and with the consciousness of acting as a social being.

My universal consciousness is only the *theoretical* form of that whose *living* form is the *real* community, the social entity, although at the present day this *universal* consciousness is an abstraction from real life and is opposed to it as an enemy. That is why the *activity* of my universal consciousness as such is my *theoretical* existence as a social being.

It is above all necessary to avoid postulating "society" once again as an abstraction confronting the individual. The individual *is* the *social being*. The manifestation of his life—even when it does not appear directly in the form of a communal manifestation, accomplished in association with other men—is therefore a manifestation and affirmation of *social life*. Individual human life and species-life are not *different things*, even though the mode of existence of individual life is necessarily either a more *specific* or a more *general* mode of species-life, or that of species-life a more *specific* or more *general* mode of individual life.

In his *species-consciousness* man confirms his real *social life*, and reproduces his real existence in thought; while conversely, species-life confirms itself in species-consciousness and exists for itself in its universality as a thinking being. Though man is a unique individual—and it is just his particularity which makes him an individual, a really *individual* communal being—he is equally the *whole*, the ideal whole, the subjective existence of society as thought and experienced. He exists in reality as the representation and the real mind of social existence, and as the sum of human manifestation of life.

Thought and being are indeed *distinct* but they also form a unity. *Death* seems to be a harsh victory of the species over the individual and to contradict their unity; but the particular individual is only a *determinate species-being* and as such he is mortal.

(4) Just as *private property* is only the sensuous expression of the fact that man is at the same time an *objective* fact for himself and becomes an alien and non-human object for himself; just as his manifestation of life is also his alienation of life and his self-realization a loss of reality, the emergence of an *alien* reality; so the positive supersession of private property, i.e., the *sensuous* appropriation of the human essence and of human life, of objective man and of human *creations*, by and for man, should not be taken only in the sense of *immediate*, exclusive *enjoyment*, or only in the sense of *possession* or *having*. Man appropriates his manifold being in an all-inclusive way, and thus as a whole man. All his *human* relations to the world—seeing, hearing, smelling, tasting, touching, thinking, observing, feeling, desiring, acting, loving—in short all the organs of his individuality, like the organs which are directly communal in form (VII) are, in their objective action (their *action in relation to the object*) the appropriation of this object, the appropriation of human reality. The way in which they react to the object is the confirmation of

human reality.[1] It is human effectiveness and human *suffering*, for suffering humanly considered is an enjoyment of the self for man.

Private property has made us so stupid and partial that an object is only *ours* when we have it, when it exists for us as capital or when it is directly eaten, drunk, worn, inhabited, etc., in short, *utilized* in some way; although private property itself only conceives these various forms of possession as *means of life*, and the life for which they serve as means is the *life* of *private property*—labor and creation of capital.

Thus *all* the physical and intellectual senses have been replaced by the simple alienation of *all* these senses; the sense of *having*. The human being had to be reduced to this absolute poverty in order to be able to give birth to all his inner wealth. (On the category of *having* see Hess in *Einundzwanzig Bogen*.)

The supersession of private property is therefore the complete *emancipation* of all the human qualities and senses. It is this emancipation because these qualities and senses have become *human*, from the subjective as well as the objective point of view. The eye has become a *human* eye when its *object* has become a *human*, social object, created by man and destined for him. The senses have therefore become directly theoreticians in practice. They relate themselves to the thing for the sake of the thing, but the thing itself is an *objective human* relation to itself and to man, and vice versa.[2] Need and enjoyment have thus lost their *egoistic* character, and nature has lost its mere *utility* by the fact that its utilization has become *human* utilization.

---

[1] It is therefore just as varied as the determinations of human nature and activities are diverse.

[2] In practice I can only relate myself in a human way to a thing when the thing is related in a human way to man.

Similarly, the senses and minds of other men have become my *own* appropriation. Thus besides these direct organs, *social* organs are constituted, in the form of society; for example, activity in direct association with others has become an organ for the manifestation of life and a mode of appropriation of *human* life.

It is evident that the human eye appreciates things in a different way from the crude, non-human eye, the human *ear* differently from the crude ear. As we have seen, it is only when the object becomes a *human* object, or objective *humanity*, that man does not become lost in it. This is only possible when the object becomes a *social* object, and when he himself becomes a social being and society becomes a being for him in this object.

On the one hand, it is only when objective reality everywhere becomes for man in society the reality of human faculties, human reality, and thus the reality of his own faculties, that all *objects* become for him the *objectification of himself.* The objects then confirm and realize his individuality, they are *his own* objects, i.e., man himself becomes the object. *The manner in which* these objects become his own depends upon the *nature of the object* and the nature of the corresponding faculty; for it is precisely the *determinate character* of this relation which constitutes the specific *real* mode of affirmation. The object is not the same for the *eye* as for the *ear*, for the ear as for the eye. The *distinctive character* of each faculty is precisely its *characteristic* essence and thus also the characteristic mode of its objectification, of its *objectively real*, living *being*. It is therefore not only in thought, (VIII) but through *all* the senses that man is affirmed in the objective world.

Let us next consider the subjective aspect. Man's musical sense is only awakened by music. The most beautiful music has no meaning for the non-musical ear, is not an object for it, because my object can only be the confirmation of one of my own faculties. It can only be so for me in so far as my faculty exists for itself as a subjective capacity, because the meaning of an object for me extends only as far as the sense extends (only makes sense for an appropriate sense). For this reason, the *senses* of social man are *different* from those of non-social man. It is only through the objectively deployed wealth of the human being that the wealth of subjective *human* sensibility (a musical ear, an eye which is sensitive to the beauty of form, in short, senses which are capable of human satisfaction and which confirm themselves as human faculties) is cultivated or created. For it is not only the five senses, but also the so-called spiritual senses, the practical senses (desiring, loving, etc.), in brief, human sensibility and the human character of the senses, which can only come into being through the existence of *its* object, through humanized nature. The cultivation of the five senses is the work of all previous history. Sense which is subservient to crude needs has only a restricted meaning. For a starving man the human form of food does not exist, but only its abstract character as food. It could just as well exist in the most crude form, and it is impossible to say in what way this feeding-activity would differ from that of animals. The needy man, burdened with cares, has no appreciation of the most beautiful spectacle. The dealer in minerals sees only their commercial value, not their beauty or their particular characteristics; he has no mineralogical sense. Thus, the objectification of the human essence, both theoretically and practically, is necessary in order to *humanize* man's *senses*, and also to create the *human senses* corresponding to all the wealth of human and natural being.

Just as society at its beginnings finds, through the

development of *private property* with its wealth and poverty (both intellectual and material), the materials necessary for this *cultural development, so* the fully constituted society produces man in all the plenitude of his being, the wealthy man endowed with all the senses, as an enduring reality. It is only in a social context that subjectivism and objectivism, spiritualism and materialism, activity and passivity, cease to be antinomies and thus cease to exist as such antinomies. The resolution of the *theoretical* contradictions is possible *only* through *practical* means, only through the practical energy of man. Their resolution is not by any means, therefore, only a problem of knowledge, but is a *real* problem of life which philosophy was unable to solve precisely because it saw there a purely theoretical problem.

It can be seen that the history of *industry* and industry as it *objectively* exists is an *open* book of the *human faculties*, and a human *psychology* which can be sensuously apprehended. This history has not so far been conceived in relation to human *nature*, but only from a superficial utilitarian point of view, since in the condition of alienation it was only possible to conceive real human faculties and *human* species-action in the form of general human existence, as religion, or as history in its abstract, general aspect as politics, art and literature, etc. *Everyday material industry* (which can be conceived as part of that general development; or equally, the general development can be conceived as a *specific* part of industry since all human activity up to the present has been labor, i.e., industry, self-alienated activity) shows us, in the form of *sensuous useful objects*, in an alienated form, the *essential human faculties* transformed into objects. No psychology for which this book, i.e., the most sensibly present and accessible part of history, remains closed, can become a *real* science with a genuine content.

What is to be thought of a science which stays aloof from this enormous field of human labor and which does not feel its own inadequacy even though this great wealth of human activity means nothing to it except perhaps what can be expressed in the single phrase— "need", "common need"?

The *natural sciences* have developed a tremendous activity and have assembled an ever-growing mass of data. But philosophy has remained alien to these sciences just as they have remained alien to philosophy. Their momentary *rapprochement* was only a *fantastic* illusion. There was a desire for union but the power to effect it was lacking. Historiography itself only takes natural science into account incidentally, regarding it as a factor making for enlightenment, for practical utility and for particular great discoveries. But natural science has penetrated all the more *practically* into human life through industry. It has transformed human life and prepared the emancipation of humanity even though its immediate effect was to accentuate the dehumanization of man. *Industry* is the actual historical relationship of nature, and thus of natural science, to man. If industry is conceived as the *exoteric* manifestation of the essential human *faculties*, the *human* essence of nature and the *natural* essence of man can also be understood. Natural science will then abandon its abstract materialist, or rather idealist, orientation, and will become the basis of a *human* science, just as it has already become— though in an alienated form—the basis of actual human life. One basis for life and another for science is *a priori* a falsehood. Nature, as it develops in human history, in the act of genesis of human society, is the *actual* nature of man; thus nature, as it develops through industry, though in an *alienated* form, is truly *anthropological* nature.

Sense experience (see Feuerbach) must be the basis of all science. Science is only *genuine* science when it proceeds from sense experience, in the two forms of *sense perception* and *sensuous* need; i.e., only when it proceeds from nature. The whole of history is a preparation for "man" to become an object of *sense perception*, and for the development of human needs (the needs of man as such). History itself is a *real* part of *natural history*, of the development of nature into man. Natural science will one day incorporate the science of man, just as the science of man will incorporate natural science; there will be a *single* science.

Man is the direct object of natural science, because directly *perceptible nature* is for man directly human sense experience (an identical expression) as the *other person* who is directly presented to him in a sensuous way. His own sense experience only exists as human sense experience for himself through the *other person*. But *nature* is the direct object of the *science of man*. The first object for man—man himself—is nature, sense experience; and the particular sensuous human faculties, which can only find objective realization in *natural* objects, can only attain self-knowledge in the science of natural being. The element of thought itself, the element of the living manifestation of thought, *language*, is sensuous in nature. The *social* reality of nature and *human* natural science or the *natural science of man*, are identical expressions.

It will be seen from this how, in place of the *wealth* and *poverty* of political economy, we have the *wealthy* man and the plenitude of *human* need. The wealthy man is at the same time one who *needs* a complex of human manifestations of life, and whose own self-realization exists as an inner necessity, a *need*. Not only the *wealth* but also the *poverty* of man acquires, in a socialist per-

spective, a *human* and thus a social meaning. Poverty
is the passive bond which leads man to experience a
need for the greatest wealth, the *other* person. The sway
of the objective entity within me, the sensuous outbreak
of my life-activity, is the passion which here becomes
the *activity* of my being.

(5) A being does not regard himself as independent
unless he is his own master, and he is only his own master
when he owes his existence to himself. A man who lives
by the favor of another considers himself a dependent
being. But I live completely by another person's favor
when I owe to him not only the continuance of my life
but also *its creation*; when he is its *source*. My life has
necessarily such a cause outside itself if it is not my own
creation. The idea of *creation* is thus one which it is
difficult to eliminate from popular consciousness. This
consciousness is *unable to conceive* that nature and man
exist on their own account, because such an existence
contradicts all the tangible facts of practical life.

The idea of the creation of the *earth* has received a
severe blow from the science of geogeny, i.e., from the
science which portrays the formation and development
of the earth as a process of spontaneous generation.
Generatio aequivoca (spontaneous generation) is the
only practical refutation of the theory of creation.

But it is easy indeed to say to the particular individual what Aristotle said: You are engendered by your
father and mother, and consequently it is the coitus of
two human beings, a human species-act, which has produced the human being. You see therefore that even
in a physical sense man owes his existence to man. Consequently, it is not enough to keep in view only one of
the two aspects, the *infinite* progression, and to ask
further: who engendered my father and my grandfather?
You must also keep in mind the *circular movement* which

is perceptible in that progression, according to which man, in the act of generation reproduces himself; thus *man* always remains the subject. But you will reply: I grant you this circular movement, but you must in turn concede the progression, which leads even further to the point where I ask: who created the first man and nature as a whole? I can only reply: your question is itself a product of abstraction. Ask yourself how you arrive at that question. Ask yourself whether your question does not arise from a point of view to which I cannot reply because it is a perverted one. Ask yourself whether that progression exists as such for rational thought. If you ask a question about the creation of nature and man you abstract from nature and man. You suppose them *nonexistent* and you want me to demonstrate that they *exist*. I reply: give up your abstraction and at the same time you abandon your question. Or else, if you want to maintain your abstraction, be consistent, and if you think of man and nature as non-existent (XI) think of yourself too as non-existent, for you are also man and nature. Do not think, do not ask me any questions, for as soon as you think and ask questions your *abstraction* from the existence of nature and man becomes meaningless. Or are you such an egoist that you conceive everything as non-existent and yet want to exist yourself?

You may reply: I do not want to conceive the nothingness of nature, etc.; I only ask you about the act of its creation, just as I ask the anatomist about the formation of bones, etc.

Since, however, for socialist man, the *whole of what is called world history* is nothing but the creation of man by human labor, and the emergence of nature for man, he therefore has the evident and irrefutable proof of his *self-creation*, of his own *origins*. Once the essence of man and of nature, man as a natural being and nature as a human reality, has become evident in practical life, in sense experience, the quest for an *alien* being, a being above man and nature (a quest which is an avowal of the unreality of man and nature) becomes impossible in practice. *Atheism*, as a denial of this unreality, is no longer meaningful, for atheism is a *negation of God* and seeks to assert by this negation the *existence of man*. Socialism no longer requires such a roundabout method; it begins from the *theoretical* and *practical sense perception* of man and nature as essential beings. It is positive human *self-consciousness*, no longer a self-consciousness attained through the negation of religion; just as the *real life* of man is positive and no longer attained through the negation of private property, through *communism*. Communism is the phase of negation of the negation and is, consequently, for the next stage of historical development, a real and necessary factor in the emancipation and rehabilitation of man. Communism is the necessary form and the dynamic principle of the immediate future, but communism is not itself the goal of human development —the form of human society.

(NEEDS, PRODUCTION, AND DIVISION OF LABOR)

(XIV) (7) We have seen what importance should be attributed, in a socialist perspective, to the *wealth of* human needs, and consequently also to a *new mode of production* and to a new *object* of production. A new manifestation of *human* powers and a new enrichment of the human being. Within the system of private property it has the opposite meaning. Every man speculates upon creating a *new* need in another in order to force

him to a new sacrifice, to place him in a new dependence, and to entice him into a new kind of pleasure and
thereby into economic ruin. Everyone tries to establish
over others an *alien* power in order to find there the
satisfaction of his own egoistic need. With the mass of
objects, therefore, there also increases the realm of alien
entities to which man is subjected. Every new product
is a new *potentiality* of mutual deceit and robbery. Man
becomes increasingly poor as a man; he has increasing
need of *money* in order to take possession of the hostile
being. The power of his *money* diminishes directly with
the growth of the quantity of production, i.e., his need
increases with the increasing *power* of money. The need
for money is therefore the real need created by the
modern economy, and the only need which it creates.
The *quantity* of money becomes increasingly its only
important quality. Just as it reduces every entity to its
abstraction, so it reduces itself in its own development
to a *quantitative* entity. Excess and immoderation become its true standard. This is shown subjectively, partly in the fact that the expansion of production and of
needs becomes an *ingenious* and always *calculating* subservience to inhuman, depraved, unnatural, and *imaginary* appetites. Private property does not know how to
change crude need into *human* need; its *idealism* is
fantasy, caprice and *fancy*. No eunuch flatters his tyrant
more shamefully or seeks by more infamous means to
stimulate his jaded appetite, in order to gain some favor,
than does the eunuch of industry, the entrepreneur, in
order to acquire a few silver coins or to charm the gold
from the purse of his dearly beloved neighbor. (Every
product is a bait by means of which the individual tries
to entice the essence of the other person, his money.
Every real or potential need is a weakness which will
draw the bird into the lime. Universal exploitation of

human communal life. As every imperfection of man is a bond with heaven, a point from which his heart is accessible to the priest, so every want is an opportunity for approaching one's neighbor, with an air of friendship, and saying, "Dear friend, I will give you what you need, but you know the *conditio sine qua non.* You know what ink you must use in signing yourself over to me. I shall swindle you while providing your enjoyment.") The entrepreneur accedes to the most depraved fancies of his neighbor, plays the role of pander between him and his needs, awakens unhealthy appetites in him, and watches for every weakness in order, later, to claim the remuneration for this labor of love.

This alienation is shown in part by the fact that the refinement of needs and of the means to satisfy them produces as its counterpart a bestial savagery, a complete, primitive and abstract simplicity of needs; or rather, that it simply reproduces itself in its opposite sense. For the worker even the need for fresh air ceases to be a need. Man returns to the cave dwelling again, but it is now poisoned by the pestilential breath of civilization. The worker has only a *precarious* right to inhabit it, for it has become an alien dwelling which may suddenly not be available, or from which he may be evicted if he does not pay the rent. He has to *pay* for this mortuary. The dwelling full of light which Prometheus, in Aeschylus, indicates as one of the great gifts by which he has changed savages into men, ceases to exist for the worker. Light, air, and the simplest *animal* cleanliness cease to be human needs. *Filth,* this corruption and putrefaction which runs in the *sewers* of civilization (this is to be taken literally) becomes the *element in which man lives.* Total and *unnatural* neglect, putrified nature, becomes the *element in which he lives.* None of his senses exist any longer, either in a human form, or even in a *non-human*, animal form. The crudest *methods* (and *instruments*) of human labor re-appear; thus the *tread-mill* of the Roman slaves has become the mode of production and mode of existence of many English workers. It is not enough that man should lose his human needs; even animal needs disappear. The Irish no longer have any need but that of *eating—eating potatoes,* and then only the worst kind, *mouldy potatoes.* But France and England already possess in every industrial town a *little* Ireland. Savages and animals have at least the need for hunting, exercise and companionship. But the simplification of machinery and of work is used to make workers out of those who are just growing up, who are still immature, *children*, while the worker himself has become a child deprived of all care. Machinery is adapted to the weakness of the human being, in order to turn the weak human being into a machine.

The fact that the growth of needs and of the means to satisfy them results in a lack of needs and of means is demonstrated in several ways by the economist (and by the capitalist; in fact, it is always *empirical* businessmen we refer to when we speak of economists, who are their *scientific* self-revelation and existence). First, by reducing the needs of the worker to the miserable necessities required for the maintenance of his physical existence, and by reducing his activity to the most abstract mechanical movements, the economist asserts that man has no needs, for activity or enjoyment, beyond that; and yet he declares that this kind of life is a *human* way of life. Secondly, by reckoning as the general standard of life (general because it is applicable to the mass of men) the *most impoverished* life conceivable, he turns the worker into a being who has neither senses nor needs, just as he turns his activity into a pure abstraction from all activity. Thus all working class *luxury* seems to him blameworthy, and everything which goes beyond the most abstract need (whether it be a passive enjoyment or a manifestation of personal activity) is regarded as a *luxury*. Political economy, the science of *wealth*, is therefore, at the same time, the science of renunciation, of privation and of saving, which actually succeeds in depriving man of fresh *air* and of physical *activity*. This science of a marvelous industry is at the same time the science of *asceticism*. Its true ideal is the *ascetic* but *usurious* miser and the *ascetic* but *productive* slave. Its moral ideal is the *worker* who takes a part of his wages to the savings bank. It has even found a servile art to embody this favorite idea, which has been produced in a sentimental manner on the stage. Thus, despite its worldly and pleasure-seeking appearance, it is a truly moral science, the most moral of all sciences. Its principal thesis is the renunciation of life and of human needs. The less you eat, drink, buy books, go to the theatre or to balls, or to the public house, and the less you think, love, theorize, sing, paint, fence, etc. the more you will be able to save and the *greater* will become your treasure which neither moth nor rust will corrupt— your *capital*. The less you *are*, the less you express your life, the more you *have*, the greater is your *alienated* life and the greater is the saving of your alienated being. Everything which the economist takes from you in the way of life and humanity, he restores to you in the form of *money* and *wealth*. And everything which you are unable to do, your money can do for you; it can eat, drink, go to the ball and to the theatre. It can acquire art, learning, historical treasures, political power; and it can travel. It *can* appropriate all these things for you, can purchase everything; it is the true *opulence*. But although it can do all this, it only *desires* to create itself, and to buy itself, for everything else is subservient to it.

When one owns the master, one also owns the servant, and one has no need of the master's servant. Thus all passions and activities must be submerged in *avarice*. The worker must have just what is necessary for him to want to live, and he must want to live only in order to have this.

It is true that some controversy has arisen in the field of political economy. Some economists (Lauderdale, Malthus, etc.) advocate luxury and condemn saving, while others (Ricardo, Say, etc.) advocate saving and condemn luxury. But the former admit that they desire luxury in order to create *work*, i.e., absolute saving, while the latter admit that they advocate saving in order to create *wealth*, i.e., luxury. The former have the romantic notion that avarice alone should not determine the consumption of the rich, and they contradict their own laws when they represent *prodigality* as being a direct means of enrichment; their opponents then demonstrate in detail and with great earnestness that prodigality diminishes rather than augments my *possessions*. The second group are hypocritical in not admitting that it is caprice and fancy which determine production. They forget the "refined needs", and that without consumption there would be no production. They forget that through competition production must become ever more universal and luxurious, that it is use which determines the value of a thing, and that use is determined by fashion. They want production to be limited to "useful things", but they forget that the production of too many useful things results in too many *useless* people. Both sides forget that prodigality and thrift, luxury and abstinence, wealth and poverty are equivalent.

You must not only be abstemious in the satisfaction of your direct senses, such as eating, etc. but also in your participation in general interests, your sympathy, trust, etc. if you wish to be economical and to avoid being ruined by illusions.

Everything which you own must be made *venal*, i.e., useful. Suppose I ask the economist: am I acting in accordance with economic laws if I earn money by the sale of my body, by prostituting it to another person's lust (in France, the factory workers call the prostitution of their wives and daughters the *n*th hour of work, which is literally true); or if I sell my friend to the Moroccans (and the direct sale of men occurs in all civilized countries in the form of trade in conscripts)? He will reply: you are not acting contrary to my laws, but you must take into account what Cousin Morality and Cousin Religion have to say. My *economic* morality and religion have no objection to make, but . . . But whom then should we believe, the economist or the moralist? The morality of political economy is *gain*, work, thrift and sobriety—yet political economy promises to satisfy my needs. The political economy of morality is the riches of a good conscience, of virtue, etc., but how can I be virtuous if I am not alive and how can I have a good conscience if I am not aware of anything? The nature of alienation implies that each sphere applies a different and contradictory norm, that morality does not apply the same norm as political economy, etc., because each of them is a particular alienation of man; (XVII) each is concentrated upon a specific area of alienated activity and is itself alienated from the other.

Thus M. Michel Chevalier reproaches Ricardo with leaving morals out of account. But Ricardo lets political economy speak its own language; he is not to blame if this language is not that of morals. M. Chevalier ignores political economy in so far as he concerns himself with morals, but he really and necessarily ignores morals when he is concerned with political economy; for the bearing of political economy upon morals is either arbitrary and accidental and thus lacking any scientific basis or character, a mere *sham*, or it is *essential* and can then only be a relation between economic laws and morals. If there is no such relation, can Ricardo be held responsible? Moreover, the antithesis between morals and political economy is itself only *apparent*; there is an antithesis and equally no antithesis. Political economy expresses, *in its own fashion*, the moral laws.

The absence of needs, as the principle of political economy, is shown in the most *striking* way in its *theory of population*. There are *too many* men. The very existence of man is a pure luxury, and if the worker is *"moral"* he will be *economical* in procreation. (Mill proposes that public commendation should be given to those who show themselves abstemious in sexual relations, and public condemnation to those who sin against the sterility of marriage. Is this not the moral doctrine of asceticism?) The production of men appears as a public misfortune.

The significance which production has in relation to the wealthy is *revealed* in the significance which it has for the poor. At the top its manifestation is always refined, concealed, ambiguous, an appearance; at the bottom it is rough, straightforward, candid, a reality. The *crude* need of the worker is a much greater source of profit than the *refined* need of the wealthy. The cellar dwellings in London bring their landlords more than do the palaces; i.e., they constitute *greater wealth* as far as the landlord is concerned and thus, in economic terms, greater *social* wealth.

Just as industry speculates upon the refinement of needs so also it speculates upon their *crudeness*, and upon their artificially produced crudeness whose true soul therefore is *self-stupefaction*, the *illusory* satisfaction of needs, a civilization *within* the crude barbarism of need. The English gin-shops are therefore *symbolical* representations of private property. Their *luxury* reveals the real relation of industrial luxury and wealth to man. They are therefore rightly the only Sunday enjoyment of the people, treated mildly at least by the English police.

We have already seen how the economist establishes the unity of labor and capital in various ways: (1) capital is *accumulated* labor; (2) the purpose of capital within production—partly the reproduction of capital with profit, partly capital as raw material (material of labor), partly capital as itself a *working instrument* (the machine is fixed capital which is identical with labor)—is *productive work*; (3) the worker is capital; (4) wages form part of the costs of capital; (5) for the worker, labor is the reproduction of his life-capital; (6) for the capitalist, labor is a factor in the activity of his capital.

Finally (7) the economist postulates the original unity of capital and labor as the unity of capitalist and worker. This is the original paradisaical condition. How these two factors, (XIX) as two persons, spring at each other's throats is for the economist a *fortuitous* occurrence, which therefore requires only to be explained by external circumstances (see Mill).

The nations which are still dazzled by the sensuous glitter of precious metals and who thus remain fetishists of metallic money are not yet fully developed money nations. Contrast between France and England. The extent to which the solution of a theoretical problem is a task of practice, and is accomplished through practice, and the extent to which correct practice is the condition of a true and positive theory is shown, for example, in the case of *fetishism*. The sense perception of a fetishist differs from that of a Greek because his sensuous existence is different. The abstract hostility between sense and spirit is inevitable so long as the human sense for nature, or the human meaning of nature, and consequently the *natural* sense of *man*, has not been produced through man's own labor.

Equality is nothing but the German "Ich $=$ Ich" translated into the French, i.e., political, form. Equality as the *basis* of communism is a *political* foundation and is the same as when the German founds it upon the fact that he conceives man as *universal self-consciousness*. Of course, the transcendence of alienation always proceeds from the form of alienation which is the *dominant* power; in Germany, *self-consciousness;* in France, *equality*, because politics; in England, the real, material, self-sufficient, *practical* need. Proudhon should be appreciated and criticized from this point of view.

If we now characterize *communism* itself (for as negation of the negation, as the appropriation of human existence which mediates itself with itself through the negation of private property, it is not the *true*, self-originating position, but rather one which begins from private property) . . .[1] . . . the alienation of human life remains and a much greater alienation remains the more one is conscious of it as such) can only be accomplished by the establishment of communism. In order to supersede the *idea* of private property communist *ideas* are sufficient but *genuine* communist activity is necessary in order to supersede *real* private property. History will produce it, and the development which we already recognize in *thought* as self-transcending will in reality involve a severe and protracted process. We must however consider it an advance that we have previously acquired an

---

[1] A part of the page is torn away here, and there follow fragments of six lines which are insufficient to reconstruct the passage.—*Tr. Note*

awareness of the limited nature and the goal of the historical development and can see beyond it.

When communist *artisans* form associations, teaching and propaganda are their first aims. But their association itself creates a new need—the need for society—and what appeared to be a means has become an end. The most striking results of this practical development are to be seen when French socialist workers meet together. Smoking, eating and drinking are no longer simply means of bringing people together. Society, association, entertainment which also has society as its aim, is sufficient for them; the brotherhood of man is no empty phrase but a reality, and the nobility of man shines forth upon us from their toilworn bodies.

(XX) When political economy asserts that supply and demand always balance each other, it forgets at once its own contention (the theory of population) that the supply of *men* always exceeds the demand, and consequently, that the disproportion between supply and demand is most strikingly expressed in the essential end of production—the existence of man.

The extent to which money, which has the appearance of a means, is the real power and the unique *end*, and in general the extent to which *the* means which gives me being and possession of the alien objective being is an *end in itself*, can be seen from the fact that landed property where land is the source of life, and *horse* and *sword* where these are the *real means of life*, are also recognized as the real political powers. In the middle ages an estate becomes emancipated when it has the right to carry the *sword*. Among nomadic peoples it is the *horse* which makes me a free man and a member of the community.

We said above that man is regressing to the *cave dwelling*, but in an alienated, malignant form. The savage in his cave (a natural element which is freely offered for his use and protection) does not feel himself a stranger; on the contrary he feels as much at home as a *fish* in water. But the cellar dwelling of the poor man is a hostile dwelling, "an alien, constricting power which only surrenders itself to him in exchange for blood and sweat." He cannot regard it as his home, as a place where he might at last say, "here I am at home". Instead, he finds himself in *another person's* house, the house of a *stranger* who lies in wait for him every day and evicts him if he does not pay the rent. He is also aware of the contrast between his own dwelling and a human dwelling such as exists in *that other world,* the heaven of wealth.

Alienation is apparent not only in the fact that *my* means of life belong to *someone else,* that *my* desires are the unattainable possession of *someone else,* but that everything is *something different* from itself, that my activity is *something else,* and finally (and this is also the case for the capitalist) that *an inhuman power* rules over everything. There is a kind of wealth which is inactive, prodigal and devoted to pleasure, the beneficiary of which *behaves* as an *ephemeral,* aimlessly active individual who regards the slave labor of others, human *blood and sweat,* as the prey of his cupidity and sees mankind, and himself, as a sacrificial and superfluous being. Thus he acquires a contempt for mankind, expressed in the form of arrogance and the squandering of resources which would support a hundred human lives, and also in the form of the infamous illusion that his unbridled extravagance and endless unproductive consumption is a condition for the *labor* and *subsistence* of others. He regards the realization of the *essential powers* of man only as the realization of his own disorderly life, his whims and his capricious, bizarre ideas. Such wealth, however, which sees wealth merely as a means, as something to be consumed, and which is therefore both master and slave, generous and mean, capricious, presumptuous, conceited, refined, cultured and witty, has not yet discovered *wealth* as a wholly *alien power* but sees in it its own power and enjoyment rather than wealth . . . final aim.[2]

(XXI) . . . and the glittering illusion about the nature of wealth, produced by its dazzling sensuous appearance, is confronted by the *hard-working, sober, economical, prosaic* industrialist who is enlightened about the nature of wealth and who, while increasing the scope of the other's self-indulgence and flattering him by his products (for his products are just so many base compliments to the spendthrift's appetites) knows how to appropriate to himself, in the only *useful* way, the other's declining power. Although, therefore, industrial wealth appears at first to be the product of prodigal, fantastic wealth, it nevertheless dispossesses the latter in an active way by its own development. The fall in the *rate of interest* is a necessary consequence of industrial development. Thus the resources of the spendthrift rentier dwindle *in proportion to* the increase in the means and occasions of enjoyment. He is obliged either to consume his capital and thus ruin himself, or to become an industrial capitalist himself. . . . On the other hand, there is a constant increase in the *rent of land* in the course of industrial development, but as we have already seen there must come a time when landed property, like every other form of property, falls into the category of capital which reproduces itself through profit—and this is a result of the same industrial develop-

---

[2] The end of the page is torn and several lines of the text are missing.—*Tr. Note*

ment. Thus the spendthrift landowner must either squander his capital and ruin himself, or become the tenant farmer of his own estate—an agricultural industrialist.

The decline in the rate of interest (which Proudhon regards as the abolition of capital and as a tendency towards the socialization of capital) is thus rather a direct symptom of the complete victory of working capital over spendthrift wealth, i.e., the transformation of all private property into industrialist capital. It is the complete victory of private property over all its *apparently* human qualities, and the total subjection of the property owner to the essence of private property— *labor*. Of course, the industrial capitalist also has his pleasures. He does not by any means return to an unnatural simplicity in his needs, but his enjoyment is only a secondary matter; it is recreation subordinated to production and thus a *calculated, economic* enjoyment, for he charges his pleasures as an expense of capital and what he squanders must not be more than can be replaced with profit by the reproduction of capital. Thus enjoyment is subordinated to capital and the pleasure-loving individual is subordinated to the capital accumulating individual, whereas formerly the contrary was the case. The decline in the rate of interest is therefore only a symptom of the abolition of capital in so far as it is a symptom of its increasing domination and increasing alienation which hastens its own abolition. In general, this is the only way in which that which exists affirms its opposite.

The dispute between economists over luxury and saving is therefore only a dispute between the political economy which has become clearly aware of the nature of wealth and that political economy which is still burdened with romantic, anti-industrialist memories. Neither side, however, knows how to express the subject of the dispute in simple terms, or is able therefore to settle the issue.

Further, the *rent of land, qua* rent of land, has been demolished, for against the argument of the Physiocrats that the landowner is the only genuine producer, modern economics demonstrates rather that the landowner as such is the only completely unproductive rentier. Agriculture is the affair of the capitalist, who employs his capital in it when he can expect a normal rate of profit. The assertion of the Physiocrats that landed property as the only productive property should alone pay taxes and consequently should alone sanction them and participate in state affairs, is transformed into the contrary conviction that the taxes upon the rent of land are the only taxes upon an unproductive revenue and thus the only ones which are not detrimental to the national output. It is evident that from this point of view no political privileges for the landowners follow from their situation as the principal taxpayers.

Everything which Proudhon conceives as a movement of labor against capital is only the movement of labor in the form of capital, of *industrial capital* against that which is not consumed *as* capital, i.e., industrially. And this movement goes upon its triumphant way, the way of the victory of industrial capital. It will be seen that only when labor is conceived as the essence of private property can the real characteristics of the economic movement itself be analyzed.

Society, as it appears to the economist, is *civil society*, in which each individual is a totality of needs and only exists for another person, as another exists for him, in so far as each becomes a means for the other. The economist (like politics in its *rights of man*) reduces everything to man, i.e., to the individual, whom he deprives of all characteristics in order to classify him as a capitalist or a worker.

The *division of labor* is the economic expression of the *social character of labor* within alienation. Or, since *labor* is only an expression of human activity within alienation, of life activity as alienation of life, the *division of labor* is nothing but the *alienated* establishment of human activity as a *real species-activity* or *the activity of man as a species-being.*

The economists are very confused and self-contradictory about the nature of the *division of labor* (which of course has to be regarded as a principal motive force in the production of wealth as soon as *labor* is recognized as the *essence of private property*), i.e., about the *alienated form of human activity as species-activity.*

Adam Smith:[3] "The division of labor . . . is not originally the effect of any human wisdom . . . It is the necessary, though very slow and gradual consequence of the propensity to truck, barter and exchange one thing for another. [Whether this propensity be one of those original principles of human nature . . .] or whether, as seems more probable, it be the necessary consequence of the faculties of reason and of speech [it belongs not to our present subject to inquire.] It is common to all men, and to be found in no other race of animals . . . [In almost

---

[3] The following passages are from *The Wealth of Nations,* Book I, Chapters II, III, and IV. Marx quotes from the French translation: *Recherches sur la nature et les causes de la richesse des nations,* par Adam Smith. Traduction nouvelle, avec les notes et observations; par Germain Garnier. T. I-V. Paris 1802. Marx quotes with omissions and in a few cases paraphrases the text. In this translation I have indicated the omissions and have restored the original text, using the Everyman edition, showing the parts which were paraphrased in square brackets.—*Tr. Note*

every other race of animals the individual] when it is grown up to maturity is entirely independent . . . But man has almost constant occasion for the help of his brethren, and it is in vain for him to expect it from their benevolence only. He will be more likely to prevail if he can interest their self-love in his favor, and show them that it is for their own advantage to do for him what he requires of them. . . . We address ourselves not to their humanity but to their self-love, and never talk to them of our own necessities but of their advantages. (pp. 12-13)

"As it is by treaty, by barter, and by purchase that we obtain from one another the greater part of those mutual good offices that we stand in need of, so it is this same trucking disposition which originally gives occasion to the division of labor. In a tribe of hunters or shepherds a particular person makes bows and arrows, for example, with more readiness and dexterity than any other. He frequently exchanges them for cattle or for venison with his companions; and he finds at last that he can in this manner get more cattle and venison than if he himself went to the field to catch them. From a regard to his own interest, therefore, the making of bows and arrows grows to be his chief business . . . (pp. 13-14)

"The difference of natural talents in different men . . . is not . . . so much the cause as the effect of the division of labor. . . . Without the disposition to truck, barter and exchange, every man must have procured to himself every necessary and conveniency of life which he wanted. All must have had . . . the same work to do, and there could have been no such difference of employment as could alone give occasion to any great difference of talents. (p. 14)

"As it is this disposition which forms that difference of talents . . . among men, so it is this same disposition which renders that difference useful. Many tribes of animals . . . of the same species derive from nature a much more remarkable distinction of genius than what, antecedent to custom and education, appears to take place among men. By nature a philosopher is not in genius and in disposition half so different from a street-porter, as a mastiff is from a greyhound, or a greyhound from a spaniel, or this last from a shepherd's dog. Those different tribes of animals, however, though all of the same species, are of scarce any use to one another. The strength of the mastiff (XXXVI) is not, in the least, supported either by the swiftness of the greyhound, or . . . The effects of those different geniuses and talents, for want of the power or disposition to barter and exchange, cannot be brought into a common stock, and do not in the least contribute to the better accommodation and conveniency of the species. Each animal is still obliged to support and defend itself, separately and independently, and derives no sort of advantage from that variety of talents with which nature has distinguished its fellows. Among men, on the contrary, the most dissimilar geniuses are of use to one another; the different produces of their respective talents, by the general disposition to truck, barter and exchange, being brought, as it were, into a common stock, where every man may purchase whatever part of the produce of other men's talents he has occasion for. (pp. 14-15)

"As it is the power of exchanging that gives occasion to the division of labor, so the extent of this division must always be limited by the extent of that power, or, in other words, by the extent of the market. When the market is very small, no person can have any encouragement to dedicate himself entirely to one employment, for want of the power to exchange all that surplus part of the produce of his own labor, which is over and above his own consumption, for such parts of the produce of other men's labor as he has occasion for." (p. 15)

In an advanced state of society: "Every man thus lives by exchanging, or becomes in some measure a merchant, and the society itself grows to be what is properly a commercial society." (p. 20) (See Destutt de Tracy:[4] "Society is a series of reciprocal exchanges; commerce is the whole essence of society.") The accumulation of capital increases with the division of labor and vice versa.—Thus far Adam Smith.

"If every family produced all that it consumed society could keep going although no exchanges of any kind took place. In our advanced state of society exchange, though *not fundamental,* is indispensable."[5] "The division of labor is a skillful deployment of man's powers; it increases society's production—its power and its pleasures— but it diminishes the ability of every person taken individually. Production cannot take place without exchange."[6]—Thus J.-B. Say.

"The inherent powers of man are his intelligence and his physical capacity for work. Those which arise from the condition of society consist of the capacity to divide labor and to distribute the tasks among different people and the power to exchange the services and products which constitute the means of subsistence. The motive which impels a man to give his services to another is self-interest; he demands a return for the services rendered. The right of exclusive private property is indispensable to the establishment of exchange among men. . . . Ex-

---

[4] Destutt de Tracy, *Eléments d'idéologie. Traité de la volonté et de ses effets.* Paris 1826; pages 68, 78.

[5] Jean-Baptiste Say, *Traité d'économie politique.* 3ème édition. Paris 1817. T.I, p. 300.

[6] *ibid.,* p. 76.

change and division of labor mutually condition each other."[7]—Thus Skarbek.

Mill presents developed exchange—*trade*—as a *consequence* of the *division of labor*: "The agency of man can be traced to very simple elements. He can, in fact, do nothing more than produce motion. He can move things towards one another, (XXXVII) and he can separate them from one another: the properties of matter perform all the rest. . . . In the employment of labor and machinery, it is often found that the effects can be increased by skilful distribution, by separating all those operations which have any tendency to impede one another, and by bringing together all those operations which can be made in any way to aid one another. As men in general cannot perform many different operations with the same quickness and dexterity with which they can by practice learn to perform a few, it is always an advantage to limit as much as possible the number of operations imposed upon each. For dividing labor, and distributing the powers of men and machinery, to the greatest advantage, it is in most cases necessary to operate upon a large scale; in other words, to produce the commodities in greater masses. It is this advantage which gives existence to the great manufacturies; a few of which, placed in the most convenient situations, frequently supply not one country, but many countries, with as much as they desire of the commodity produced."[8]—Thus Mill.

---

[7] F. Skarbek, *Théorie des richesses sociales, suivie d'une bibliographie de l'économie politique*. Paris 1829. T.I., pages 25-27.

[8] James Mill, *Elements of Political Economy*. London 1821. Marx quotes from the French translation by J. T. Parisot (Paris 1823).—*Tr. Note*

The whole of modern political economy is agreed, however, upon the fact that division of labor and wealth of production, division of labor and accumulation of capital, are mutually determining; and also that liberated and autonomous private property alone can produce the most effective and extensive division of labor.

Adam Smith's argument may be summarized as follows: the division of labor confers upon labor an unlimited capacity to produce. It arises from the *propensity to exchange and barter*, a specifically human propensity which is probably not fortuitous but determined by the use of reason and speech. The motive of those who engage in exchange is not humanity but *egoism*. The diversity of human talents is more the effect than the cause of the division of labor, i.e., of exchange. Furthermore, it is only the latter which makes this diversity useful. The particular qualities of the different tribes within an animal species are by nature more pronounced than the differences between the aptitudes and activities of human beings. But since animals are not able to exchange, the diversity of qualities in animals of the same species but of different tribes is of no benefit to any individual animal. Animals are unable to combine the various qualities of their species, or to contribute to the *common* advantage and comfort of the species. It is otherwise with *men*, whose most diverse talents and forms of activity are useful to each other, *because* they can bring their *different* products together in a common stock, from which each man can buy. As the division of labor arises from the propensity to *exchange*, so it develops and is limited by the *extent of exchange*, by the *extent of the market*. In developed conditions every man is a *merchant* and society is a *commercial association*. Say regards *exchange* as fortuitous and not fundamental.

Society could exist without it. It becomes indispensable in an advanced state of society. Yet *production* cannot take place *without it.* The division of labor is a *conveni- ent* and *useful* means, a skillful deployment of human powers for social wealth, but it diminishes the *capacity of each person* taken *individually.* The last remark is an advance on the part of Say.

Skarbek distinguishes the *individual innate* powers of man, intelligence and physical capacity for work, from the powers *derived* from society—*exchange and division of labor,* which mutually determine each other. But the necessary precondition of exchange is *private property.* Skarbek here expresses objectively what Smith, Say, Ricardo, etc. say when they designate *egoism* and *self- interest* as the basis of exchange and *commercial hag- gling* as the *essential* and *adequate* form of exchange.

Mill represents *trade* as the consequence of the *divi- sion of labor.* For him, *human* activity is reduced to *mechanical motion.* The division of labor and the use of machinery promote abundance of production. Each individual must be given the smallest possible range of operations. The division of labor and the use of ma- chinery, for their part, require the mass production of wealth, i.e., of products. This is the reason for large scale manufacture.

(XXXVIII) The consideration of *division of labor* and *exchange* is of the greatest interest, since they are the *perceptible, alienated* expression of human *activity* and *capacities* as the activity and capacities *proper to a species.*

To state that *private property* is the basis of the *division of labor* and *exchange* is simply to assert that *labor* is the essence of private property; an assertion which the economist cannot prove and which we wish to prove for him. It is precisely in the fact that the *division of labor* and *exchange* are manifestations of private property that we find the proof, first that *human* life needed *private property* for its realization, and secondly, that it now requires the supersession of private property.

The *division of labor* and *exchange* are the two *phenomena* which lead the economist to vaunt the social character of his science, while in the same breath he unconsciously expresses the contradictory nature of his science—the establishment of society through unsocial, particular interests.

The factors we have to consider are as follows: the *propensity to exchange*—whose basis is egoism—is regarded as the cause of the reciprocal effect of the division of labor. Say considers exchange as being not *fundamental* to the nature of society. Wealth and production are explained by the division of labor and exchange. The impoverishment and denaturing of individual activity through the division of labor are admitted. Exchange and division of labor are recognized as the sources of the great *diversity of human talents*, a diversity which in turn becomes useful as a result of exchange. Skarbek distinguishes two parts in men's productive powers: (1) the individual and innate, his intelligence and his specific aptitudes or abilities; (2) those which are *derived* not from the real individual, but from society—the division of labor and exchange. Further, the division of labor is limited by the *market*. Human labor is simple *mechanical motion*; the major part is done by the material properties of the objects. The smallest possible number of operations must be allocated to each individual. Fission of labor and concentration of capital; the nullity of individual production and the mass production of wealth. Meaning of free private property in the division of labor.

(MONEY)

(XLI) If man's *feelings*, passions, etc. are not merely anthropological characteristics in the narrower sense, but are true *ontological* affirmations of being (nature), and if they are only really affirmed in so far as their *object* exists as an object of *sense*, then it is evident:

(1) that their mode of affirmation is not one and unchanging, but rather that the diverse modes of affirmation constitute the distinctive character of their existence, of their life. The manner in which the object exists for them is the distinctive mode of their *gratification*;

(2) where the sensuous affirmation is a direct annulment of the object in its independent form (as in drinking, eating, working up of the object, etc.) this is the affirmation of the object;

(3) in so far as man, and hence also his feelings, etc. are *human*, the affirmation of the object by another person is also his own gratification;

(4) only through developed industry, i.e., through the mediation of private property, does the ontological essence of human passions, in its totality and its humanity, come into being; the science of man itself is a product of man's self-formation through practical activity;

(5) the meaning of private property—released from its alienation—is the *existence of essential objects* for man, as objects of enjoyment and activity.

Money, since it has the *property* of purchasing everything, of appropriating objects to itself, is therefore the *object par excellence*. The universal character of this *property* corresponds to the omnipotence of money, which is regarded as an omnipotent being . . . money is the *pander* between need and object, between human life and the means of subsistence. But *that which* mediates *my* life mediates also the existence of other men for me. It is for me the *other* person.

"Why, Zounds! Both hands and feet are, truly—
And head and virile forces—thine:
Yet all that I indulge in newly,
Is't thence less wholly mine?
If I've six stallions in my stall,
Are not their forces also lent me?
I speed along completest man of all,
As though my feet were four-and-twenty.

(Goethe, *Faust*—Mephistopheles)[1]

Shakespeare in *Timon of Athens*:

"Gold? yellow, glittering, precious gold? No, gods,
I am no idle votarist: roots, you clear heavens!
Thus much of this will make black, white; foul, fair;
Wrong, right; base, noble; old, young; coward, valiant.
.... Why this
Will lug your priests and servants from your sides;
Pluck stout men's pillows from below their heads:
This yellow slave
Will knit and break religions; bless th'accurst;
Make the hoar leprosy ador'd; place thieves,
And give them title, knee, and approbation,
With senators on the bench: this is it
That makes the wappen'd widow wed again;
She whom the spital-house and ulcerous ʁores
Would cast the gorge at, this embalms and spices
To th'April day again. Come, damned earth,
Thou common whore of mankind, that putt'st odds

---

[1] Goethe, *Faust*. Part I, Scene 4. This passage is taken from the translation by Bayard Taylor; the Modern Library, New York, 1950.—*Tr. Note*

Among the rout of nations, I will make thee
Do thy right nature."[2]

And later on:

"O thou sweet king-killer, and dear divorce
'Twixt natural son and sire! Thou bright defiler
Of Hymen's purest bed! thou valiant Mars!
Thou ever young, fresh, loved, and delicate wooer,
Whose blush doth thaw the consecrated snow
That lies on Dian's lap! thou visible god,
That solder'st close impossibilities,
And mak'st them kiss! that speak'st with every tongue,
To every purpose! O thou touch of hearts!
Think, thy slave man rebels; and by thy virtue
Set them into confounding odds, that beasts
May have the world in empire!"[3]

Shakespeare portrays admirably the nature of *money*. To understand him, let us begin by expounding the passage from Goethe.

That which exists for me through the medium of *money*, that which I can pay for (i.e., which money can buy), that *I am*, the possessor of the money. My own power is as great as the power of money. The properties of money are my own (the possessor's) properties and faculties. What I *am* and *can do* is, therefore, not at all determined by my individuality. I *am* ugly, but I can buy the *most beautiful* woman for myself. Consequently, I am not *ugly*, for the effect of *ugliness*, its power to repel, is annulled by money. As an individual I am *lame*, but money provides me with twenty-four legs. Therefore, I am not lame. I am a detestable, dishonorable, un-

---

[2] Shakespeare, *Timon of Athens*. Act IV, Scene 3. Marx quotes from the Schlegel-Tieck translation.—*Tr. Note*
[3] *ibid.*

scrupulous and stupid man but money is honored and so also is its possessor. Money is the highest good, and so its possessor is good. Besides, money saves me the trouble of being dishonest; therefore, I am presumed honest. I am *stupid*, but since money is the *real mind* of all things, how should its possessor be stupid? Moreover, he can buy talented people for himself, and is not he who has power over the talented more talented than they? I who can have, through the power of money, *everything* for which the human heart longs, do I not possess all human abilities? Does not my money, therefore, transform all my incapacities into their opposites?

If *money* is the bond which binds me to *human* life, and society to me, and which links me with nature and man, is it not the bond of all *bonds*? Is it not, therefore also the universal agent of separation? It is the real means of both *separation* and *union*, the galvano-*chemical* power of society.

Shakespeare emphasizes particularly two properties of money:

(1) it is the visible deity, the transformation of all human and natural qualities into their opposites, the universal confusion and inversion of things; it brings incompatibles into fraternity;

(2) it is the universal whore, the universal pander between men and nations.

The power to confuse and invert all human and natural qualities, to bring about fraternization of incompatibles, the *divine* power of money, resides in its *character* as the alienated and self-alienating species-life of man. It is the alienated *power* of *humanity*.

What I as a *man* am unable to do, and thus what all my individual faculties are unable to do, is made possible for me by *money*. Money, therefore, turns each of these faculties into something which it is not, into its *opposite*.

If I long for a meal, or wish to take the mail coach because I am not strong enough to go on foot, money provides the meal and the mail coach; i.e., it transforms my desires from representations into *realities*, from imaginary being into *real being*. In mediating thus, money is a *genuinely creative* power.

Demand also exists for the individual who has no money, but his demand is a mere creature of the imagination which has no effect, no existence for me, for a third party, for . . . , (XLIII) and which thus remains *unreal* and *without object*. The difference between effective demand, supported by money, and ineffective demand, based upon my need, my passion, my desire, etc. is the difference between *being* and *thought*, between the merely *inner* representation and the representation which exists outside myself as a *real object*.

If I have no money for travel I have no *need*—no real and self-realizing need—for travel. If I have a *vocation* for study but no money for it, then I have *no* vocation, i.e., no *effective, genuine* vocation. Conversely, if I really have *no* vocation for study, but have money and the urge for it, then I have an *effective* vocation. *Money* is the external, universal *means* and *power* (not derived from man as man or from human society as society) to change *representation* into *reality* and *reality* into *mere representation*. It transforms *real human and natural faculties* into mere abstract representations, i.e., *imperfections* and tormenting chimeras; and on the other hand, it transforms *real imperfections and fancies*, faculties which are really impotent and which exist only in the individual's imagination, into *real faculties and powers*. In this respect, therefore, money is the general inversion of *in-*

dividualities, turning them into their opposites and associating contradictory qualities with their qualities.

Money, then, appears as a *disruptive* power for the individual and for the social bonds, which claim to be self-subsistent *entities.* It changes fidelity into infidelity, love into hate, hate into love, virtue into vice, vice into virtue, servant into master, stupidity into intelligence and intelligence into stupidity.

Since money, as the existing and active concept of value, confounds and exchanges everything, it is the universal *confusion and transposition* of all things, the inverted world, the confusion and transposition of all natural and human qualities.

He who can purchase bravery is brave, though a coward. Money is not exchanged for a particular quality, a particular thing, or a specific human faculty, but for the whole objective world of man and nature. Thus, from the standpoint of its possessor, it exchanges every quality and object for every other, even though they are contradictory. It is the fraternization of incompatibles; it forces contraries to embrace.

Let us assume *man* to be *man,* and his relation to the world to be a human one. Then love can only be exchanged for love, trust for trust, etc. If you wish to enjoy art you must be an artistically cultivated person; if you wish to influence other people you must be a person who really has a stimulating and encouraging effect upon others. Every one of your relations to man and to nature must be a *specific expression,* corresponding to the object of your will, of your *real individual* life. If you love without evoking love in return, i.e., if you are not able, by the *manifestation* of yourself as a loving person, to make yourself a *beloved person,* then your love is impotent and a misfortune.

(CRITIQUE OF HEGEL'S DIALECTIC AND GENERAL PHILOSOPHY)

(6) This is perhaps an appropriate point at which to explain and substantiate what has been said, and to make some general comments upon Hegel's dialectic, especially as it is expounded in the *Phenomenology* and *Logic*, and upon its relation to the modern critical movement.

Modern German criticism was so much concerned with the past, and was so hampered by its involvement with its subject matter, that it had a wholly uncritical attitude to the methods of criticism and completely ignored the partly formal, but in fact *essential* question— how do we now stand with regard to the Hegelian *dialectic?* This ignorance of the relationship of modern criticism to Hegel's general philosophy, and his dialectic in particular, was so great that critics such as Strauss and Bruno Bauer (the former in all his writings; the latter in his *Synoptiker*, where, in opposition to Strauss, he substitutes the "self-consciousness" of abstract man for the substance of "abstract nature", and even in *Das entdeckte Christentum*) were, at least implicitly, ensnared in Hegelian logic. Thus, for instance, in *Das entdeckte Christentum* it is argued: "As if self-consciousness in positing the world, that which is different, did not produce itself in producing its object; for it then annuls the difference between itself and what it has produced, since it exists only in this creation and movement, has its purpose only in this movement, etc.". Or again: "They (the French materialists) could not see

169

that the movement of the universe has only become real and unified in itself in so far as it is the movement of self-consciousness." These expressions not only do not differ from the Hegelian conception; they reproduce it textually.

(XII) How little these writers, in undertaking their criticism (Bauer in his *Synoptiker*) were aware of their relation to Hegel's dialectic, and how little such an awareness emerged from the criticism, is demonstrated by Bauer in his *Gute Sache der Freiheit* when, instead of replying to the indiscreet question put by Gruppe, "And now what is to be done with logic?", he transmits it to future critics.

Now that Feuerbach, in his "Thesen" in *Anecdotis* and in greater detail in his *Philosophie der Zukunft*, has demolished the inner principle of the old dialectic and philosophy, the "Critical School", which was unable to do this itself but has seen it accomplished, has proclaimed itself the pure, decisive, absolute, and finally enlightened criticism, and in its spiritual pride has reduced the whole historical movement to the relation existing between itself and the rest of the world which comes into the category of "the mass". It has reduced all dogmatic antitheses to the *single* dogmatic antithesis between its own cleverness and the stupidity of the world, between the critical Christ and mankind—*"the rabble."* At every moment of the day it has demonstrated its own excellence *vis à vis* the stupidity of the mass, and it has finally announced the critical *last judgment* by proclaiming that the day is at hand when the whole of fallen mankind will assemble before it and will be divided up into groups each of which will be handed its *testimonium paupertatis* (certificate of poverty). The Critical School has made public its superiority to all human feelings and to the world, above which it sits enthroned in sublime solitude, content to utter occasionally from its sarcastic lips the laughter of the Olympian gods. After all these entertaining antics of idealism (of Young Hegelianism) which is expiring in the form of criticism, the Critical School has not even now intimated that it was necessary to discuss critically its own source, the dialectic of Hegel; nor has it given any indication of its relation with the dialectic of Feuerbach. This is a procedure totally lacking in critical sense.

Feuerbach is the only person who has a *serious* and *critical* relation to Hegel's dialectic, who has made real discoveries in this field, and above all, who has vanquished the old philosophy. The magnitude of Feuerbach's achievement and the unassuming simplicity with which he presents his work to the world are in striking contrast with the behaviour of others.

Feuerbach's great achievement is:

(1) to have shown that philosophy is nothing more than religion brought into thought and developed by thought, and that it is equally to be condemned as another form and mode of existence of human alienation;

(2) to have founded *genuine materialism* and *positive science* by making the social relationship of "man to man" the basic principle of his theory;

(3) to have opposed to the negation of the negation which claims to be the absolute positive, a self-subsistent principle positively founded on itself.

Feuerbach explains Hegel's dialectic, and at the same time justifies taking the positive phenomenon, that which is perceptible and indubitable, as the starting point, in the following way:

Hegel begins from the alienation of substance (logically, from the infinite, the abstract universal) from the absolute and fixed abstraction; i.e., in ordinary language, from religion and theology. Secondly, he supersedes the infinite, and posits the real, the perceptible, the finite, and the particular. (Philosophy, supersession of religion and theology). Thirdly, he then supersedes the positive and re-establishes the abstraction, the infinite. (Re-establishment of religion and theology).

Thus Feuerbach conceives the negation of the negation as being *only* a contradiction within philosophy itself, which affirms theology (transcendance, etc.) after having superseded it, and thus affirms it in opposition to philosophy.

For the positing or self-affirmation and self-confirmation which is implied in the negation of the negation is regarded as a positing which is still uncertain, burdened with its contrary, doubtful of itself and thus incomplete, not demonstrated by its own existence, and implicit. (XIII) The positing which is perceptually indubitable and grounded upon itself is directly opposed to it.

In conceiving the negation of the negation, from the aspect of the positive relation inherent in it, as the only true positive, and from the aspect of the negative relation inherent in it, as the only true act and self-confirming act of all being, Hegel has merely discovered an *abstract, logical* and *speculative* expression of the historical process, which is not yet the *real* history of man as a given subject, but only the history of the *act of creation*, of the *genesis of man*.

We shall explain both the abstract form of this process and the difference between the process as conceived by Hegel and by modern criticism, by Feuerbach in *Das Wesen des Christentums*; or rather, the *critical* form of this process which is still so uncritical in Hegel.

Let us examine Hegel's system. It is necessary to begin with the *Phenomenology*, because it is there that Hegel's philosophy was born and that its secret is to be found.

Phenomenology

A. *Self-consciousness*

    I. *Consciousness* (a) Certainty in sense experience, or the "this" and *meaning*. (b) *Perception*, or the thing with its properties, and *illusion*. (c) Power and understanding, phenomena and the supersensible world.

    II. *Self-consciousness*. The truth of certainty of oneself. (a) Independence and dependence of self-consciousness, domination and servitude. (b) Freedom of self-consciousness. Stoicism, scepticism, the unhappy consciousness.

    III. *Reason*. Certainty and truth of reason. (a) Observational reason: observation of nature and of self-consciousness. (b) Self-realization of the rational self-consciousness. Pleasure and necessity. The law of the heart and the frenzy of vanity. Virtue and the way of the world. (c) Individuality which is real in and for itself. The spiritual animal kingdom and deceit, or the thing itself. Legislative reason. Reason which tests laws.

B. *Spirit*

    I. *True* spirit; customary morality

    II. Self-alienated spirit; culture

    III. Spirit certain of itself; morality

C. *Religion*

    Natural religion, the *religion of art, revealed* religion

D. *Absolute knowledge*

Hegel's *Encyclopaedia* begins with logic, with *pure speculative thought*, and ends with *absolute knowledge*, the self-conscious and self-conceiving philosophical or absolute mind, i.e. the, superhuman, abstract mind. The whole of the *Encyclopaedia* is nothing but the *extended being* of the philosophical mind, its self-objectification; and the philosophical mind is nothing but the alienated world mind thinking within the bounds of its self-alienation, i.e., conceiving itself in an abstract manner. *Logic* is the *money* of the mind, the speculative *thought-value* of man and of nature, their essence indifferent to any real determinate character and thus unreal; *thought* which is *alienated* and abstract and which ignores real nature and man. *The external character of this abstract thought . . . nature* as it exists for this abstract thought. Nature is external to it, loss of itself, and is only conceived as something external, as abstract thought, but alienated abstract thought. Finally, spirit, this thought which returns to its own origin and which, as anthropological, phenomenological, psychological, customary, artistic-religious spirit, is not valid for itself until it discovers itself and relates itself to itself as absolute knowledge in the absolute (i.e., abstract) spirit, and so receives its conscious and fitting existence. For its real mode of existence is *abstraction*.

Hegel commits a double error. The first appears most clearly in the *Phenomenology*, the birthplace of his philosophy. When Hegel conceives wealth, the power of the state, etc. as entities alienated from the human being, he conceives them only in their thought form. They are entities of thought and thus simply an alienation of *pure* (i.e., abstract philosophical) thought. The whole movement, therefore, ends in absolute knowledge. It is precisely abstract thought from which these objects are alienated, and which they confront with their presumptuous reality. The *philosopher*, himself an abstract form of alienated man, sets himself up as the *measure* of the alienated world. The whole *history of alienation*, and of the *retraction* of alienation, is therefore only the *history of the production* of abstract thought, i.e., of absolute, logical, speculative thought. *Estrangement*, which thus forms the real interest of this alienation and of the super-session of this alienation, is the opposition of *in itself* and *for itself*, of *consciousness* and *self-consciousness*, of *object* and *subject*, i.e., the opposition in thought itself between abstract thought and sensible reality or real sensuous existence. All other contradictions and movements are merely the *appearance*, the *cloak*, the *exoteric* form of these two opposites which are alone important and which constitute the *significance* of the other, profane contradictions. It is not the fact that the human being *objectifies* himself *inhumanly*, in opposition to himself, but that he *objectifies* himself by *distinction* from and in *opposition* to abstract thought, which constitutes alienation as it exists and as it has to be transcended.

(XVIII) The appropriation of man's objectified and alienated faculties is thus, in the first place, only an *appropriation* which occurs in *consciousness*, in *pure thought*, i.e., in *abstraction*. It is the appropriation of these objects as *thoughts* and as *movements of thought*. For this reason, despite its thoroughly negative and critical appearance, and despite the genuine criticism which it contains and which often anticipates later developments, there is already implicit in the *Phenomenology*, as a germ, as a potentiality and a secret, the uncritical positivism and uncritical idealism of Hegel's later works—the philosophical dissolution and restoration of the existing empirical world. *Secondly*, the vindication of the objective world for man (for example, the recognition that *sense* perception is not *abstract* sense perception but *human* sense perception, that religion, wealth, etc. are only the alienated reality of *human* objectification, of *human* faculties put to work, and are therefore a *way* to genuine *human* reality) this appropriation, or the insight into this process, appears in Hegel as the recognition of *sensuousness, religion,* state power, etc. as *mental* phenomena, for *mind* alone is the *true* essence of man, and the true form of mind is thinking mind, the logical, speculative mind. The *human character* of nature, of historically produced nature, of man's products, is shown by their being *products* of abstract mind, and thus phases of *mind, entities of thought.* The *Phenomenology* is a concealed, unclear and mystifying criticism, but in so far as it grasps the *alienation* of man (even though man appears only as mind) *all* the elements of criticism are contained in it, and are often *presented* and *worked out* in a manner which goes far beyond Hegel's own point of view. The sections devoted to the "unhappy consciousness", the "honest consciousness", the struggle between the "noble" and the "base" consciousness, etc., etc. contain the *critical* elements (though still in an alienated form) of whole areas such as religion, the state, civil life, etc. Just as the *entity,* the *object,* appears as an entity of thought, so also the *subject* is always *consciousness* or *self-consciousness;* or rather, the object appears only as *abstract* consciousness and man as *self-consciousness.* Thus the distinctive forms of alienation which are manifested are only different forms of consciousness and self-consciousness. Since abstract consciousness (the form in which the object is conceived) is in *itself* merely a distinctive moment of self-consciousness, the outcome of the movement is the identity of self-consciousness and consciousness—absolute knowledge —the movement of abstract thought not directed outwards but proceeding within itself; i.e., the dialectic of pure thought is the result.

(XXIII) The outstanding achievement of Hegel's *Phenomenology*—the dialectic of negativity as the moving and creating principle—is, first, that Hegel grasps the self-creation of man as a process, objectification as loss of the object, as alienation and transcendence of this alienation, and that he therefore grasps the nature of *labor*, and conceives objective man (true, because real man) as the result of his *own labor*. The *real*, active orientation of man to himself as a species-being, or the affirmation of himself as a real species-being (i.e., as a human being) is only possible so far as he really brings forth all his *species-powers* (which is only possible through the co-operative endeavors of mankind and as an outcome of history) and treats these powers as objects, which can only be done at first in the form of alienation.

We shall next show in detail Hegel's one-sidedness and limitations, as revealed in the final chapter of the *Phenomenology*, on absolute knowledge, a chapter which contains the concentrated spirit of the *Phenomenology*, its relation to the dialectic, and also Hegel's *consciousness* of both and of their interrelations.

For the present, let us make these preliminary observations: Hegel's standpoint is that of modern political economy. He conceives *labor* as the *essence*, the self-confirming essence of man; he observes only the positive side of labor, not its negative side. Labor is *man's coming to be for himself* within *alienation*, or as an *alienated* man. Labor as Hegel understands and recognizes it is *abstract mental* labor. Thus, that which above all constitutes the *essence* of philosophy, the *alienation of man knowing himself*, or *alienated* science *thinking* itself, Hegel grasps as its essence. Consequently he is able to bring together the separate elements of earlier philosophy and to present his own as *the* philosophy. What other philosophers did, that is, to conceive separate elements of nature and of human life as phases of self-consciousness and indeed of abstract self-consciousness,

Hegel *knows* by *doing* philosophy; therefore, his science is absolute.

Let us now turn to our subject.

Absolute knowledge.

The final chapter of the Phenomenology.

The main point is that the *object of consciousness* is nothing else but *self-consciousness*, that the object is only *objectified self-consciousness*, self-consciousness as an object. (Positing man = self-consciousness.)

It is necessary, therefore, to surmount the *object of consciousness. Objectivity* as such is regarded as an *alienated* human relationship which does not correspond with the *essence of man*, self-consciousness. The re-appropriation of the objective essence of man, which was produced as something alien and determined by alienation, signifies the supersession not only of *alienation* but also of *objectivity;* that is, man is regarded as a *non-objective, spiritual* being.

The process of *overcoming the object of consciousness* is described by Hegel as follows: The *object* does not reveal itself only as *returning* into the Self (according to Hegel that is a *one-sided* conception of the movement, considering only one aspect). Man is equated with self. The Self, however, is only man conceived *abstractly* and produced by abstraction. Man is self-referring. His eye, his ear, etc. are *self-referring*; every one of his faculties has this quality of *self-reference*. But it is entirely false to say on that account, "*Self-consciousness* has eyes, ears, faculties". Self-consciousness is rather a quality of human nature, of the human eye, etc.; human nature is not a quality of (XXIV) *self-consciousness*.

The Self, abstracted and determined for itself, is man as an *abstract egoist*, purely abstract *egoism* raised to the level of thought. (We shall return to this point later).

For Hegel, *human life, man,* is equivalent to *self-consciousness.* All alienation of human life is therefore *nothing* but *alienation of self-consciousness.* The alienation of self-consciousness is not regarded as the *expression,* reflected in knowledge and thought, of the *real* alienation of human life. Instead, *actual* alienation, that which appears real, is in its *innermost* hidden nature (which philosophy first discloses) only the *phenomenal being* of the alienation of real human life, of *self-consciousness.* The science which comprehends this is therefore called *Phenomenology.* All re-appropriation of alienated objective life appears therefore as an incorporation in self-consciousness. The person who takes possession of his being is only the self-consciousness which takes possession of objective being; the return of the object into the Self is therefore the re-appropriation of the object.

Expressed in a *more comprehensive way* the *supersession of the object of consciousness* means: (1) that the object as such presents itself to consciousness as something disappearing; (2) that it is the alienation of self-consciousness which establishes 'thinghood'; (3) That this alienation has *positive* as well as *negative* significance; (4) that it has this significance not only *for us* or in itself, but also *for self-consciousness itself;* (5) that *for self-consciousness* the negative of the object, its self-supersession, has *positive* significance, or self-consciousness *knows* thereby the nullity of the object in that self-consciousness alienates itself, for in this alienation it establishes *itself* as object or, for the sake of the indivisible unity of *being-for-itself,* establishes the object as itself; (6) that, on the other hand, this other 'moment' is equally present, that self-consciousness has superseded and re-absorbed this alienation and objectively, and is thus *at home* in its other being *as such;* (7) that this is the movement of consciousness, and consciousness is therefore the totality of its 'moments'; (8) that similarly, consciousness must have related itself to the object in all its determinations, and have conceived it in terms of each of them. This totality of determinations makes the object *intrinsically* a *spiritual being,* and it becomes truly so for consciousness by the apprehension of every one of these determinations as the Self, or by what was called earlier the *spiritual* attitude toward them.

ad (1) That the object as such presents itself to consciousness as something disappearing is the above-mentioned *return of the object into the Self.*

ad (2) *The alienation of self-consciousness* establishes '*thinghood.*' Because man equals self-consciousness, his alienated objective being or '*thinghood*' is equivalent to *alienated self-consciousness,* and 'thinghood' is established by this alienation. ('Thinghood' is that which is *an object for him,* and an object for him is really only that which is an essential object, consequently his *objective* essence. And since it is not the *real man,* nor *nature*— man being *human nature*—who becomes as such a subject, but only an abstraction of man, self-consciousness, 'thinghood' can only be *alienated self-consciousness*). It it quite understandable that a living, natural being endowed with objective (i.e., material) faculties should have *real natural objects* of its being, and equally that its self-alienation should be the establishment of a *real,* objective world, but in the form of *externality,* as a world which does not belong to, and dominates, his being. There is nothing incomprehensible or mysterious about this. The converse, rather, would be mysterious. But it is equally clear that a *self-consciousness,* i.e., its alienation, can only establish '*thinghood*', i.e., only an abstract thing, a thing created by abstraction and not a *real* thing. It is (XXVI) clear, moreover, that 'thinghood' is totally lacking in *independence,* in *being, vis à vis* self-consciousness; it is a mere *construct* established by self-consciousness. And what is established is not self-confirming; it is the confirmation of the act of establishing, which for an instant, but only for an instant, fixes its energy as a product and *apparently* confers upon it the role of an independent, real being.

When real, corporeal *man*, with his feet firmly planted on the solid ground, inhaling and exhaling all the powers of nature, *posits* his real objective *faculties*, as a result of his alienation, as alien objects, the *positing* is not the subject of this act but the subjectivity of *objective* faculties whose action must also therefore be *objective*. An objective being acts objectively, and it would not act objectively if objectivity were not part of its essential being. It creates and establishes *only objects because* it is established by objects, and because it is fundamentally *natural*. In the act of establishing it does not descend from its "pure activity" to the *creation of objects;* its *objective* product simply confirms its *objective* activity, its activity as an objective, natural being.

We see here how consistent naturalism or humanism is distinguished from both idealism and materialism, and at the same time constitutes their unifying truth. We see also that only naturalism is able to comprehend the process of world history.

Man is directly a *natural being*. As a natural being, and as a living natural being he is, on the one hand, endowed with *natural powers* and *faculties*, which exist in him as tendencies and abilities, as *drives*. On the other hand, as a natural, embodied, sentient, objective being he is a *suffering*, conditioned and limited being, like animals and plants. The *objects* of his drives exist outside himself as *objects* independent of him, yet they are *objects* of his *needs*, essential *objects* which are indispensable to the exercise and confirmation of his faculties.

The fact that man is an *embodied*, living, real, sentient, objective being with natural powers, means that he has *real, sensuous objects* as the objects of his being, or that he can only express his being in real, sensuous objects. *To be* objective, natural, sentient and at the same time to have object, nature and sense outside oneself, or to be oneself object, nature and sense for a third person, is the same thing. *Hunger* is a natural *need*; it requires therefore a *nature* outside itself, an *object* outside itself, in order to be satisfied and stilled. Hunger is the objective need of a body for an *object* which exists outside itself and which is essential for its integration and the expression of its nature. The sun is an *object*, a necessary and life-assuring object, for the plant, just as the plant is an object for the sun, an *expression* of the sun's life-giving power and *objective* essential powers.

A being which does not have its nature outside itself is not a *natural* being and does not share in the being of nature. A being which has no object outside itself is not an objective being. A being which is not itself an object for a third being has no being for its *object*, i.e., it is not objectively related and its being is not objective.

(XXVII) A non-objective being is a *non-being*. Suppose a being which neither is an object itself nor has an object. In the first place, such a being would be the *only* being; no other being would exist outside itself and it would be solitary and alone. For as soon as there exist objects outside myself, as soon as I am not *alone*, I am *another, another reality* from the object outside me. For this third object I am thus an *other reality* than itself, i.e., *its object*. To suppose a being which is not the object of another being would be to suppose that *no* objective being exists. As soon as I have an object, this object has me for its object. But a *non-objective* being is an unreal, non-sensuous, merely conceived being; i.e., a merely imagined being, an abstraction. To be *sensuous*, i.e., real, is to be an object of sense or *sensuous* object, and thus to have sensuous objects outside oneself, objects of one's sensations. To be sentient is to *suffer* (to experience).

Man as an objective sentient being is a *suffering* being, and since he feels his suffering, a *passionate* being. Passion is man's faculties striving to attain their object.

But man is not merely a natural being; he is a *human* natural being. He is a being for himself, and therefore a *species-being*; and as such he has to express and authenticate himself in being as well as in thought. Consequently, *human* objects are not natural objects as they present themselves directly, nor is *human sense*, as it is immediately and objectively *given*, *human* sensibility and human objectivity. Neither objective nature nor subjective nature is directly presented in a form adequate to the *human* being. And as everything natural must have its *origin* so *man* has his process of genesis, *history*, which is for him, however, a conscious process and thus one which is consciously self-transcending. (We shall return to this point later).

Thirdly, since this establishment of 'thinghood' is itself only an appearance, an act which contradicts the nature of pure activity, it has to be annulled again and 'thinghood' has to be denied.

ad 3, 4, 5, 6. (3) This alienation of consciousness has not only a negative but also a positive significance, and (4) it has this positive significance not only *for us* or in itself, but for consciousness itself. (5) *For consciousness* the negation of the object, or its annulling of itself by that means, has *positive* significance; it *knows* the nullity of the object by the fact that it alienates *itself*, for in this alienation it *knows* itself as the object or, for the sake of the indivisible unity of *being-for-self*, knows the object as itself. (6) On the other hand, this other 'moment' is equally present, that consciousness has superseded and re-absorbed this alienation and objectivity and is thus *at home in its other being as such.*

We have already seen that the appropriation of alienated objective being, or the supersession of objectivity in the condition of *alienation* (which has to develop from indifferent otherness to real antagonistic alienation) signifies for Hegel also, or primarily, the supersession of *objectivity*, since it is not the determinate character of the object but its *objective* character which is the scandal of alienation for self-consciousness. The object is therefore negative, self-annulling, a *nullity*. This nullity of the object has a *positive* as well as a negative significance for consciousness, for *it* is the self-*confirmation* of the non-objectivity, (XXVIII) the *abstract* character of itself. For *consciousness itself*, therefore, the nullity of the object has a positive significance because it *knows* this nullity, objective being, as its *self-alienation,* and knows that this nullity exists only through its self-alienation. . . .

The way in which consciousness is, and in which something is for it, is *knowing.* Knowing is its only act. Thus something comes to exist for consciousness so far as it *knows* this *something.* Knowing is its only objective relation. It knows, then, the nullity of the object (i.e., knows the non-existence of the distinction between itself and the object, the non-existence of the object for it) because it knows the object as its *self-alienation.* That is to say, it knows itself (knows knowing as an object), because the object is only the *semblance* of an object, a deception, which is intrinsically nothing but knowing itself which has confronted itself with itself, has established in face of itself a *nullity,* a 'something' which has *no* objective existence outside the knowing itself. Knowing knows that in relating itself to an object it is only *outside* itself, alienates itself, and that *it* only *appears* to itself as an object; or in other words, that that which appears to it as an object is only itself.

On the other hand, Hegel says, this other 'moment' is present at the same time; namely, that consciousness has equally superseded and re-absorbed this alienation and objectivity, and consequently is *at home in its other being as such*.

In this discussion all the illusions of speculation are assembled.

First, consciousness—self-consciousness—is *at home in its other being as such*. It is therefore—if we abstract from Hegel's abstraction and substitute the self-consciousness of man for self-consciousness—*at home in its other being as such*. This implies, first, that consciousness (knowing as knowing, thinking as thinking) claims to be directly the *other* of itself, the sensuous world, reality, life; it is thought over-reaching itself in thought (Feuerbach). This aspect is contained in it, in so far as consciousness as mere consciousness is offended not by the alienated objectivity but by *objectivity as such*.

Secondly, it implies that self-conscious man, in so far as he has recognized and superseded the spiritual world (or the universal spiritual mode of existence of his world) then confirms it again in this alienated form and presents it as his true existence; he re-establishes it and claims to *be at home in his other being*. Thus, for example, after superseding religion, when he has recognized religion as a product of self-alienation, he then finds a confirmation of himself in *religion as religion*. *This is* the root of Hegel's *false* positivism, or of his merely *apparent* criticism; what Feuerbach calls the positing, negation and re-establishment of religion or theology, but which has to be conceived in a more general way. Thus reason is at home in unreason as such. Man, who has recognized that he leads an alienated life in law, politics, etc. leads his true human life in this alienated life as such. Self-affirmation, *in contradiction* with itself, and with the knowledge and the nature of the object, is thus the true *knowledge* and *life*.

There can no longer be any question about Hegel's compromise with religion, the state, etc. for this lie is the lie of his whole argument.

(XXIX) If I *know* religion as *alienated* human self-consciousness what I know in it as religion is not my self-consciousness but my alienated self-consciousness confirmed in it. Thus my own self, and the self-consciousness which is its essence, is not confirmed in *religion* but in the *abolition* and *supersession* of religion.

In Hegel, therefore, the negation of the negation is not the confirmation of true being by the negation of illusory being. It is the confirmation of illusory being, or of self-alienating being in its denial; or the denial of this illusory being as an objective being existing outside man and independently of him, and its transformation into a subject.

The act of *supersession* plays a strange part in which *denial* and preservation, denial and affirmation, are linked together. Thus, for example, in Hegel's *Philosophy of Right, private right* superseded equals *morality*, morality superseded equals *the family*, the family superseded equals *civil society*, civil society superseded equals the *state* and the state superseded equals *world history*. But in *actuality* private right, morality, the family, civil society, the state, etc. remain; only they have become 'moments,' modes of existence of man, which have no validity in isolation but which mutually dissolve and engender one another. *They are moments of the movement.*

In their actual existence this *mobile* nature is concealed. It is first revealed in thought, in philosophy; consequently, my true religious existence is my existence in the *philosophy of religion*, my true political existence is my existence in the *philosophy of right*, my true natural existence is my existence in the *philosophy of nature*, my true artistic existence is my existence in the *philosophy of art*, and my true human existence is my existence in *philosophy*. In the same way, the true existence of religion, the state, nature and art, is the *philosophy* of religion, of the state, of nature, and of art. But if the philosophy of religion is the only true existence of religion I am only truly religious as a *philosopher of religion*, and I deny *actual* religious sentiment and the actual *religious* man. At the same time, however, I *confirm* them, partly in my own existence or in the alien existence with which I confront them (for this *is* only their *philosophical* expression), and partly in their own original form, since they are for me the merely *apparent* other being, allegories, the lineaments of their own true existence (i.e., of my *philosophical* existence) concealed by sensuous draperies.

In the same way, *quality* superseded equals *quantity*, quantity superseded equals *measure*, measure superseded equals *being*, being superseded equals *phenomenal being*, phenomenal being superseded equals *actuality*, actuality superseded equals the *concept*, the concept superseded equals *objectivity*, objectivity superseded equals the *absolute idea*, the absolute idea superseded equals *nature*, nature superseded equals *subjective* spirit, subjective spirit superseded equals *ethical* objective spirit, ethical spirit superseded equals *art*, art superseded equals *religion*, and religion superseded equals *absolute knowledge*.

On the one hand, this supersession is supersession of an entity of thought; thus, private property *as thought* is superseded in the *thought* of morality. And since thought imagines itself to be, without mediation, the other aspect of itself, namely *sensuous reality*, and takes its own action for *real, sensuous action*, this supersession in thought, which leaves its object in existence in the real world believes itself to have really overcome it. On the other hand, since the object has now become for it a 'moment' of thought, it is regarded in its real existence as a confirmation of thought, of self-consciousness, of abstraction.

(XXX) From the one aspect the existent which Hegel *supersedes* in philosophy is not therefore the *actual* religion, state, or nature, but religion itself as an object of knowledge, i.e., *dogmatics*; and similarly with *jurisprudence, political science,* and *natural science.* From this aspect, therefore, he stands in opposition both to the *actual* being and to the direct, non-philosophical science (or the non-philosophical *concepts*) of this being. Thus he contradicts the conventional conceptions.

From the other aspect, the religious man, etc. can find in Hegel his ultimate confirmation.

We have now to consider the *positive* moments of Hegel's dialectic, within the condition of alienation.

(a) *Supersession* as an objective movement which *re-absorbs* alienation into itself. This is the insight, expressed within alienation, into the *appropriation* of the objective being through the supersession of its alienation. It is the alienated insight into the *real objectification* of man, into the real appropriation of his objective being by the destruction of the *alienated* character of the objective world, by the annulment of its alienated mode of existence. In the same way, atheism as the annulment of God is the emergence of theoretical humanism, and communism as the annulment of private property is the vindication of real human life as man's property. The latter is also the emergence of practical humanism, for atheism is humanism mediated to itself by the annulment of religion, while communism is humanism mediated to itself by the annulment of private property. It is only by the supersession of this mediation (which is, however, a necessary pre-condition) that the self-originating *positive* humanism can appear.

But atheism and communism are not flight or abstraction from, or loss of, the objective world which men have created by the objectification of their faculties. They are not an impoverished return to unnatural, primitive simplicity. They are rather the first real emergence, the genuine actualization, of man's nature as something real.

Thus Hegel, in so far as he sees the *positive* significance of the self-referring negation (though in an alienated mode), conceives man's self-estrangement, alienation of being, loss of objectivity and reality, as self-discovery, change of nature, objectification and realization. In short, Hegel conceives labor as man's *act of self-creation* (though in abstract terms); he grasps man's relation to himself as an alien being and the emergence of *species consciousness* and *species-life* as the demonstration of his alien being.

(b) But in Hegel, apart from, or rather as a consequence of, the inversion we have already described, this act of genesis appears, in the first place, as one which is merely *formal*, because it is abstract, and because human nature itself is treated as merely *abstract, thinking nature*, as self-consciousness.

Secondly, because the conception is *formal* and *abstract* the annulment of alienation becomes a confirmation of alienation. For Hegel, this movement of *self-creation* and *self-objectification* in the form of *self-estrangement* is the *absolute* and hence final *expression of human life*, which has its end in itself, is at peace with itself and at one with its own nature.

This movement, in its abstract (XXXI) form as dialectic, is regarded therefore as *truly human life*, and since it is nevertheless an abstraction, an alienation of human life, it is regarded as a *divine process* and thus as the divine process of mankind; it is a process which man's abstract, pure, absolute being, as distinguished from himself, traverses.

Thirdly, this process must have a bearer, a subject; but the subject first emerges as a result. This result, the subject knowing itself as absolute self-consciousness, is therefore *God, absolute spirit, the self-knowing and self-manifesting idea.* Real man and real nature become mere predicates, symbols of this concealed unreal man and unreal nature. Subject and predicate have therefore an inverted relation to each other; a *mystical subject-object,* or a *subjectivity reaching beyond the object,* the *absolute subject* as a *process of self-alienation* and of return from alienation into itself, and at the same time of re-absorption of this alienation, the *subject* as this process; pure, *unceasing* revolving within itself.

First, the formal and abstract conception of man's act of self-creation or self-objectification.

Since Hegel equates man with self-consciousness, the alienated object, the alienated real being of man, is simply *consciousness,* merely the thought of alienation, its abstract and hence vacuous and unreal expression, the *negation.* The annulment of alienation is also, therefore, merely an abstract and vacuous annulment of this empty abstraction, the *negation of the negation.* The replete, living, sensuous, concrete activity of self-objectification is therefore reduced to a mere abstraction, *absolute negativity,* an abstraction which is then crystallized as such and is conceived as an independent activity, as activity itself. Since this so-called negativity is merely the *abstract, vacuous* form of that real living act, its content can only be a *formal* content produced by abstraction from all content. These are, therefore, general, abstract *forms of abstraction* which refer to any content and are thus neutral towards, and valid for, any content; forms of thought, logical forms which are detached from *real* spirit and *real* nature. (We shall expound later the *logical* content of absolute negativity).

Hegel's positive achievement in his speculative logic is to show that the *determinate concepts*, the universal *fixed thought-forms*, in their independence from nature and spirit, are a necessary result of the general alienation of human nature and also of human thought, and to depict them as a whole as moments in the process of abstraction. For example, being superseded is essence, essence superseded is concept, the concept superseded is . . . the absolute idea. But what is the absolute idea? It must supersede itself if it does not want to traverse the whole process of abstraction again from the beginning and to rest content with being a totality of abstractions or a self-comprehending abstraction. But the self-comprehending abstraction knows itself to be nothing; it must abandon itself, the abstraction, and so arrives at an entity which is its exact opposite, *nature*. The whole *Logic* is, therefore, a demonstration that abstract thought is nothing for itself, that the absolute idea is nothing for itself, that only *nature* is something.

(XXXII) The absolute idea, the *abstract* idea which "*regarded* from the aspect of its unity with itself, is *intuition*" (Hegel's *Encyclopaedia*, 3rd ed. p. 222) and which "in its own absolute truth *resolves* to let the moment of its particularity or of initial determination and other-being, the *immediate idea*, as its reflection, *emerge freely from itself as nature*". (*ibid*); this whole idea which behaves in such a strange and fanciful way and which has given the Hegelians such terrible headaches is throughout nothing but *abstraction*, i.e., the abstract thinker. It is abstraction which, made wise by experience and enlightened about its own truth, resolves under various (false and still abstract) conditions to *abandon* itself, and to establish its other being, the particular, the determinate, in place of its self-absorption, non-being, universality and indeterminateness; and which resolves to let nature, which it concealed within itself only as an abstraction, as an entity of thought, *emerge freely from itself*. That is, it decides to forsake abstraction and to observe nature *free* from abstraction. The abstract idea, which without mediation becomes *intuition*, is nothing but abstract thought which abandons itself and decides for *intuition*. This whole transition from logic to the philosophy of nature is simply the transition from *abstracting* to *intuiting*, a transition which is extremely difficult for the abstract thinker to accomplish and which he therefore describes in such strange terms. The *mystical* feeling which drives the philosopher from abstract thinking to intuition is *ennui*, the longing for a content.

(Man alienated from himself is also the thinker alienated from his *being*, i.e., from his natural and human life. His thoughts are consequently spirits existing outside nature and man. In his *Logic* Hegel has imprisoned all these spirits together, and has conceived each of them first as negation, i.e., as *alienation of human* thought, and secondly as negation of the negation, i.e., as the supersession of this alienation and as the *real* expression of human thought. But since this negation of the negation is itself still confined within the alienation, it is in part a restoration of these fixed spiritual forms in their alienation, in part an immobilization in the final act, the act of self-reference, as the true being of these spiritual forms.[1] Further, in so far as this abstraction conceives itself, and experiences an increasing weariness of itself, there appears in Hegel an abandonment of abstract thought which moves solely in the sphere of thought and is devoid of eyes, ears, teeth, everything, and a resolve to recognize *nature* as a being and to go over to intuition.)

(XXXIII) But *nature* too, taken abstractly, for itself, and rigidly separated from man, is *nothing* for man. It goes without saying that the abstract thinker who has committed himself to intuition, intuits nature abstractly. As nature lay enclosed in the thinker in a form which was obscure and mysterious even to himself, as absolute idea, as an entity of thought, so in truth, when he let it emerge from himself it was still only *abstract nature*, nature as an *entity of thought*, but now with the significance that it is the other being of thought, is real, intuited nature, distinguished from abstract thought. Or, to speak in human language, the abstract thinker discovers from intuiting nature that the entities which he thought to create out of nothing, out of pure abstraction, to create in the divine dialectic as the pure products of

---

[1] That is, Hegel substitutes the act of abstraction revolving within itself, for these fixed abstractions. In so doing, he has first of all the merit of having indicated the source of all these inappropriate concepts which originally belonged to different philosophies, and having brought them together and established the comprehensive range of abstractions, instead of some particular abstraction, as the object of criticism. We shall see later why Hegel separates thought from the *subject*. It is already clear, however, that if man is not human the expression of his nature cannot be human, and consequently, thought itself could not be conceived as an expression of man's nature, as the expression of a human and natural subject, with eyes, ears, etc. living in society, in the world, and in nature.

thought endlessly shuttling back and forth in itself and never regarding external reality, are simply *abstractions* from *natural characteristics*. The whole of nature, therefore, reiterates to him the logical abstractions, but in a sensuous, external form. He *analyzes* nature and these abstractions again. His intuition of nature is therefore simply the act of confirmation of his abstraction from the intuition of nature; his conscious re-enactment of the process of generating his abstraction. Thus, for example, Time equals Negativity which refers to itself (*loc. cit.* p. 238). In the natural form, superseded Movement as Matter corresponds to superseded Becoming as Being. In the *natural* form Light is *Reflection-in-itself*. Body as *Moon* and *Comet* is the *natural* form of the antithesis which, according to the *Logic*, is on the one hand the *positive grounded upon itself*, and on the other hand, the *negative* grounded upon itself. The Earth is the *natural* form of the logical *ground*, as the negative unity of the antithesis, etc.

Nature as nature, i.e., so far as it is sensuously distinguished from that secret sense concealed within it, nature separated and distinguished from these abstractions is *nothing* (a *nullity demonstrating its nullity*), is *devoid of sense*, or has only the sense of an external thing which has been superseded.

"In the finite-*teleological* view is to be found the correct premise that nature does not contain within itself the absolute purpose" (*loc. cit.* p. 225). Its purpose is the confirmation of abstraction. "Nature has shown itself to be the idea in the *form* of *other-being*. Since the *idea* is in this form the negative of itself, or *external to itself*, nature is not just relatively external *vis à vis* this idea, but *externality* constitutes the form in which it exists as nature." (*loc. cit.* p. 227)

Externality should not be understood here as the *self-externalizing world of sense*, open to the light and to man's senses. It has to be taken here in the sense of alienation, an error, a defect, that which ought not to be. For that which is true is still the idea. Nature is merely the *form* of its *other-being*. And since abstract thought is *being*, that which is external to it is by its nature a merely *external thing*. The abstract thinker recognizes at the same time that *sensuousness, externality* in contrast to thought which shuttles back and forth *within itself*, is the essence of nature. But at the same time he expresses this antithesis in such a way that this *externality of nature*, and its *contrast* with thought, appears as a *deficiency*, and that nature distinguished from abstraction appears as a deficient being. (XXXIV) A being which is deficient, not simply for me or in my eyes, but in itself, has something outside itself which it lacks. That is to say, its being is something other than itself. For the abstract thinker, nature must therefore supersede itself, because it is already posited by him as a potentially *superseded* being.

"*For us*, spirit has *nature as its premise*, being the *truth* of nature and thereby its *absolute primus*. In this truth nature has *vanished*, and spirit has surrendered itself as the idea which has attained being-for-itself, whose *object*, as well as the *subject*, is the *concept*. This identity is *absolute negativity*, for whereas in nature the concept has its perfect external objectivity, here its alienation has been superseded and the concept has become identical with itself. It is this identity only so far as it is a return from nature." (*loc. cit.* p. 392)

"*Revelation*, as the *abstract* idea, is unmediated transition to, the *coming-to-be* of, nature; as the revelation of the spirit, which is free, it is the *establishment* of nature as *its own* world, an establishment which, as reflection, is simultaneously the *presupposition* of the world as independently existing nature. Revelation in conception is the creation of nature as spirit's own being, in which it acquires the *affirmation* and *truth* of its freedom." *"The absolute is spirit*; this is the highest definition of the absolute."

From GERMAN IDEOLOGY
KARL MARX

The fact is . . . that definite individuals who are productively active in a definite way enter into . . . definite
social and political relations. Empirical observation must
in each separate instance bring out empirically, and without any mystification and speculation, the connection of
the social and political structure with production. The
social structure and the State are continually evolving
out of the life-process of definite individuals, but individuals, not as they may appear in their own or other
people's imagination, but as they really are; i.e., as they
are effective, produce materially, and are active under
definite material limits, presuppositions and conditions
independent of their will.

The production of ideas, of conceptions, of consciousness, is at first directly interwoven with the material activity and the material intercourse of men, the language
of real life. Conceiving, thinking, the mental intercourse
of men, appear at this stage as the direct efflux of their
material behavior. The same applies to mental production as expressed in the language of the politics, laws,
morality, religion, metaphysics of a people. Men are the
producers of their conceptions, ideas, etc.—real, active
men, as they are conditioned by a definite development
of their productive forces and of the intercourse corresponding to these, up to its furthest forms. Consciousness
can never be anything else than conscious existence, and
the existence of men is their actual life-process. If in all
ideology men and their circumstances appear upside
down as in a *camera obscura,* this phenomenon arises

just as much from their historical life-process as the inversion of objects on the retina does from their physical
life-process.

In direct contrast to German philosophy which descends from heaven to earth, here we ascend from earth
to heaven. That is to say, we do not set out from what
men say, imagine, conceive, nor from men as narrated,
thought of, imagined, conceived, in order to arrive at
men in the flesh. We set out from real, active men, and
on the basis of their real life-process we demonstrate
the development of the ideological reflexes and echoes of
this life-process. The phantoms formed in the human
brain are also, necessarily, sublimates of their material
life-process, which is empirically verifiable and bound
to material premises. Morality, religion, metaphysics, all
the rest of ideology and their corresponding forms of
consciousness, thus no longer retain the semblance of
independence. They have no history, no development;
but men, developing their material production and their
material intercourse, alter, along with this their real
existence, their thinking and the products of their thinking. Life is not determined by consciousness, but consciousness by life. In the first method of approach the
starting-point is consciousness taken as the living individual; in the second it is the real living individuals
themselves, as they are in actual life, and consciousness
is considered solely as *their* consciousness.

This method of approach is not devoid of premises.
It starts out from the real premises and does not abandon them for a moment. Its premises are men, not in
any fantastic isolation or abstract definition, but in their
actual, empirically perceptible process of development
under definite conditions. As soon as this active life-process is described, history ceases to be a collection of dead
facts as it is with the empiricists (themselves still ab-

stract), or an imagined activity of imagined subjects, as with the idealists.

Where speculation ends—in real life—there real, positive science begins: the representation of the practical activity, of the practical process of development of men. Empty talk about consciousness ceases, and real knowledge has to take its place. When reality is depicted, philosophy as an independent branch of activity loses its medium of existence. At the best its place can only be taken by a summing-up of the most general results, abstractions which arise from the observation of the historical development of men. Viewed apart from real history, these abstractions have in themselves no value whatsoever. They can only serve to facilitate the arrangement of historical material, to indicate the sequence of its separate strata. But they by no means afford a recipe or schema, as does philosophy, for neatly trimming the epochs of history. On the contrary, our difficulties begin only when we set about the observation and the arrangement — the real depiction — of our historical material, whether of a past epoch or of the present. The removal of these difficulties is governed by premises which it is quite impossible to state here, but which only the study of the actual life-process and the activity of the individuals of each epoch will make evident. We shall select here some of these abstractions, which we use to refute the ideologists, and shall illustrate them by historical examples.

(a) History

Since we are dealing with the Germans, who do not postulate anything, we must begin by stating the first premise of all human existence, and therefore of all history, the premise namely that men must be in a position to live in order to be able to "make history." But life involves before everything else eating and drinking, a habitation, clothing and many other things. The first historical act is thus the production of the means to satisfy these needs, the production of material life itself. And indeed this is an historical act, a fundamental condition of all history, which to-day, as thousands of years ago, must daily and hourly be fulfilled merely in order to sustain human life. Even when the sensuous world is reduced to a minimum, to a stick as with Saint Bruno, it presupposes the action of producing the stick. The first necessity therefore in any theory of history is to observe this fundamental fact in all its significance and all its implications and to accord it its due importance. This, as is notorious, the Germans have never done, and they have never therefore had an earthly basis for history and consequently never a historian. The French and the English, even if they have conceived the relation of this fact with so-called history only in an extremely one-sided fashion, particularly as long as they remained in the toils of political ideology, have nevertheless made the first attempts to give the writing of history a materialistic basis by being the first to write histories of civil society, of commerce and industry.

The second fundamental point is that as soon as a need is satisfied, (which implies the action of satisfying, and the acquisition of an instrument), new needs are made; and this production of new needs is the first historical act. Here we recognize immediately the spiritual ancestry of the great historical wisdom of the Germans who, when they run out of positive material and when they can serve up neither theological nor political nor literary rubbish, do not write history at all, but invent the "prehistoric era." They do not, however, enlighten us as to how we proceed from this nonsensical "pre-history" to history proper; although, on the other hand, in their historical speculation they seize upon this "pre-history" with especial eagerness because they imagine themselves safe there from interference on the part of "crude facts," and, at the same time, because there they can give full rein to their speculative impulse and set up and knock down hypotheses by the thousand.

The third circumstance which, from the very first, enters into historical development, is that men, who daily remake their own life, begin to make other men, to prop-agate their kind: the relation between man and wife, parents and children, the *family*. The family which to begin with is the only social relationship, becomes later, when increased needs create new social relations and the increased population new needs, a subordinate one (ex-cept in Germany), and must then be treated and ana-lyzed according to the existing empirical data,[1] not ac-cording to "the concept of the family," as is the custom in Germany. These three aspects of social activity are not of course to be taken as three different stages, but just, as I have said, as three aspects or, to make it clear to the Germans, three "moments," which have existed simultaneously since the dawn of history and the first men, and still assert themselves in history to-day.

The production of life, both of one's own in labor and

---

[1] The building of houses. With savages each family has of course its own cave or hut like the separate family tent of the nomads. This separate domestic economy is made only the more necessary by the further development of private property. With the agricultural peoples a communal domestic economy is just as impossible as a communal cultivation of the soil. A great advance was the building of towns. In all previous periods, however, the abolition of individual econ-omy, which is inseparable from the abolition of private prop-erty, was impossible for the simple reason that the material conditions governing it were not present. The setting-up of a communal domestic economy presupposes the development

of fresh life in procreation, now appears as a double relationship: on the one hand as a natural, on the other as a social relationship. By social we understand the co-operation of several individuals, no matter under what conditions, in which manner and to what end. It follows from this that a certain mode of production, or industrial stage, is always combined with a certain mode of co-operation, or social stage, and this mode of co-operation is itself a "productive force." Further, that the multitude of productive forces accessible to men determines the nature of society, hence that the "history of humanity" must always be studied and treated in relation to the history of industry and exchange. But it is also clear how in Germany it is impossible to write this sort of history, because the Germans lack not only the necessary power of comprehension and the material but also the "evidence of their senses," for across the Rhine you cannot have any experience of these things since history has stopped happening. Thus it is quite obvious from the start that there exists a materialistic connection of men with one another, which is determined by their needs and their mode of production, and which is as old as men themselves. This connection is ever taking on new forms, and thus presents a "history" independently of

---

of machinery, of the use of natural forces and of many other productive forces—e.g., of water-supplies, of gas-lighting, steam-heating, etc., the removal of the antagonism of town and country. Without these conditions a communal economy would not in itself form a new productive force; lacking any material basis and resting on a purely theoretical foundation, it would be a mere freak and would end in nothing more than a monastic economy.—What was possible can be seen in the formation of towns and the erection of communal buildings for various definite purposes (prisons, barracks, etc.). That the abolition of individual economy is inseparable from the abolition of the family is self-evident.

the existence of any political or religious nonsense which would hold men together on its own.

Only now, after having considered four moments, four aspects of the fundamental historical relationships, do we find that man also possesses "consciousness"; but, even so, not inherent, not "pure" consciousness. From the start the "spirit" is afflicted with the curse of being "burdened" with matter, which here makes its appearance in the form of agitated layers of air, sounds, in short of language. Language is as old as consciousness, language is practical consciousness, as it exists for other men, and for that reason is really beginning to exist for me personally as well; for language, like consciousness only arises from the need, the necessity, of intercourse with other men. Where there exists a relationship, it exists for me: the animal has no "relations" with anything, cannot have any. For the animal, its relation to others does not exist as a relation. Consciousness is therefore from the very beginning a social product, and remains so as long as men exist at all. Consciousness is at first, of course, merely consciousness concerning the immediate sensuous environment and consciousness of the limited connection with other persons and things outside the individual who is growing self-conscious. At the same time it is consciousness of nature, which first appears to men as a completely alien, all-powerful and unassailable force, with which men's relations are purely animal and by which they are overawed like beasts; it is thus a purely animal consciousness of nature (natural religion).

We see here immediately: this natural religion or animal behavior towards nature is determined by the form of society and *vice versa*. Here, as everywhere, the identity of nature and man appears in such a way that the restricted relation of men to nature determines their restricted relation to one another, and their restricted relation to one another determines men's restricted relation to nature, just because nature is as yet hardly modified historically; and, on the other hand, man's consciousness of the necessity of associating with the individuals around him is the beginning of the consciousness that he is living in society at all. This beginning is as animal as social life itself at this stage. It is mere hard-consciousness, and at this point man is only distinguished from sheep by the fact that with him consciousness takes the place of instinct or that his instinct is a conscious one.

This sheep-like or tribal consciousness receives its further development and extension through increased productivity, the increase of needs, and, what is fundamental to both of these, the increase of population. With these there develops the division of labor, which was originally nothing but the division of labor in the sexual act, then that division of labor which develops spontaneously or "naturally" by virtue of natural pre-disposition (e.g., physical strength), needs, accidents, etc., etc. Division of labor only becomes truly such from the moment when a division of material and mental labor appears. From this moment onwards consciousness *can* really flatter itself that it is something other than consciousness of existing practice, that it is *really* conceiving something without conceiving something *real*; from now on consciousness is in a position to emancipate itself from the world and to proceed to the formation of "pure" theory, theology, philosophy, ethics, etc. But even if this theory, theology, philosophy, ethics, etc. comes into contradiction with the existing relations, this can only occur as a result of the fact that existing social relations have come into contradiction with existing forces of production; this, moreover, can also occur in a particular national sphere of relations through the appearance of the contradiction, not within the national orbit, but between this national consciousness and the practice of other nations, i.e., between the national and the general consciousness of a nation.

Moreover, it is quite immaterial what consciousness starts to do on its own: out of all such muck we get only the one inference that these three moments, the forces of production, the state of society, and consciousness, can and must come into contradiction with one another, because the division of labor implies the possibility, nay the fact that intellectual and material activity—enjoyment and labor, production and consumption—devolve on different individuals, and that the only possibility of their not coming into contradiction lies in the negation in its turn of the division of labor. It is self-evident, moreover, that "spectres," "bonds," "the higher being," "concept," "scruple," are merely the idealistic, spiritual expression, the conception apparently of the isolated individual, the image of very empirical fetters and limitations, within which the mode of production of life, and the form of intercourse coupled with it, move.

With the division of labor, in which all these contradictions are implicit, and which in its turn is based on the natural division of labor in the family and the separation of society into individual families opposed to one another, is given simultaneously the distribution, and indeed the unequal distribution, (both quantitative and qualitative), of labor and its products, hence property: the nucleus, the first form, of which lies in the family, where wife and children are the slaves of the husband. This latent slavery in the family, though still very crude, is the first property, but even at this early stage it corresponds perfectly to the definition of modern economists who call it the power of disposing of the labor-power of others. Division of labor and private property are, moreover, identical expressions: in the one the same thing is affirmed with reference to activity as is affirmed in the other with reference to the product of the activity.

Further, the division of labor implies the contradiction between the interest of the separate individual or the individual family and the communal interest of all individuals who have intercourse with one another. And indeed, this communal interest does not exist merely in the imagination, as "the general good," but first of all in reality, as the mutual interdependence of the individuals among whom the labor is divided. And finally, the division of labor offers us the first example of how, as long as man remains in natural society, that is as long as a cleavage exists between the particular and the common interest, as long therefore as activity is not voluntarily, but naturally, divided, man's own deed becomes an alien power opposed to him, which enslaves him instead of being controlled by him. For as soon as labor is distributed, each man has a particular, exclusive sphere of activity, which is forced upon him and from which he cannot escape. He is a hunter, a fisherman, a shepherd, or a critical critic, and must remain so if he does not want to lose his means of livelihood; while in communist society, where nobody has one exclusive sphere of activity but each can become accomplished in any branch he wishes, society regulates the general production and thus makes it possible for me to do one thing to-day and another to-morrow, to hunt in the morning, fish in the afternoon, rear cattle in the evening, criticize after dinner, just as I have a mind, without ever becoming hunter, fisherman, shepherd or critic.

This crystallization of social activity, this consolidation of what we ourselves produce into an objective power above us, growing out of our control, thwarting our expectations, bringing to naught our calculations, is one of the chief factors in historical development up till now. And out of this very contradiction between the interest of the individual and that of the community the latter takes an independent form as the *State*, divorced from the real interests of individual and community, and at the same time as an illusory communal life, always based, however, on the real ties existing in every family and tribal conglomeration (such as flesh and blood, language, division of labor on a larger scale, and other interests) and especially, as we shall enlarge upon later, on the classes, already determined by the division of labor, which in every such mass of men separate out, and of which one dominates all the others. It follows from this that all struggles within the State, the struggle between democracy, aristocracy and monarchy, the struggle for the franchise, etc., etc., are merely the illusory forms in which the real struggles of the different classes are fought out among one another (of this the German theoreticians have not the faintest inkling, although they have received a sufficient introduction to the subject in *The German-French Annals* and *The Holy Family*).

Further, it follows that every class which is struggling for mastery, even when its domination, as is the case with the proletariat, postulates the abolition of the old form of society in its entirety and of mastery itself, must first conquer for itself political power in order to represent its interest in turn as the general interest, a step to which in the first moment it is forced. Just because individuals seek *only* their particular interest, i.e., that not coinciding with their communal interest (for the "general good" is the illusory form of communal life), the latter will be imposed on them as an interest "alien" to them, and "independent" of them, as in its turn a particular, peculiar "general interest"; or they must meet face to face in this antagonism, as in democracy. On the other hand too, the *practical* struggle of these particular interests, which constantly *really* run counter to the communal and illusory communal interests, make *practical* intervention and control necessary through the illusory "general-interest" in the form of the State. The social power, i.e., the multiplied productive force, which arises through the cooperation of different individuals as it is determined within the division of labor, appears to these individuals, since their co-operation is not voluntary but natural, not as their own united power but as an alien force existing outside them, of the origin and end of which they are ignorant, which they thus cannot control, which on the contrary passes through a peculiar series of phases and stages independent of the will and the action of man, nay even being the prime governor of these.

This "estrangement" (to use a term which will be comprehensible to the philosophers) can, of course, only be abolished given two *practical* premises. For it to become an "intolerable" power, i.e., a power against which men make a revolution, it must necessarily have rendered the great mass of humanity "propertyless," and produced, at the same time, the contradiction of an existing world of wealth and culture, both of which conditions presuppose a great increase in productive power, a high degree of its development. And, on the other hand, this development of productive forces (which itself implies the actual empirical existence of men in their *world-historical*, instead of local, being) is absolutely necessary as a practical premise: firstly, for the reason that without it only *want* is made general, and with want the struggle for necessities and all the old filthy business would necessarily be reproduced; and secondly, because only with this universal development of productive forces is a *universal* intercourse between men established, which produces in all nations simultaneously the phenomenon of the "propertyless" mass (universal competition), makes each nation dependent on the revolutions of the others, and finally has put *world-historical*, empirically universal individuals in place of local ones. Without this, (1) Communism could only exist as a local event; (2) The forces of intercourse themselves could not have developed as universal, hence intolerable powers: they would have remained home-bred superstitious conditions; and (3) Each extension of intercourse would abolish local communism. Empirically, communism is only possible as the act of the dominant peoples "all at once" or simultaneously, which presupposes the universal development of productive forces and the world-intercourse bound up with them. How otherwise could property have had a history at all, have taken on different forms, and landed property, for instance, according to the different premises given, have proceeded in France from parcellation to centralization in the hands of a few, in England from centralization in the hands of a few to parcellation, as is actually the case today? Or how does it happen that trade, which after all is nothing more than the exchange of products of various individuals and countries, rules the whole world through the relation of supply and demand—a relation which, as an English economist says, hovers over the earth like the Fate of the Ancients, and with invisible hand allots fortune and misfortune to men, sets up empires and overthrows empires, causes nations to rise and to disappear—while with the abolition of the basis of private property, with the communistic regulation of production (and, implicit in this, the destruction of the alien relation between men and what they themselves produce), the power of the relation of supply and demand is dissolved into nothing, and men get exchange, production, the mode of their mutual relation, under their own control again?

Communism is for us not a stable state which is to be

established, an *ideal* to which reality will have to adjust itself. We call communism the *real* movement which abolishes the present state of things. The conditions of this movement result from the premises now in existence. Besides, the world market is presupposed by the mass of propertyless workers—labor-power cut off as a mass from capital or from even a limited satisfaction—and therefore no longer by the mere precariousness of labor, which, not giving an assured livelihood, is often lost through competition. The proletariat can thus only exist *world-historically*, just as communism, its movement, can only have a "world-historical" existence. World-historical existence of individuals, i.e., existence of individuals which is directly linked up with world history.

The form of intercourse determined by the existing productive forces at all previous historical stages, and in its turn determining these, is *civil society*. This, as is clear from what we have said above, has as its premises and basis the simple family and the multiple, the so-called tribe, the more precise determinants of which are enumerated in our remarks above. Already here we see how this civil society is the true source and theatre of all history, and how nonsensical is the conception of history held hitherto, which neglects the real relationships and confines itself to high-sounding dramas of princes and states. Civil society embraces the whole material intercourse of individuals within a definite stage of the development of productive forces. It embraces the whole commercial and industrial life of this stage and, in so far, transcends the State and the nation, though, on the other hand again, it must assert itself towards foreign peoples as nationality, and inwardly must organize itself as State. The word "civil society" emerged in the eighteenth century, when property relationships had already extricated themselves from the ancient and medieval communal society. Civil society as such only develops with the bourgeoisie; the social organization evolving directly out of production and commerce, which in all ages forms the basis of the State and of the rest of the idealistic superstructure, has, however, always been designated by the same name. . . .

History is nothing but the succession of the separate generations, each of which exploits the materials, the forms of capital, the productive forces handed down to it by all preceding ones, and thus on the one hand continues the traditional activity in completely changed circumstances and, on the other, modifies the old circumstances with a completely changed activity. This can be speculatively distorted so that later history is made the goal of earlier history, e.g., the goal ascribed to the discovery of America is to further the eruption of the French Revolution. Thereby history receives its own special aims and becomes "a person ranking with other persons" (to wit: "self-consciousness, criticism, the Unique," etc.), while what is designated with the words "destiny," "goal," "germ," or "idea" of earlier history is nothing more than an abstraction formed from later history, from the active influence which earlier history exercises on later history. The further the separate spheres, which interact on one another, extend in the course of this development, the more the original isolation of the separate nationalities is destroyed by the developed mode of production and intercourse and the division of labor naturally brought forth by these, the more history becomes world-history. Thus, for instance, if in England a machine is invented, which in India or China deprives countless workers of bread, and overturns the whole form of existence of these empires, this invention becomes a world-historical fact. Or again, take the case of sugar and coffee which have proved their world-historical importance in the nineteenth century by the fact that the lack of these products occasioned by the Napoleonic Continental system, caused the Germans to rise against Napoleon, and thus became the real basis of the glorious Wars of Liberation of 1813. From this it follows that this transformation of history into world-history is not indeed a mere abstract act on the part of the "self-consciousness," the world-spirit, or of any other metaphysical spectre, but a quite material empirically verifiable act, an act the proof of which every individual furnishes as he comes and goes, eats, drinks and clothes himself.

The ideas of the ruling class are in every epoch the ruling ideas: i.e., the class, which is the ruling material force of society, is at the same time its ruling intellectual force. The class which has the means of material production at its disposal, has control at the same time over the means of mental production, so that thereby, generally speaking, the ideas of those who lack the means of mental production are subject to it. The ruling ideas are nothing more than the ideal expression of the dominant material relationships, the dominant material relationships grasped as ideas; hence of the relationships which make the one class the ruling one, therefore the ideas of its dominance. The individuals composing the ruling class possess among other things consciousness, and therefore think. In so far, therefore, as they rule as a class and determine the extent and compass of an epoch, it is self-evident that they do this in their whole range, hence among other things rule also as thinkers, as producers of ideas, and regulate the production and distribution of the ideas of their age: thus their ideas are the ruling ideas of the epoch. For instance, in an age and in a country where royal power, aristocracy and

bourgeoisie are contending for mastery and where, therefore, mastery is shared, the doctrine of the separation of
powers proves to be the dominant idea and is expressed
as an "eternal law." The division of labor, which we saw
above as one of the chief forces of history up till now,
manifests itself in the ruling class as the division of
mental and material labor, so that inside this class one
part appears as the thinkers of the class (its active, con-
ceptive ideologists, who make the perfecting of the illusion of the class about itself their chief source of livelihood), while the others' attitude to these ideas and illusions is more passive and receptive, because they are in
reality the active members of this class and have less
time to make up illusions and ideas about themselves.
Within this class this cleavage can even develop into a
certain opposition and hostility between the two parts,
which, however, in the case of a practical collision, in
which the class itself is endangered, automatically comes
to nothing, in which case there also vanishes the semblance that the ruling ideas were not the ideas of the
ruling class and had a power distinct from the power of
this class. The existence of revolutionary ideas in a particular period presupposes the existence of a revolutionary class; about the premises for the latter sufficient has
already been said above.

If now in considering the course of history we detach
the ideas of the ruling class from the ruling class itself
and attribute to them an independent existence, if we
confine ourselves to saying that these or those ideas were
dominant, without bothering ourselves about the conditions of production and the producers of these ideas, if
we then ignore the individuals and world conditions
which are the source of the ideas, we can say, for instance, that during the time that the aristocracy was dominant, the concepts honor, loyalty, etc., were dominant,

during the dominance of the bourgeoisie the concepts freedom, equality, etc. The ruling class itself on the whole imagines this to be so. This conception of history, which is common to all historians, particularly since the eighteenth century, will necessarily come up against the phenomenon that increasingly abstract ideas hold sway, i.e., ideas which increasingly take on the form of universality. For each new class which puts itself in the place of one ruling before it, is compelled, merely in order to carry through its aim, to represent its interest as the common interest of all the members of society, put in an ideal form; it will give its ideas the form of universality, and represent them as the only rational, universally valid ones. The class making a revolution appears from the very start, merely because it is opposed to a *class*, not as a class but as the representative of the whole of society; it appears as the whole mass of society confronting the one ruling class. It can do this because, to start with, its interest really is more connected with the common interest of all other non-ruling classes, because under the pressure of conditions its interest has not yet been able to develop as the particular interest of a particular class. Its victory, therefore, benefits also many individuals of the other classes which are not winning a dominant position, but only in so far as it now puts these individuals in a position to raise themselves into the ruling class. When the French bourgeoisie overthrew the power of the aristocracy, it thereby made it possible for many proletarians to raise themselves above the proletariat, but only in so far as they become bourgeois. Every new class, therefore, achieves its hegemony only on a broader basis than that of the class ruling previously, in return for which the opposition of the non-ruling class against the new ruling class later develops all the more sharply and profoundly. Both these things determine the fact that the struggle to be waged against this new ruling class, in its turn, aims at a more decided and radical negation of the previous conditions of society than could all previous classes which sought to rule.

This whole semblance, that the rule of a certain class is only the rule of certain ideas, comes to a natural end, of course, as soon as society ceases at last to be organized in the form of class-rule, that is to say as soon as it is no longer necessary to represent a particular interest as general or "the general interest" as ruling.

Once the ruling ideas have been separated from the ruling individuals and, above all, from the relationships which result from a given stage of the mode of production, and in this way the conclusion has been reached that history is always under the sway of ideas, it is very easy to abstract from these various ideas "the idea," "die Idee," etc., as the dominant force in history, and thus to understand all these separate ideas and concepts as "forms of self-determination" on the part of *the* concept developing in history. It follows then naturally, too, that all the relationships of men can be derived from the concept of man, man as conceived, the essence of man, *man*. This has been done by the speculative philosophers. Hegel himself confesses at the end of *The Philosophy of History* that he "has considered the progress of *the concept* only" and has represented in history "the true theodicy." Now one can go back again to the "producers of the concept," to the theoreticians, ideologists and philosophers, and one comes then to the conclusion that the philosophers, the thinkers as such, have at all times been dominant in history: a conclusion, as we see, already expressed by Hegel. The whole trick of proving the hegemony of the spirit in history (hierarchy, Stirner calls it) is thus confined to the following three tricks.

1. One must separate the ideas of those ruling for

empirical reasons, under empirical conditions and as empirical individuals, from these actual rulers, and thus recognize the rule of ideas or illusions in history.

2. One must bring an order into this rule of ideas, prove a mystical connection among the successive ruling ideas, which is managed by understanding them as "acts of self-determination on the part of the concept" (this is possible because by virtue of their empirical basis these ideas are really connected with one another and because, conceived as *mere* ideas, they become self-distinctions, distinctions made by thought).

3. To remove the mystical appearance of this "self-determining concept" it is changed into a person—"self-consciousness"—or, to appear thoroughly materialistic, into a series of persons, who represent the "concept" in history, into the "thinkers," the "philosophers" the ideologists, who again are understood as the manufacturers of history, as "the council of guardians," as the rulers. Thus the whole body of materialistic elements has been removed from history and now full rein can be given to the speculative steed.

While in ordinary life every shopkeeper is very well able to distinguish between what somebody professes to be and what really is, our historians have not yet won even this trivial insight. They take every epoch at its word and believe that everything it says and imagines about itself is true.

This historical method which reigned in Germany, (and especially the reason why), must be understood from its connection with the illusion of ideologists in general, e.g., the illusions of the jurists, politicians (of the practical statesmen among them, too), from the dogmatic dreamings and distortions of these fellows; this illusion is explained perfectly easily from their practical position in life, their job, and the division of labor.

PREFACE TO A CONTRIBUTION TO THE KARL MARX CRITIQUE OF POLITICAL ECONOMY

. . . My investigations led to the conclusion that legal relations as well as forms of State could not be understood from themselves, nor from the so-called general development of the human mind, but, on the contrary, are rooted in the material conditions of life, the aggregate of which Hegel, following the precedent of the English and French of the eighteenth century, grouped under the name of "civil society"; but that the anatomy of civil society is to be found in political economy. My study of the latter, begun in Paris, was continued in Brussels, whither I migrated in consequence of an expulsion order issued by M. Guizot. The general conclusion I arrived at—and once reached, it served as the guiding thread in my studies—can be briefly formulated as follows: In the social production of their means of existence men enter into definite, necessary relations which are independent of their will, productive relationships which correspond to a definite stage of development of their material productive forces. The aggregate of these productive relationships constitutes the economic structure of society, the real basis on which a juridical and political superstructure arises, and to which definite forms of social consciousness correspond. The mode of production of the material means of existence conditions the whole process of social, political and intellectual life. It is not the consciousness of men that determines their existence, but, on the contrary, it is their social exist-

ence that determines their consciousness. At a certain
stage of their development the material productive forces
of society come into contradiction with the existing productive relationships, or, what is but a legal expression
for these, with the property relationships within which
they had moved before. From forms of development of
the productive forces these relationships are transformed
into their fetters. Then an epoch of social revolution
opens. With the change in the economic foundation the
whole vast superstructure is more or less rapidly transformed. In considering such revolutions it is necessary
always to distinguish between the material revolution
in the economic conditions of production, which can be
determined with scientific accuracy, and the juridical,
politial, religious, aesthetic or philosophic—in a word,
ideological forms wherein men become conscious of this
conflict and fight it out. Just as we cannot judge an individual on the basis of his own opinion of himself, so
such a revolutionary epoch cannot be judged from its
own consciousness; but on the contrary this consciousness must be explained from the contradictions of material life, from the existing conflict between social productive forces and productive relationships. A social system never perishes before all the productive forces have
developed for which it is wide enough; and new, higher
productive relationships never come into being before
the material conditions for their existence have been
brought to maturity within the womb of the old society
itself. Therefore, mankind always sets itself only such
problems as it can solve; for when we look closer we
will always find that the problem itself only arises when
the material conditions for its solution are already present or at least in the process of coming into being. In
the modern bourgeois modes of production can be indicated as progressive epochs in the economic system

of society. Bourgeois productive relationships are the last antagonistic form of the social process of production—antagonistic in the sense not of individual antagonism, but of an antagonism arising out of the conditions of the social life of individuals; but the productive forces developing within the womb of bourgeois society at the same time create the material conditions for the solution of this antagonism. With this social system, therefore, the pre-history of human society comes to a close. . . .

From MARX'S "INTRODUCTION TO THE CRITIQUE
OF HEGEL'S PHILOSOPHY OF LAW. CRITIQUE
OF RELIGION"

The critique has plucked the imaginary flowers off
the chain not in order that man wears the unimaginative,
desolate chain, but in order that he throws off the chain
and plucks the living flower. The critique of religion
disappoints man for the purpose that he should think,
act, create his reality like a disappointed man who has
come to his senses in order that he moves around himself and thus around his real sun. Religion is only an
illusory sun which moves around man as long as he does
not move around himself. . . .

The weapons of critique indeed cannot replace the
critique of weapons; material force must be overthrown
by material force, but the theory too becomes a material force once it gets hold of men. Theory is capable
of getting hold of men once it demonstrates its truth
with regard to man, once it becomes radical. *To be
radical is to grasp something at its roots. But for man
the root is man himself.* . . . The critique of religion ends
with the idea that man is a supreme being for man.
Hence with the categorical imperative change all circumstances in which man is a humiliated, enslaved,
abandoned, contemptuous being. . . . The theory is realized in a nation only to the extent to which it is a
realization of its true needs.

REMINISCENCES OF MARX

Paul Lafargue

> He was a man, take him for all in all,
> I shall not look upon his like again.
>
> *(Hamlet,* Act I, Sc. 2)

I met Karl Marx for the first time in February 1865. The First International had been founded on September 28, 1864 at a meeting in Saint Martin's Hall, London, and I went to London from Paris to give Marx news of the development of the young organization there. M. Tolain, now a senator in the bourgeois republic, gave me a letter of introduction.

I was then 24 years old. As long as I live I shall remember the impression that first visit made on me. Marx was not well at the time. He was working on the first book of *Capital,* which was not published until two years later, in 1867. He feared he would not be able to finish his work and was therefore glad of visits from young people. "I must train men to continue communist propaganda after me," he used to say.

Karl Marx was one of the rare men who could be leaders in science and public life at the same time: these two aspects were so closely united in him that one can understand him only by taking into account both the scholar and the socialist fighter.

Marx held the view that science must be pursued for itself, irrespective of the eventual results of research, but at the same time that a scientist could only debase himself by giving up active participation in public life or shutting himself up in his study or laboratory like a maggot in cheese and holding aloof from the life and political struggle of his contemporaries.

"Science must not be a selfish pleasure," he used to say. "Those who have the good fortune to be able to devote themselves to scientific pursuits must be the first to place their knowledge at the service of humanity." One of his favorite sayings was: "Work for humanity."

Although Marx sympathized profoundly with the sufferings of the working classes, it was not sentimental considerations but the study of history and political economy that led him to communist views. He maintained that any unbiased man, free from the influence of private interests and not blinded by class prejudices, must necessarily come to the same conclusions.

Yet while studying the economic and political development of human society without any preconceived opinion, Marx wrote with no other intention than to propagate the results of his research and with a determined will to provide a scientific basis for the socialist movement, which had so far been lost in the clouds of utopianism. He gave publicity to his views only to promote the triumph of the working class, whose historic mission is to establish communism as soon as it has achieved political and economic leadership of society.

Marx did not confine his activity to the country he was born in. "I am a citizen of the world," he used to say; "I am active wherever I am." And in fact, no matter what country events and political persecution drove him to—France, Belgium, England—he took a prominent part in the revolutionary movements which developed there.

However, it was not the untiring and incomparable socialist agitator but rather the scientist that I first saw in his study in Mailand Park Road. That study was the center to which Party comrades came from all parts of the civilized world to find out the opinion of the master of socialist thought. One must know that historic room before one can penetrate into the intimacy of Marx's spiritual life.

It was on the first floor, flooded by light from a broad window that looked out on to the park. Opposite the window and on either side of the fireplace the walls were lined with bookcases filled with books and stacked up to the ceiling with newspapers and manuscripts. Opposite the fireplace on one side of the window were two tables piled up with papers, books, and newspapers; in the middle of the room, well in the light, stood a small, plain desk (three foot by two) and a wooden armchair; between the armchair and the bookcase, opposite the window, was a leather sofa on which Marx used to lie down for a rest from time to time. On the mantelpiece were more books, cigars, matches, tobacco boxes, paperweights and photographs of Marx's daughters and wife, Wilhelm Wolff and Frederick Engels.

Marx was a heavy smoker. *"Capital,"* he said to me once, "will not even pay for the cigars I smoked writing it." But he was still heavier on matches. He so often forgot his pipe or cigar that he emptied an incredible number of boxes of matches in a short time to relight them.

He never allowed anybody to put his books or papers in order—or rather in disorder. The disorder in which they lay was only apparent, everything was really in its intended place so that it was easy for him to lay his hand on the book or notebook he needed. Even during conversations he often paused to show in the book a quotation or figure he had just mentioned. He and his study were one: the books and papers in it were as much under his control as his own limbs.

Marx had no use for formal symmetry in the arrangement of his books: volumes of different sizes and pamphlets stood next to one another. He arranged them according to their contents, not their size. Books were tools for his mind, not articles of luxury. "They are my slaves and they must serve me as I will," he used to say. He paid no heed to size or binding, quality of paper or type; he would turn down the corners of the pages, make pencil marks in the margin and underline whole lines. He never wrote on books, but sometimes he could not refrain from an exclamation or question mark when the author went too far. His system of underlining made it easy for him to find any passage he needed in any book. He had the habit of going through his notebooks and reading the passages underlined in the books after intervals of many years in order to keep them fresh in his memory. He had an extraordinarily reliable memory which he had cultivated from his youth according to Hegel's advice by learning by heart verse in a foreign language he did not know.

He knew Heine and Goethe by heart and often quoted them in his conversations; he was an assiduous reader of poets in all European languages. Every year he read Aeschylus in the Greek original. He considered him and Shakespeare as the greatest dramatic geniuses humanity ever gave birth to. His respect for Shakespeare was boundless: he made a detailed study of his works and knew even the least important of his characters. His whole family had a real cult for the great English dramatist; his three daughters knew many of his works by heart. When after 1848 he wanted to perfect his knowledge of English, which he could already read, he sought out and classified all Shakespeare's original expressions. He did the same with part of the polemical works of William Cobbett, of whom he had a high opinion. Dante and Robert Burns ranked among his favorite poets and he would listen with great pleasure to his daughters reciting or singing the Scottish poet's satires or ballads.

Cuvier, an untirable worker and past master in the sciences, had a suite of rooms, arranged for his personal use, in the Paris Museum, of which he was director. Each room was intended for a particular pursuit and contained the books, instruments, anatomic aids, etc. required for the purpose. When he felt tired of one kind of work he would go into the next room and engage in another; this simple change of mental occupation, it is said, was a rest for him.

Marx was just as tireless a worker as Cuvier, but he had not the means to fit out several studies. He would rest by pacing up and down the room. A strip was worn out from the door to the window, as sharply defined as a track across a meadow.

From time to time he would lie down on the sofa and read a novel; he sometimes read two or three at a time, alternating one with another. Like Darwin, he was a great reader of novels, his preference being for those of the eighteenth century, particularly Fielding's *Tom Jones*. The more modern novelists whom he found most interesting were Paul de Kock, Charles Lever, Alexander Dumas senior and Walter Scott, whose *Old Mortality* he considered a masterpiece. He had a definite preference for stories of adventure and humor.

He ranked Cervantes and Balzac above all other novelists. In *Don Quixote* he saw the epic of dying-out chivalry whose virtues were ridiculed and scoffed at in the emerging bourgeois world. He admired Balzac so much that he wished to write a review of his great work *La Comédie humaine* as soon as he had finished his book on economics. He considered Balzac not only as the historian of his time, but as the prophetic creator of characters which were still in the embryo in the days of Louis Philippe and did not fully develop until after his death, under Napoleon III.

Marx could read all European languages and write in three: German, French and English, to the admiration of language experts. He liked to repeat the saying: "A foreign language is a weapon in the struggle of life."

He had a great talent for languages which his daughters inherited from him. He took up the study of Russian when he was already 50 years old, and although that language had no close affinity to any of the modern or ancient languages he knew, in six months he knew it well enough to derive pleasure from reading Russian poets and prose writers, his preference going to Pushkin, Gogol and Shchedrin. He studied Russian in order to be able to read the documents of official inquiries which were hushed over by the Russian Government because of the political revelations they made. Devoted friends got the documents for Marx and he was certainly the only political economist in Western Europe who had knowledge of them.

Besides the poets and novelists, Marx had another remarkable way of relaxing intellectually—mathematics, for which he had a special liking. Algebra even brought him moral consolation and he took refuge in it in the most distressing moments of his eventful life. During his wife's last illness he was unable to devote himself to his usual scientific work and the only way in which he could shake off the oppression caused by her sufferings was to plunge into mathematics. During that time of moral suffering he wrote a work on infinitesimal calculus which, according to the opinion of experts, is of great scientific value and will be published in his collected works. He saw in higher mathematics the most logical and at the same time the simplest form of dialectical movement. He held the view that a science is not really developed until it has learned to make use of mathematics.

Although Marx's library contained over a thousand volumes carefully collected during his lifelong research work, it was not enough for him, and for years he regularly attended the British Museum, whose catalogue he appreciated very highly.

Even Marx's opponents were forced to acknowledge his extensive and profound erudition, not only in his own specialty—political economy—but in history, philosophy and the literature of all countries.

In spite of the late hour at which Marx went to bed he was always up between eight and nine in the morning, had some black coffee, read through his newspapers and then to his study, where he worked till two or three in the morning. He interrupted his work only for meals and, when the weather allowed, for a walk on Hampstead Heath in the evening. During the day he sometimes slept for an hour or two on the sofa. In his youth he often worked the whole night through.

Marx had a passion for work. He was so absorbed in it that he often forgot his meals. He had often to be called several times before he came down to the dining-room and hardly had he eaten the last mouthful than he was back in his study.

He was a very light eater and even suffered from lack of appetite. This he tried to overcome by highly flavored food—ham, smoked fish, caviare, pickles. His stomach had to suffer for the enormous activity of his brain. He sacrificed his whole body to his brain; thinking was his greatest enjoyment. I often heard him repeat the words of Hegel, the philosophy master of his youth: "Even the criminal thought of a malefactor has more grandeur and nobility than the wonders of the heavens."

His physical constitution had to be good to put up with this unusual way of life and exhausting mental work. He was, in fact, of powerful build, more than average height, broad-shouldered, deep-chested, and had well-proportioned limbs, although the spinal column was rather long in comparison with the legs, as is often the case with Jews. Had he practiced gymnastics in his youth he would have become a very strong man. The only physical exercise he ever pursued regularly was walking: he could ramble or climb hills for hours, chatting and smoking, and not feel at all tired. One can say that he even worked walking in his room, only sitting down for short periods to write what he thought out while walking. He liked to walk up and down while talking, stopping from time to time when the explanation became for animated or the conversation serious.

For many years I went with him on his evening walks on Hampstead Heath and it was while strolling over the meadows with him that I got my education in economics. Without noticing it he expounded to me the whole contents of the first book of *Capital* as he wrote it.

On my return home I always noted as well as I could all I had heard. At first it was difficult for me to follow Marx's profound and complicated reasoning. Unfortunately I have lost those precious notes, for after the Commune the police ransacked and burned my papers in Paris and Bordeaux.

What I regret most is the loss of the notes I took on the evening when Marx, with the abundance of proof and considerations which was typical of him, expounded his brilliant theory of the development of human society. It was as if scales fell from my eyes. For the first time I saw clearly the logic of world history and could trace the apparently so contradictory phenomena of the development of society and ideas to their material origins. I felt dazzled, and the impression remained for years.

The Madrid Socialists[1] had the same impression when I developed to them as well as my feeble powers would allow that most magnificent of Marx's theories, which is beyond doubt one of the greatest ever elaborated by the human brain.

Marx's brain was armed with an unbelievable stock of facts from history and natural science and philosophical theories. He was remarkably skilled in making use of the knowledge and observations accumulated during years of intellectual work. You could question him at any time on any subject and get the most detailed answer you could wish for, always accompanied by philosophical reflexions of general application. His brain was like a man-of-war in port under steam, ready to launch into any sphere of thought.

There is no doubt that *Capital* reveals to us a mind of astonishing vigor and superior knowledge. But for me, as for all those who knew Marx intimately, neither *Capital* nor any other of his works shows all the magnitude of his genius or the extent of his knowledge. He was highly superior to his own works.

I worked with Marx; I was only the scribe to whom he dictated, but that gave me the opportunity of observing his manner of thinking and writing. Work was easy for him,. and at the same time difficult. Easy because his mind found no difficulty in embracing the relevant facts and considerations in their completeness. But that very completeness made the exposition of his ideas a matter of long and arduous work.

---

[1] After the defeat of the Paris Commune Lafargue emigrated to Spain, charged by Marx and the General Council of the First International with the fight against the anarchist Bakuninists.—*Ed.*

Vico said: "The thing is a body only for God, who knows everything; for man, who knows only the exterior, it is only surface." Marx grasped things after the fashion of Vico's god. He saw not only the surface, but what lay beneath it. He examined all the constituent parts in their mutual action and reaction; he isolated each of those parts and traced the history of its development. Then he went on from the thing to its surroundings and observed the reaction of one upon the other. He traced the origin of the object, the changes, evolutions and revolutions it went through, and proceeded finally to its remotest effects. He did not see a thing singly, in itself and for itself, separate from its surroundings: he saw a highly complicated world in continual motion.

His intention was to disclose the whole of that world in its manifold and continually varying action and reaction. Men of letters of Flaubert's and the Goncourts' school complain that it is so difficult to render exactly what one sees; yet all they wish to render is the surface, the impression that they get. Their literary work is child's play in comparison with Marx's: it required extraordinary vigor of thought to grasp reality and render what he saw and wanted to make others see. Marx was never satisfied with his work—he was always making some improvements and he always found his rendering inferior to the idea he wished to convey. . . .

Marx had the two qualities of a genius: he had an incomparable talent for dissecting a thing into its constituent parts, and he was past master at reconstituting the dissected object out of its parts, with all its different forms of development, and discovering their mutual inner relations. His demonstrations were not abstractions —which was the reproach made to him by economists who were themselves incapable of thinking; his method was not that of the geometrician who takes his definitions from the world around him but completely disregards reality in drawing his conclusions. *Capital* does not give isolated definitions or isolated formulas; it gives a series of most searching analyses which bring out the most evasive shades and the most elusive gradations.

Marx begins by stating the plain fact that the wealth of a society dominated by the capitalist mode of production presents itself as an enormous accumulation of commodities; the commodity, which is a concrete object, not a mathematical abstraction, is therefore the element, the cell, of capitalist wealth. Marx now seizes on the commodity, turns it over and over and inside out, and pries out of it one secret after another that official economists were not in the least aware of, although those secrets are more numerous and profound than all the mysteries of the Catholic religion. Having examined the commodity in all its aspects, Marx considers it in its relation to its fellow commodity, in exchange. Then he goes on to its production and the historic prerequisites for its production. He considers the forms which commodities assume and shows how they pass from one to another, how one form is necessarily engendered by the other. He expounds the logical course of development of phenomena with such perfect art that one could think he had imagined it. And yet it is a product of reality, a reproduction of the actual dialectics of the commodity.

Marx was always extremely conscientious about his work: he never gave a fact or figure that was not borne out by the best authorities. He was never satisfied with second-hand information, he always went to the source itself, no matter how tedious the process. To make sure of a minor fact he would go to the British Museum and consult books there. His critics were never able to prove that he was negligent or that he based his arguments on facts which did not bear strict checking.

His habit of always going to the very source made him read authors who were very little known and whom he was the only one to quote. *Capital* contains so many quotations from little-known authors that one might think Marx wanted to show off how well-read he was. He had no intention of the sort. "I administer historical justice," he said. "I give each one his due." He considered himself obliged to name the author who had first expressed an idea or formulated it most correctly, no matter how insignificant and little known he was.

Marx was just as conscientious from the literary as from the scientific point of view. Not only would he never base himself on a fact he was not absolutely sure of, he never allowed himself to talk of a thing before he had studied it thoroughly. He did not publish a single work without repeatedly revising it until he had found the most appropriate form. He could not bear to appear in public without thorough preparation. It would have been a torture for him to show his manuscripts before giving them the finishing touch. He felt so strongly about this that he told me one day that he would rather burn his manuscripts than leave them unfinished.

His method of working often imposed upon him tasks the magnitude of which the reader can hardly imagine. Thus, in order to write the twenty pages or so on English factory legislation in *Capital* he went through a whole library of Blue Books containing reports of commissions and factory inspectors in England and Scotland. He read them from cover to cover, as can be seen from the pencil marks in them. He considered those reports as the most important and weighty documents for the study of the capitalist mode of production. He had such a high opinion of those in charge of them that he doubted the possibility of finding in another country in Europe "men as competent, as free from partisanship and respect of persons as are the English factory inspectors." He paid them this brilliant tribute in the Preface to *Capital.*

From these Blue Books Marx drew a wealth of factual information. Many members of Parliament to whom they are distributed use them only as shooting targets, judging the striking power of the gun by the number of pages pierced. Others sell them by the pound, which is the most reasonable thing they can do, for this enabled Marx to buy them cheap from the old paper dealers in Long Acre whom he used to visit to look through their old books and papers. Professor Beesley said that Marx was the man who made the greatest use of English official inquiries and brought them to the knowledge of the world. He did not know that before 1845 Engels took numerous documents from the Blue Books in writing his book on the condition of the working class in England.

2

To get to know and love the heart that beat within the breast of Marx the scholar you had to see him when he had closed his books and notebooks and was surrounded by his family, or again on Sunday evenings in the society of his friends. He then proved the pleasantest of company, full of wit and humor, with a laugh that came straight from the heart. His black eyes under the arches of his bushy brows sparkled with pleasure and malice whenever he heard a witty saying or a pertinent repartee.

He was a loving, gentle and indulgent father. "Children should educate their parents," he used to say. There was never even a trace of the bossy parent in his relations with his daughters, whose love for him was extraordinary. He never gave them an order, but asked them to do what he wished as a favor or made them feel that they should not do what he wanted to forbid them. And yet a father could seldom have had more docile children than he. His daughters considered him as their friend and treated him as a companion; they did not call him "father," but "Moor"—a nickname that he owed to his dark complexion and jet-black hair and beard. The members of the Communist League, on the other hand, called him "Father Marx" before 1848, when he was not even thirty years of age. . . .

Marx used to spend hours playing with his children. These still remember the sea battles in a big basin of water and the burning of the fleets of paper ships that he made for them and set on fire to their great joy.

On Sundays his daughters would not allow him to work, he belonged to them for the whole day. If the weather was fine, the whole family would go for a walk in the country. On their way they would stop at a modest inn for bread and cheese and ginger beer. When his daughters were small he would make the long walk seem shorter to them by telling them endless fantastic tales which he made up as he went, developing and tensening the complications according to the distance they had to go, so that the little ones forgot their weariness listening.

He had an incomparably fertile imagination: his first literary works were poems. Mrs. Marx carefully preserved the poetry her husband wrote in his youth but never showed it to anybody. His family had dreamt of him being a man of letters or a professor and thought he was debasing himself by engaging in socialist agitation and political economy, which was then disdained in Germany.

Marx had promised his daughters to write a drama on the Gracchi for them. Unfortunately he was unable to keep his word. It would have been interesting to see how he, who was called "the knight of the class struggle," would have dealt with that terrible and magnificent episode in the class struggle of the ancient world. Marx fostered a lot of plans which were never carried out. Among other works he intended to write a Logis and a History of Philosophy, the latter having been his favorite subject in his younger days. He would have needed to live to a hundred to carry out all his literary plans and present the world with a portion of the treasure hidden in his brain.

Marx's wife was his lifelong helpmate in the truest and fullest sense of the word. They had known each other as children and grown up together. Marx was only seventeen at the time of his engagement. Seven long years the young couple had to wait before they were married in 1843. After that they never parted.

Mrs. Marx died shortly before her husband. Nobody ever had a greater sense of equality than she, although she was born and bred in a German aristocratic family. No social differences or classifications existed for her. She entertained working people in their working clothes in her house and at her table with the same politeness and consideration as if they had been dukes or princes. Many workers of all countries enjoyed her hospitality and I am convinced that not one of them ever dreamt that the woman who received them with such homely and sincere cordiality descended in the female line from the family of the Dukes of Argyll and that her brother was a minister of the King of Prussia. That did not worry Mrs. Marx; she had given up everything to follow her Karl and never, not even in times of dire need, was she sorry she had done so.

She had a clear and brilliant mind. Her letters to her friends, written without constraint or effort, are masterly achievements of vigorous and original thinking. It was a treat to get a letter from Mrs. Marx. Johann Philipp Becker published several of her letters. Heine, a pitiless satirist as he was, feared Marx's irony, but he was full of admiration for the penetrating sensitive mind of his wife; when the Marxes were in Paris he was one of their regular visitors.

Marx had such respect for the intelligence and critical sense of his wife that he showed her all his manuscripts and set great store by her opinion, as he himself told me in 1866. Mrs. Marx copied out her husband's manuscripts before they were sent to the print-shop.

Mrs. Marx had a number of children. Three of them died at a tender age during the period of hardships that the family went through after the 1848 Revolution. At that time they lived as emigrants in London in two small rooms in Dean Street, Soho Square. I only knew the three daughters. When I was introduced to Marx in 1865 his youngest daughter, now Mrs. Aveling, was a charming child with a sunny disposition. Marx used to say his wife had made a mistake as to sex when she brought her into the world. The other two daughters formed a most surprising and harmonious contrast. The eldest, Mrs. Longuet, had her father's dark and vigorous complexion, dark eyes and jet-black hair. The second, Mrs. Lafargue, was fair-haired and rosy-skinned, her rich curly hair had a golden shimmer as if it had caught the rays of the setting sun: she was like her mother.

Another important member of the Marx household was Hélène Demuth. Born of a peasant family, she entered the service of Mrs. Marx long before the latter's wedding, when hardly more than a child. When her mistress got married she remained with her and devoted herself with complete self-oblivion to the Marx family. She accompanied her mistress and her husband on all their journeys over Europe and shared their exile. She was the good genius of the house and could always find a way out of the most difficult situations. It was thanks to her sense of order, her economy and skill that the Marx family were at least never short of the bare essentials. There was nothing she could not do: she cooked, kept the house, dressed the children, cut clothes for them and sewed them with Mrs. Marx. She was housekeeper and *major domo* at the same time: she ran the whole house. The children loved her like a mother and her maternal feelings towards them gave her a mother's authority. Mrs. Marx considered her as her bosom friend and Marx fostered a particular friendship towards her; he played chess with her and often enough lost to her.

Hélène loved the Marx family blindly: anything they did was good in her eyes and could not be otherwise; whoever criticized Marx had to deal with her. She extended her motherly protection to everyone who was admitted to intimacy with the Marxes. It was as though she had adopted all of the Marx family. She outlived Marx and his wife and transferred her care to Engels's household. She had known him since she was a girl and extended to him the attachment she had for the Marx family.

Engels was, so to speak, a member of the Marx family. Marx's daughters called him their second father. He was Marx's *alter ego*. For a long time the two names were never separated in Germany and they will be for ever united in history.

Marx and Engels were the personification in our time of the ideal of friendship portrayed by the poets of antiquity. From their youth they developed together and parallel to each other, lived in intimate fellowship of ideas and feelings and shared the same revolutionary agitation; as long as they could live together they worked in common. Had events not parted them for about twenty years they would probably have worked together their whole life. But after the defeat of the 1848 Revolution

Engels had to go to Manchester, while Marx was obliged to remain in London. Even so, they continued their common intellectual life by writing to each other almost daily, giving their views on political and scientific events and their work. As soon as Engels was able to free himself from his work he hurried from Manchester to London, where he set up his home only ten minutes away from his dear Marx. From 1870 to the death of his friend not a day went by but the two men saw each other, sometimes at one's house, sometimes at the other's.

It was a day of rejoicing for the Marxes when Engels informed them that he was coming from Manchester. His pending visit was spoken of long beforehand, and on the day of his arrival Marx was so impatient that he could not work. The two friends spent the whole night smoking and drinking together and talking over all that had happened since their last meeting.

Marx appreciated Engels' opinion more than anybody else's, for Engels was the man he considered capable of being his collaborator. For him Engels was a whole audience. No effort could have been too great for Marx to convince Engels and win him over to his ideas. For instance, I have seen him read whole volumes over and over to find the fact he needed to change Engels' opinion on some secondary point that I do not remember concerning the political and religious wars of the Albigenses. It was a triumph for Marx to bring Engels round to his opinion.

Marx was proud of Engels. He took pleasure in enumerating to me all his moral and intellectual qualities. He once specially made the journey to Manchester with me to introduce me to him. He admired the versatility of his knowledge and was alarmed at the slightest thing that could befall him. "I always tremble," he said to me, "for fear he should meet with an accident at the chase.

He is so impetuous; he goes galloping over the fields with slackened reins, not shying at any obstacle."

Marx was as good a friend as he was a loving husband and father. In his wife and daughters, Hélène and Engels, he found worthy objects of love for a man such as he was.

3

Having started as leader of the radical bourgeoisie, Marx found himself deserted as soon as his opposition became too resolute and looked upon as an enemy as soon as he became a Socialist. He was baited and expelled from Germany after being decried and calumniated, and then there was a conspiracy of silence against him and his work. *The Eighteenth Brumaire*, which proves that Marx was the only historian and politician of 1848 who understood and disclosed the real nature of the causes and results of the *coup d'état* of December 2, 1851, was completely ignored. In spite of the actuality of the work not a single bourgeois newspaper even mentioned it.

The Poverty of Philosophy, an answer to the *Philosophy of Poverty*, and *A Contribution to the Critique of Political Economy* were likewise ignored. The First International and the first book of *Capital* broke this conspiracy of silence after it had lasted fifteen years. Marx could no longer be ignored: the International developed and filled the world with the glory of its achievements. Although Marx kept in the background and let others act it was soon discovered who the man behind the scenes was.

The Social-Democratic Party was founded in Germany and became a power that Bismarck courted before he attacked it. Schweitzer, a follower of Lassalle, published a series of articles, which Marx highly praised, to bring

Capital to the knowledge of the working public. On a motion by Johann Philipp Becker the Congress of the International adopted a resolution directing the attention of Socialists in all countries to *Capital* as to the "Bible of the working class."[2]

After the rising on March 18, 1871, in which people tried to see the work of the International, and after the defeat of the Commune, which the General Council of the First International took it upon itself to defend against the rage of the bourgeois press in all countries; Marx's name became known to the whole world. He was acknowledged as the greatest theoretician of scientific socialism and the organizer of the first international working-class movement.

Capital became the manual of socialists in all countries. All socialist and working-class papers spread its scientific theories. During a big strike which broke out in New York extracts from *Capital* were published in the form of leaflets to inspire the workers to endurance and show them how justified their claims were.

Capital was translated into the main European languages—Russian, French and English, and extracts were published in German, Italian, French, Spanish and Dutch. Every time attempts were made by opponents in Europe or America to refute its theories, the economists immediately got a socialist reply which closed their mouths. *Capital* is really today what it was called by the Congress of the international—*the Bible of the working class.*

The share Marx had to take in the international socialist movement took time from his scientific activity. The death of his wife and that of his eldest daughter, Mrs. Longuet, also had an adverse effect upon it.

---

[2] This resolution was adopted by the Brussels Congress of the First International in September 1868.—*Ed.*

Marx's love for his wife was profound and intimate. Her beauty had been his pride and his joy, her gentleness and devotedness had lightened for him the hardships necessarily resulting from his eventful life as a revolutionary Socialist. The disease which led to the death of Jenny Marx also shortened the life of her husband. During her long and painful illness Marx, exhausted by sleeplessness and lack of exercise and fresh air and morally weary, contracted the pneumonia which was to snatch him away.

On December 2, 1881, Mrs. Marx died as she had lived, a communist and a materialist. Death had no terrors for her. When she felt her end approach she exclaimed: "Karl, my strength is ebbing!" Those were her last intelligible words.

She was buried in Highgate Cemetery, in unconsecrated ground, on December 5. Conforming to the habits of her life and Marx's, all care was taken to avoid her funeral being made a public one and only a few close friends accompanied her to her last resting-place. Marx's old friend Engels delivered the address over her grave.

After the death of his wife, Marx's life was a succession of physical and moral sufferings which he bore with great fortitude. They were aggravated by the sudden death of his eldest daughter, Mrs. Longuet, a year later. He was broken, never to recover.

He died at his desk on March 14, 1883, at the age of sixty-four.

First published in *Die Neue Zeit,* Vol. 1, 1890-91. Translated from the German.

JENNY MARX TO JOSEPH WEYDEMEYER

London, May 20, 1850

Dear Herr Weydemeyer,

It will soon be a year since I was given such friendly and cordial hospitality by you and your dear wife, since I felt so comfortably at home in your house. All that time I have not given you a sign of life: I was silent when your wife wrote me such a friendly letter and did not even break that silence when we received the news of the birth of your child. My silence has often oppressed me, but most of the time I was unable to write and even today I find it hard, very hard.

Circumstances, however, force me to take up my pen. I beg you *to send us as soon as possible any money that has been or will be received* from the *Revue*.[1] *We need it very, very much.* Certainly nobody can reproach us with ever having made much case of the sacrifices we have been making and bearing for years, the public has never or almost never been informed of our circumstances; my husband is very sensitive in such matters and he would rather sacrifice his last than resort to democratic begging like officially recognized "great men." But he could have expected active and energetic support for his *Revue* from his friends, particularly those in Cologne. He could have expected such support first of all from where his sacrifices for *Rheinische Zeitung* were known. But instead of that the business has been

---

[1] *Neue Rheinische Zeitung. Politisch-ökonomische Revue.* —*Ed.*

completely ruined by negligent and disorderly manage-
ment, and one cannot say whether the delays of the
bookseller or of the business managers or acquaintances
in Cologne or the attitude of the Democrats on the
whole were the most ruinous.

Here my husband is almost overwhelmed with the
paltry worries of life in so revolting a form that it has
taken all his energy, all his calm, clear, quiet sense of
dignity to maintain him in that daily, hourly struggle.
You know, dear Herr Weydemeyer, the sacrifices my
husband has made for the paper. He put thousands in
cash into it, he took over proprietorship, talked into it by
worthy Democrats who would otherwise have had to
answer for the debts themselves, at a time when there
was little prospect of success. To save the paper's political honor and the civic honor of his Cologne acquaintances he took upon himself the whole responsibility; he
sacrificed his printing-press, he sacrificed all income, and
before he left he even borrowed 300 thalers to pay the
rent of the newly hired premises and the outstanding
salaries of the editors, etc. And he was to be turned out
by force. You know that we kept nothing for ourselves.
I went to Frankfurt to pawn my silver—the last that we
had—and I had my furniture in Cologne sold because I
was in peril of having my linen and everything sequestrated. At the beginning of the unhappy period of the
counter-revolution my husband went to Paris and I
followed him with my three children. Hardly had he
settled down in Paris when he was expelled and even
my children and I were refused permission to reside
there any longer. I followed him again across the sea. A
month later our fourth child was born. You have to
know London and conditions here to understand what
it means to have three children and give birth to a

fourth. For rent alone we had to pay 42 thalers a month. We were able to cope with this out of money which we received, but our meager resources were exhausted when the *Revue* was published. Contrary to the agreement, we were not paid, and later only in small sums, so that our situation here was most alarming.

I shall describe to you just *one* day of that life, exactly as it was, and you will see that few emigrants, perhaps, have gone through anything like it. As wet-nurses here are too expensive I decided to feed my child myself in spite of continual terrible pains in the breast and back. But the poor little angel drank in so much worry and hushed-up anxiety that he was always poorly and suffered horribly day and night. Since he came into the world he has not slept a single night, two or three hours at the most and that rarely. Recently he has had violent convulsions, too, and has always been between life and death. In his pain he sucked so hard that my breast was chafed and the skin cracked and the blood often poured into his trembling little mouth. I was sitting with him like that one day when our housekeeper came in. We had paid her 250 thalers during the winter and had an agreement to give the money in the future not to her but to her landlord, who had a bailiff's warrant against her. She denied the agreement and demanded five pounds that we still owed her. As we did not have the money at the time (Naut's letter did not arrive until later) two bailiffs came and sequestrated all my few possessions—linen, beds, clothes—everything, even my poor child's cradle and the best toys of my daughters, who stood there weeping bitterly. They threatened to take everything away in two hours. I would then have had to lie on the bare floor with my freezing children and my bad breast. Our friend Schramm hurried to town to get help for us. He got into a cab, but the horses bolted and he jumped out and was brought bleeding back to the house, where I was wailing with my poor shivering children.

We had to leave the house the next day. It was cold, rainy and dull. My husband looked for accommodation for us. When he mentioned the four children nobody would take us in. Finally a friend helped us, we paid our rent and I hastily sold all my beds to pay the chemist, the baker, the butcher and the milkman who, alarmed at the sight of the sequestration, suddenly besieged me with their bills. The beds which we had sold were taken out and put on a cart. What was happening? It was well after sunset. We were contravening English law. The landlord rushed up to us with two constables, maintaining that there might be some of his belongings among the things, and that we wanted to make away abroad. In less than five minutes there were two or three hundred persons loitering around our door—the whole Chelsea mob. The beds were brought in again—they could not be delivered to the buyer until after sunrise next day. When we had sold all our possessions we were in a position to pay what we owed to the last farthing. I went with my little darlings to the two small rooms we are now occupying in the German Hotel, 1, Leicester St., Leicester Square. There for £5 a week we were given a human reception.

Forgive me, dear friend, for being so long and wordy in describing a single day of our life here. It is indiscreet, I know, but my heart is bursting this evening, and I must at least once unload it to my oldest, best and truest friend. Do not think that these paltry worries have bowed me down: I know only too well that our struggle is not an isolated one and that I, in particular, am one of the chosen, happy, favored ones, for my dear husband, the prop of my life, is still at my side. What really tortures my very soul and makes my heart bleed is that he had to suffer so much from paltry things, that so little could be done to help him, and that he who willingly and gladly helped so many others was so helpless himself. But do not think, dear Herr Weydemeyer, that we make demands on anybody. The only thing that my husband could have asked of those to whom he gave his ideas, his encouragement and his support was to show more energy in business and more support for his *Revue*. I am proud and bold to make that assertion. That little was his due. I do not think that would have been unfair to anybody. That is what grieves me. But my husband is of a different opinion. Never, not even in the most frightful moments, did he lose his confidence in the future or even his cheery humor, and he was satisfied when he saw me cheerful and our loving children cuddling close to their dear mother. He does not know, dear Herr Weydemeyer, that I have written to you in such detail about our situation. That is why I ask you not to refer to these lines. All he knows is that I have asked you in his name to hasten as much as you can the collection and sending of our money.

Farewell, dear friend. Give your wife my most affectionate remembrances and kiss your little angel for a mother who has shed many a tear over her baby. Our three eldest children are doing splendidly for all that, for all that. The girls are pretty, healthy, cheerful and good, and our chubby little boy is full of good humor and the most amusing notions. The little goblin sings the whole day long with astonishing feeling in a thunderous voice. The house shakes when he rings out in a fearful voice the words of Freiligrath's Marseillaise:

> Come, June, and bring us noble feats!
> To deeds of fame our heart aspires.

Perhaps it is the historic destiny of that month, as of its two predecessors,[1] to open the gigantic struggle in which we shall all join hands again. Farewell!

---

[1] The reference is to June 1848—the defeat of the Paris proletariat, and June 1849—the failure of the campaign for a Reich Constitution in southwest Germany.—*Ed.*

Printed in *Die Neue Zeit*, Vol. 2, 1906-7. Translated from the German according to the text of the journal checked with a photocopy of the manuscript.

KARL MARX
Eleanor Marx-Aveling
(A Few Stray Notes)

My Austrian friends ask me to send them some recollections of my father. They could not well have asked me for anything more difficult. But Austrian men and women are making so splendid a fight for the cause for which Karl Marx lived and worked, that one cannot say nay to them. And so I will even try to send them a few stray, disjointed notes about my father.

Many strange stories have been told about Karl Marx, from that of his "millions" (in pounds sterling, of course, no smaller coin would do), to that of his having been subventioned by Bismarck, whom he is supposed to have constantly visited in Berlin during the time of the International (!). But after all, to those who knew Karl Marx no legend is funnier than the common one which pictures him a morose, bitter, unbending, unapproachable man, a sort of Jupiter Tonans, ever hurling thunder, never known to smile, sitting aloof and alone in Olympus. This picture of the cheeriest, gayest soul that ever breathed, of a man brimming over with humor and good-humor, whose hearty laugh was infectious and irresistible, of the kindliest, gentlest, most sympathetic of companions, is a standing wonder—and amusement—to those who knew him.

In his home life, as in his intercourse with friends, and even with mere acquaintances, I think one might say that Karl Marx's main characteristics were his unbounded good-humor and his unlimited sympathy. His kindness and patience were really sublime. A less sweet-

248

tempered man would have often been driven frantic by the constant interruptions, the continual demands made upon him by all sorts of people. That a refugee of the Commune—a most unmitigated old bore, by the way—who had kept Marx three mortal hours, when at last told that time was pressing, and much work still had to be done, should reply "*Mon cher Marx, je vous excuse*" is characteristic of Marx's courtesy and kindness.

As to this old bore, so to any man or woman whom he believed honest (and he gave of his precious time to not a few who sadly abused his generosity), Marx was always the most friendly and kindly of men. His power of "drawing out" people, of making them feel that he was interested in what interested them was marvellous. I have heard men of the most diverse callings and positions speak of his peculiar capacity for understanding them and their affairs. When he thought anyone really in earnest his patience was unlimited. No question was too trivial for him to answer, no argument too childish for serious discussion. His time and his vast learning were always at the service of any man or woman who seemed anxious to learn.

*   *   *

But it was in his intercourse with children that Marx was perhaps most charming. Surely never did children have a more delightful playfellow. My earliest recollection of him is when I was about three years old, and "Mohr" (the old home name will slip out) was carrying me on his shoulder round our small garden in Grafton Terrace, and putting convolvulus flowers in my brown curls. Mohr was admittedly a splendid horse. In earlier days—I cannot remember them, but have heard tell of them—my sisters and little brother—whose death just

after my own birth was a lifelong grief to my parents—
would "harness" Mohr to chairs which they "mounted,"
and that he had to pull. . . . Personally—perhaps because
I had no sisters of my own age—I preferred Mohr as a
riding-horse. Seated on his shoulders, holding tight by
his great mane of hair, then black, with but a hint of
grey, I have had magnificent rides round our little garden, and over the fields—now built over—that surrounded
our house in Grafton Terrace.

One word as to the name "Mohr." At home we all
had nicknames. (Readers of *Capital* will know what a
hand at giving them Marx was.) "Mohr" was the regular,
almost official, name by which Marx was called, not only
by us, but by all the more intimate friends. But he was
also our "Challey" (originally I presume a corruption of
Charley!) and "Old Nick." My mother was always our
"Mohme." Our dear old friend Hélène Demuth—the lifelong friend of my parents, became after passing through
a series of names—our "Nym." Engels, after 1870, became our "General." A very intimate friend—Lina Schöler
—our "Old Mole." My sister Jenny was "Qui Qui, Emperor of China" and "Di." My sister Laura (Madame
Lafargue) "the Hottentot" and "Kakadou." I was "Tussy"
—a name that has remained—and "Quo Quo, Successor
to the Emperor of China," and for a long time the "Ge-
twerg Alberich" (from the *Niebelungen Lied*).

But if Mohr was an excellent horse, he had a still
higher qualification. He was a unique, an unrivalled
story-teller. I have heard my aunts say that as a little
boy he was a terrible tyrant to his sisters, whom he would
"drive" down the Markusberg at Trier full speed, as his
horses, and worse, would insist on their eating the
"cakes" he made with dirty dough and dirtier hands. But
they stood the "driving" and ate the "cakes" without a
murmur, for the sake of the stories Karl would tell them

as a reward for their virtue. And so many and many a year later Marx told stories to his children. To my sisters—I was then too small—he told tales as they went for walks, and these tales were measured by miles not chapters. "Tell us another mile," was the cry of the two girls. For my part, of the many wonderful tales Mohr told me, the most wonderful, the most delightful one, was "Hans Röckle." It went on for months and months; it was a whole series of stories. The pity no one was there to write down these tales so full of poetry, of wit, of humor! Hans Röckle himself was a Hoffmann-like magician, who kept a toyshop, and who was always "hard up." His shop was full of the most wonderful things—of wooden men and women, giants and dwarfs, kings and queens, workmen and masters, animals and birds as numerous as Noah got into the Ark, tables and chairs, carriages, boxes of all sorts and sizes. And though he was a magician, Hans could never meet his obligations either to the devil or the butcher, and was therefore— much against the grain—constantly obliged to sell his toys to the devil. These then went through wonderful adventures—always ending in a return to Hans Röckle's shop. Some of these adventures were as grim, as terrible, as any of Hoffmann's; some were comic; all were told with inexhaustible verve, wit and humor.

And Mohr would also read to his children. Thus to me, as to my sisters before me, he read the whole of Homer, the whole *Niebelungen Lied, Gudrun, Don Quixote*, the *Arabian Nights*, etc. As to Shakespeare he was the Bible of our house, seldom out of our hands or mouths. By the time I was six I knew scene upon scene of Shakespeare by heart.

On my sixth birthday Mohr presented me with my first novel—the immortal *Peter Simple*. This was followed by a whole course of Marryat and Cooper. And my father actually read every one of the tales as I read them, and gravely discussed them with his little girl. And when that little girl, fired by Marryat's tales of the sea, declared she would become a "Post-Captain" (whatever that may be) and consulted her father as to whether it would not be possible for her "to dress up as a boy" and "run away to join a man-of-war" he assured her he thought it might very well be done, only they must say nothing about it to anyone until all plans were well matured. Before these plans could be matured, however, the Scott mania had set in, and the little girl heard to her horror that she herself partly belonged to the detested clan of Campbell. Then came plots for rousing the Highlands, and for reviving "the forty-five." I should add that Scott was an author to whom Marx again and again returned, whom he admired and knew as well as he did Balzac and Fielding. And while he talked about these and many other books he would, all unconscious though she was of it, show his little girl where to look for all that was finest and best in the works, teach her—though she never thought she was being taught, to that she would have objected—to try and think, to try and understand for herself.

And in the same way this "bitter" and "embittered" man would talk "politics" and "religion" with the little girl. How well I remember, when I was perhaps some five or six years old, feeling certain religious qualms and (we had been to a Roman Catholic Church to hear the beautiful music) confiding them, of course, to Mohr, and how he quietly made everything clear and straight, so that from that hour to this no doubt could ever cross my mind again. And how I remember his telling me the story—I do not think it could ever have been so told before or since—of the carpenter whom the rich men killed, and many and many a time saying, "After all we can forgive Christianity much, because it taught us the worship of the child."

And Marx could himself have said "suffer little children to come unto me" for wherever he went there children somehow would turn up also. If he sat on the Heath at Hampstead—a large open space in the north of London, near our old home—if he rested on a seat in one of the parks, a flock of children would soon be gathered round him on the most friendly and intimate terms with the big man with the long hair and beard, and the good brown eyes. Perfectly strange children would thus come about him, would stop him in the street. . . . Once, I remember, a small schoolboy of about ten, quite unceremoniously stopping the dreaded "chief of the International" in Maitland Park and asking him to "swop knives." After a little necessary explanation that "swop" was schoolboy for "exchange," the two knives were produced and compared. The boy's had only one blade; the man's had two, but these were undeniably blunt. After much discussion a bargain was struck, and the knives exchanged, the terrible "chief of the International" adding a penny in consideration of the bluntness of his blades.

How I remember, too, the infinite patience and sweetness with which, the American war and Blue Books having for the time ousted Marryat and Scott, he would answer every question, and never complain of an interruption. Yet it must have been no small nuisance to have a small child chattering while he was working at his great book. But the child was never allowed to think she was in the way. At this time too, I remember, I felt absolutely convinced that Abraham Lincoln badly needed my advice as to the war, and long letters would I indite to him, all of which Mohr, of course, had to read and post. Long long years after he showed me those childish letters that he had kept because they had amused him.

And so through the years of childhood and girlhood Mohr was an ideal friend. At home we were all good comrades, and he always the kindest and best humored. Even through the years of suffering when he was in constant pain, suffering from carbuncles, even to the end. . . .

*   *   *

I have jotted down these few disjointed memories, but even these would be quite incomplete if I did not add a word about my mother. It is no exaggeration to say that Karl Marx could never have been what he was without Jenny von Westphalen. Never were the lives of two people—both remarkable—so at one, so complementary one of the other. Of extraordinary beauty—a beauty in which he took pleasure and pride to the end, and that had wrung admiration from men like Heine and Herwegh and Lassalle—of intellect and wit as brilliant as her beauty, Jenny von Westphalen was a woman in a million. As little boy and girl Jenny and Karl played together; as youth and maiden—he but seventeen, she twenty-one,—they were betrothed, and as Jacob for Rachel he served for her seven years before they were wed. Then through all the following years of storm and stress, of exile, bitter poverty, calumny, stern struggle and strenuous battle, these two, with their faithful and trusty friend, Hélène Demuth, faced the world, never flinching, never shrinking, always at the post of duty and of danger. Truly he could say of her in Browning's words:

Therefore she is immortally my bride,
Chance cannot change my love nor time impair.

And I sometimes think that almost as strong a bond between them as their devotion to the cause of the workers was their immense sense of humor. Assuredly two people never enjoyed a joke more than these two. Again and again—especially if the occasion were one demanding decorum and sedateness, have I seen them laugh till tears ran down their cheeks, and even those inclined to be shocked at such awful levity could not choose but laugh with them. And how often have I seen them not daring to look at one another, each knowing that once a glance was exchanged uncontrollable laughter would result. To see these two with eyes fixed on anything but one another, for all the world like two school children, suffocating with suppressed laughter that at last despite all efforts would well forth, is a memory I would not barter for all the millions I am sometimes credited with having inherited. Yes, in spite of all the suffering, the struggles, the disappointments, they were a merry pair, and the embittered Jupiter Tonans a figment of bourgeois imagination. And if in the years of struggle there were many disillusions, if they met with strange ingratitude, they had what is given to few—true friends. Where the name of Marx is known there too is known that of Frederick Engels. And those who knew Marx in his home remember also the name of as noble a woman as ever lived, the honored name of Hélène Demuth.

To those who are students of human nature it will not seem strange that this man, who was such a fighter, should at the same time be the kindliest and gentlest of men. They will understand that he could hate so fiercely only because he could love so profoundly; that if his trenchant pen could as surely imprison a soul in hell as Dante himself it was because he was so true and tender; that if his sarcastic humor could bite like a corrosive acid, that same humor could be as balm to those in trouble and afflicted.

My mother died in the December of 1881. Fifteen months later he who had never been divided from her in life had joined her in death. After life's fitful fever they sleep well. If she was an ideal woman, he—well, he "was a man, take him for all in all, we shall not look upon his like again."

Printed from the manuscript   Written in English

CONFESSION

Your favorite virtue: *Simplicity*
Your favorite virtue in man: *Strength*
Your favorite virtue in woman: *Weakness*
Your chief characteristic: *Singleness of purpose*
Your idea of happiness: *To fight*
Your idea of misery: *Submission*
The vice you excuse most: *Gullibility*
The vice you detest most: *Servility*
Your aversion: *Martin Tupper*
Favorite occupation: *Bookworming*
Favorite poet: *Shakespeare, Aeschylus, Goethe*
Favorite prose-writer: *Diderot*
Favorite hero: *Spartacus, Kepler*
Favorite heroine: *Gretchen*
Favorite flower: *Daphne*
Favorite color: *Red*
Favorite name: *Laura, Jenny*
Favorite dish: *Fish*
Favorite maxim: *Nihil humani a me alienum puto*
Favorite motto: *De omnibus dubitandum*

KARL MARX

From a manuscript by Marx's daughter Laura

Written in English

KARL MARX'S FUNERAL

Frederick Engels

On Saturday, March 17, Marx was laid to rest in Highgate Cemetery, in the same grave in which his wife had been buried fifteen months earlier.

At the graveside *G. Lemke* laid two wreaths with red ribbons on the coffin in the name of the editorial board and dispatching service of *Sozialdemokrat* and in the name of the *London Workers' Educational Society.*

Frederick Engels then made the following speech in *English:*

"On the 14th of March, at a quarter to three in the afternoon, the greatest living thinker ceased to think. He had been left alone for scarcely two minutes, and when we came back we found him in his armchair, peacefully gone to sleep—but forever.

"An immeasurable loss has been sustained both by the militant proletariat of Europe and America, and by historical science, in the death of this man. The gap that has been left by the departure of this mighty spirit will soon enough make itself felt.

"Just as Darwin discovered the law of development of organic nature, so Marx discovered the law of development of human history: the simple fact, hitherto concealed by an overgrowth of ideology, that mankind must first of all eat, drink, have shelter and clothing, before it can pursue politics, science, art, religion, etc.; that therefore the production of the immediate material means of subsistence and consequently the degree of economic development attained by a given epoch form the foundation upon which the state institutions, the legal conceptions, art, and even the ideas on religion, of the people concerned have been evolved, and in the light of which they must, therefore, be explained, instead of vice versa, as had hitherto been the case.

"But that is not all. Marx also discovered the special law of motion governing the present-day capitalist mode of production and the bourgeois society that this mode of production has created. The discovery of surplus value suddenly threw light on the problem, in trying to solve which all previous investigations, of both bourgeois economists and socialist critics, had been groping in the dark.

"Two such discoveries would be enough for one lifetime. Happy the man to whom it is granted to make even one such discovery. But in every single field which Marx investigated—and he investigated very many fields, none of them superficially—in every field, even in that of mathematics, he made independent discoveries.

"Such was the man of science. But this was not even half the man. Science was for Marx a historically dynamic, revolutionary force. However great the joy with which he welcomed a new discovery in some theoretical science whose practical application perhaps it was as yet quite impossible to envisage, he experienced quite another kind of joy when the discovery involved immediate revolutionary changes in industry and in historical development in general. For example, he followed closely the development of the discoveries made in the field of electricity and recently those of Marcel Deprez.

"For Marx was before all else a revolutionist. His real mission in life was to contribute, in one way or another, to the overthrow of capitalist society and of the state institutions which it brought into being, to contribute to the liberation of the modern proletariat, which *he* was the first to make conscious of its own position and its needs, conscious of the conditions of its emancipation. Fighting was his element. And he fought with a passion, a tenacity and a success such as few could rival. His work on the first *Rheinische Zeitung* (1842), the Paris *Vorwärts*[1] (1844), *Deutsche - Brüsseler Zeitung* (1847), the *Neue Rheinische Zeitung* (1848-49), the *New York Tribune* (1852-61), and in addition to these a host of militant pamphlets, work in organizations in Paris, Brussels and London, and finally, crowning all, the formation of the great International Working Men's Association—this was indeed an achievement of which its founder might well have been proud even if he had done nothing else.

"And, consequently, Marx was the best hated and most calumniated man of his time. Governments, both absolutist and republican, deported him from their territories. Bourgeois, whether conservative or ultra-democratic, vied with one another in heaping slanders upon him. All this he brushed aside as though it were cobweb, ignoring it, answering only when extreme necessity compelled him. And he died beloved, revered and mourned by millions of revolutionary fellow-workers—from the mines of Siberia to California, in all parts of Europe and America—and I make bold to say that though he may have had many opponents he had hardly one personal enemy.

"His name will endure through the ages, and so also will his work!"

---

[1] *Vorwärts*—a German newspaper which appeared in Paris 1844. Under the influence of Marx, who took part in the editing of it from summer 1844, it began to develop a communist tendency.—*Ed.*

AFTERWORD

When this book was published in 1961 the author hoped that it might help to restore a proper understanding of Marx's philosophy. This was considered as being of special importance for the English-speaking public who had had little opportunity to read Marx's philosophical writings in English translation. The many printings issued since 1961 are evidence that to some extent the book has fulfilled the author's hopes.

There have in the interim been many other important factors which, in turn, have tended to increase the interest in Marx's ideas. The most notable of these, in my opinion, are the increasing significance of humanist thought within Christian thinking on the one hand, and that within Marxist socialist thinking on the other. As to the new importance of humanism within the Roman Catholic Church, one need only mention the names of such men as Pope John XXIII, Teilhard de Chardin, and of theologians such as Karl Rahner and Hans Küng; in the Protestant Church we should mention theologians such as Paul Tillich and Albert Schweitzer.

At the other end of the philosophical spectrum there is evidence of a new humanism among Marxist thinkers, especially among the Marxist philosophers in Yugoslavia, Poland, and Czechoslovakia, but also in Western Europe and America. Names such as those of Georg Lukács, Adam Schaff, Veljko Korać, Ernst Bloch, and many others give expression to this rise of socialist humanism.[1]

---

[1] For an expression of thirty-six humanists, mostly Marxists, and some non-Marxists, see *Socialist Humanism,* an international symposium edited by Erich Fromm (New York: Doubleday & Co., Inc., 1965).

In spite of the fact that Christian and Marxist thinkers do not share identical views—there are sharp differences between the two groups—it is perfectly clear that there is a common core of thought and feeling that unites them: humanism. This is not the place to discuss the nature of humanism. Suffice to say that it is a system of thought and feeling centered upon man, his growth, integrity, dignity, freedom; upon man as an end in himself, and not as a means toward anything; upon his capacity to be active not only as an individual but as a participant in history; and upon the fact that every man carries within himself all of humanity.

Among the great humanists of the past were Buddha, the Hebrew Prophets, Jesus Christ, Socrates, the philosophers of the Renaissance, and those of the Enlightenment down to Goethe and Marx. There is an unbroken tradition of humanism which reaches back some 2500 years and which is now growing in the most divergent fields of thought, mostly in those of Christianity and Marxism, but also among thinkers who belong to neither camp, such as Bertrand Russell, Camus, and Einstein.

How can one explain this renaissance of humanism? It is a reaction to the ever-increasing threat to man. This threat is twofold. In the first place there is the threat to his spiritual existence resulting from an industrial society in which man becomes increasingly alienated, a mere *homo consumens*, a thing among things, subordinate to the interests of the state and to economic production. In the second, there is the threat to his physical existence by an ever-increasing nuclear arms race. These threats have evoked in many men and women, philosophers and theologians as well as in laymen, a deep and passionate desire to fight the danger by putting the concern for man in the center of their thoughts and actions.

It is this growth of humanism that has led to the beginning of a dialogue between Marxists and Christian theologians. An increasing number of such dialogues have been taking place in Europe, in the United States, and in Mexico. But, one might ask, what have Christians and Marxists to talk about to each other, when their basic beliefs, especially in relation to God and salvation, are so contradictory? The answer lies in two factors. First of all, the participants in such dialogues approach each other in a humanist spirit, that is to say, with love and respect; and without fanaticism. Secondly, while the participants by no means tend to minimize their differences, they are also convinced that in addition to their different concepts there is still another dimension—the human reality which paradoxically in its fullness is itself inexpressible, although it can be expressed to a limited degree in different and even contradictory concepts.

I hope that this book, which contains Marx's concept of man, will continue to help toward an understanding of Marx and thus serve as a corrective to the distortion and corruption of his ideas by "anti-Marxists" and by many who call themselves Marxists. At the same time I hope that it may be helpful to the humanist renaissance that is taking place today, upon the success of which not only philosophy but also the physical survival of man to a large extent depends.

Erich Fromm